The History of Ideas

The History of Ideas:

A BIBLIOGRAPHICAL INTRODUCTION

Volume I:
CLASSICAL ANTIQUITY

by
Jeremy L. Tobey

Clio Books
American Bibliographical Center—Clio Press, Inc.
Santa Barbara   Oxford

Library of Congress Catalog Card Number 74-83160
ISBN 0-87436-143-5

Publishing history:
First printing, May, 1975
Second Printing, July, 1978

American Bibliographical Center—Clio Press
2040 Alameda Padre Serra, Riviera Campus, Box 4379
Santa Barbara, California 93103

European Bibliographical Centre—Clio Press, Ltd.
Woodside House, Hinksey Hill
Oxford OX1 5BE, England

Manufactured in the United States of America

Acknowledgments

I wish to thank the library staffs of Harvard University for their valuable assistance. I am especially grateful for the generosity of the Harvard Theological School library. The bulk of the research for this volume was done during a sabbatical granted by California State University in Sacramento. The final manuscript was expertly typed by Mrs. Gladys Kornweibel. Finally, I am grateful to Professor David S. Berkowitz of Brandeis University for introducing me to the history of ideas in antiquity and to the science of bibliography.

For Marilyn

Contents

x   *Contents*

Chapter 1:   Introduction

Part I: The History of Ideas

On the Definition of the History of Ideas

SCHOLARS DEFINE THE history of ideas or intellectual history in various overlapping and even contradictory ways. In this bibliography the history of ideas means the study of the ideas used by educated people in each era to comprehend the universe and rationalize their social institutions, arts, and religions. This definition generally follows the understanding of Arthur Lovejoy, one of the American pioneers in the development of the discipline. Lovejoy was most interested in the study of important "unit ideas" in the development of western thought. In part the study of these unit ideas was the study of basic themes or theories consistently articulated in civilized speculation, as for instance the idea of plenitude or the "great chain of being" so brilliantly analyzed by Lovejoy himself. But for Lovejoy the province of the history of ideas ranged beyond consciously articulated important themes to study such elements as the presuppositions of rational thought, the emotional forces which attracted thinkers to particular ideas, the conflicting and ill-coordinated elements in the thought of individuals, and the role of semantic change and confusion in the history of thought. For Lovejoy the field was also especially interested in the migration of ideas from one field to another and the uses made of an idea when transplanted into a novel intellectual environment. This understanding of the history of ideas makes it clear that its practitioners must range over various areas of human thought, especially over the areas of philosophy, science, theology, and aesthetics, looking for those themes and ideas which contribute to the world view of the educated classes. The chief purpose of this bibliography is to provide for the lay person and the student (1) a convenient summary of bibliographical guides, reference works, and periodicals in the four most important specialized fields relevant to the history of ideas, (2) references to the most important works in each field, and (3) references to the most important studies of ideas and themes which encompass all fields and contribute to the world view of each era.

Many scholars argue that the history of ideas must include the study of the ideas held by the uneducated as well as by the educated people of any era and analyze the ways in which ideas influence social action. Without doubt these areas of history are vitally important, but they are logically part of social history or the sociology of knowledge rather than the history of ideas. This does not mean that the history of ideas must restrict itself to great or first-rank ideas of the past. On the contrary, the history of ideas takes a special interest in ideas of the second rank entertained by educated peoples and in the peculiar, even illogical, uses of great ideas. Thus the fact that patristic speculation on nature or medicine was of a low calibre or that British poets misunderstood the implications of Newtonian physics in no way lessens the interest of the historian of ideas in these themes. Nor does this mean that the history of ideas involves no interest at all in the social, economic, and political environment of thought. Actually, an appreciation of the social background to ideas is essential to understanding the meaning and intellectual influence of those ideas, just as an understanding of economic interests or technology is essential for the study of political or military history. This field of study, however, focuses on the interplay of ideas in history regardless of their social consequences and on the efforts of educated people to think about the world—however unsuccessful those efforts have often been.

A fairly extensive literature is now available for the student interested in the various understandings of the history of ideas. Perhaps the best starting place is Crane Brinton, *European Intellectual History*, a pamphlet for the American Historical Association's Service Center for Teachers which explains some alternative definitions of the field and comments on illustrative histories of western ideas. Lovejoy's approach is outlined in the introduction on "The Study of the History of Ideas" in his *The Great Chain of Being* and in two articles: "The Historiography of Ideas" (pp. 1–14) in his *Essays in the History of Ideas* and "Reflections on the History of Ideas" (pp. 3–24) in *Ideas in Cultural Perspective*, edited by Philip Wiener and Aaron Noland. Lovejoy's general approach is also illustrated by a short work written by his colleague and coauthor, George Boas, *The History of Ideas: An Introduction*. Joseph A. Mazzeo's recent article, "Some Interpretations of the History of Ideas," in the *Journal of the History of Ideas* 33 (1972):379–395, ranges widely over attitudes in modern Europe toward the history of ideas and has a number of comments directly on Lovejoy's interpretation. Other discussions generally compatible with Lovejoy's approach can be found in H. Stuart Hughes, *Consciousness and Society* (pp. 3–33); Paul O. Kristeller, "The History of Philosophy and the History of Ideas," *The Journal of the History of Philosophy* 2 (1964):1–14; and Franklin L. Baumer, "Intellectual History and Its Problems," *Journal of Modern History* 21 (1949):191–203. Also see "Intellectual History: Its Aims and Methods," *Daedalus* (1971):80–98, wherein Felix Gilbert recommends a more modest approach for the history of ideas, focusing on the attempt to "reconstitute the mind of an individual or of groups at the times when a past event happened or an advance was achieved." The attempt to define the entire *Zeitgeist* of an era should be given up because it is an impossible task and because it gives the false impression that there was unity of thought among the educated people of past ages.

John Higham, "Intellectual History and Its Neighbors" (pp. 81–93), in Wiener and Noland, *Ideas in Cultural Perspective*, distinguishes between an "internalist" approach to the history of ideas, whose proponents (e.g., Lovejoy) focus on the influence of "thought on thought," and an externalist approach, whose proponents focus on the interaction of ideas and their social environment. The latter school tends to be interested in the ideas of average people as well as the highly educated: in "Little Orphan Annie as well as Adam Smith." Crane Brinton argues that the history of ideas is primarily the study of the effects of ideas on people's actions in the introduction to *Ideas and Men* (pp. 3–29) and in his article on intellectual history for the *International Encyclopedia of the Social Sciences* 2:462–467. Brinton also emphasizes that the role of the historian of ideas is to condense and simplify the work of specialists in one field so that it can be understood by scholars and students in other fields.

Other useful essays on the history of ideas and its relationship to other areas of study appear in George Boas et al., *Studies in Intellectual History,* especially the Boas article, "Some Problems of Intellectual History" (pp. 3–22); Maurice Mandelbaum, "The History of Ideas, Intellectual History, and the History of Philosophy" (pp. 33–66), in "Beiheft" 5 (1965) of *History and Theory;* Quentin Skinner, "Meaning and Understanding in the History of Ideas" (pp. 3–53), in *History and Theory* 8 (1969); John Dunn, "The Identity of the History of Ideas" (pp. 85–104), in *Philosophy* 43 (1968); Hajo Holborne, "The History of Ideas," in the *American Historical Review* 73 (1968):683–695; and a series of exchanges in volumes 1 and 2 of the now defunct *The History of Ideas Newsletter* (1954–1960). The most recent general review of the character of the field is Leonard Krieger's "The Autonomy of Intellectual History" in the *Journal of the History of Ideas* 34 (1973):499–517.

Surveys of the History of Ideas

The range and complexity of the history of ideas precludes the compilation of an ideal one-volume survey of the field. All of the surveys omit some important areas in order to briefly encompass the field. Unfortunately for the reader interested in the history of ideas in the classical world of Greece and Rome, one of the most common measures for restricting surveys to manageable proportions is the omission of comments on the ancient world. There are some exceptions to this habit. Harry E. Barnes, *The Intellectual and Cultural History of the West,* is a good reference-style survey which includes all of the important names and developments without extended treatment. Chapters 1–6 of volume 1 cover the ancient world and reflect Barnes's healthy rationalism in dealing with the "reign of the supernatural" in the ancient world. Crane Brinton, *Ideas and Men: The Story of Western Thought,* devotes chapters 2–5 to the ancient world, but the treatment is barely satisfactory. Brinton advocates emphasizing the influence of ideas on human action, and consequently he largely ignores the formal structure of philosophy and science. Even his descriptions of the general character of Greek and Roman civilization are often superficial. His discussion of the modern period is better, but there is little reason to recommend his work to the reader as an introduction to the ancient history of ideas.

A number of other surveys cover the ancient and medieval worlds by tracing the development of a key idea or cluster of ideas. Arthur Lovejoy, *The Great Chain of Being,* and Herschel Baker, *The Image of Man: A Study of the Idea of Human Dignity in Classical Antiquity, the Middle Ages, and the Renaissance,* are obvious examples, and others are cited under different headings throughout this bibliography.

There is need for a survey by a specialist in medieval thought, which has been recognized by Frederick Herr in *The Intellectual History of Europe.* Unfortunately, however, that work is disappointing. Herr gives more information on the medieval mind than the student normally finds in a text, and he includes a number of interesting comments on such polarities as the conflict between the educated and the uneducated classes throughout European history. His treatment of the history of the development of modern thought, however, is superficial and misleading and employs psychological guesswork in his analysis of intellectual movements. For example, he uses a psychological hammer on Calvinism and its attitude toward nature which leaves the anvil, hammer, and concept unrecognizable. More importantly, Herr's survey leaves the reader the impression that the development of modern science is worth little comment. Leonard Krieger's review of Herr in the *Journal of the History of Ideas* 31 (1970):305–312 provides good general comments on the writing of histories of ideas. Another approach to the history of medieval thought as part of the general history of western ideas can be found in Philippe Wolff, *The Awakening of Europe,* volume 1 of the *Pelican History of European Thought.*

Other major surveys of the history of ideas do not deal extensively with either classical or medieval civilization. One of the most popular texts has been John Herman Randall, *The Making of the Modern Mind.* Randall's survey is a fairly clear and detailed history which briefly summarizes the beginnings of the medieval period and proceeds to the present. Its emphasis on scientific thought, its good, lengthy quotations, and its bibliographical suggestions are especially strong; however, Randall tends to oversimplify the evolution of thought and he relies too much on middle-class interests in explanation. Preserved Smith, *A History of Modern Culture* (2 vols.), topically organizes an immense amount of information, but it is probably more suited to reference work than textbook use. Smith intended to encompass modern thought to Darwin's period, but his early death terminated the study at 1776. Roland Stromberg, *Intellectual History of Modern Europe,* surveys the history of ideas from the Renaissance to the present. The survey is accurate in detail, judicious in judgment, and well designed for use as a textbook in undergraduate courses. Its lengthy bibliography is uneven and less reliable in its recommendations. Wilson H. Coates and Hayden V. White, *Western Intellectual History* (2 vols.), emphasizes the rise of "liberal humanism," a critical attitude inherited from the Greeks. Despite its political focus it gives good accounts of developments in other areas of the history of ideas. Jacob Bronowski and Bruce Mazlish use a rather different approach in their *The Western Intellectual Tradition from Leonardo to Hegel.* They concentrate on social and scientific ideas and illustrate major ideas by discussing typical figures and groups. Their treatment, which places the history of ideas into a general cultural context, is excellent, but their survey is not as systematic as Stromberg's.

Some scholarly journals have broad enough interests to encompass the entire history of ideas. The standard journal in the field is the *Journal of the History of Ideas,* a quarterly founded in 1940 by Arthur O. Lovejoy and Philip O. Wiener. It publishes excellent articles on all areas of the history of ideas, but its bibliographical value is limited because of its limited number of book reviews and surveys of scholarship in particular areas. No other wide-ranging journal is as valuable as the *Journal of the History of Ideas,* but *Saeculum: Jahrbuch für Universalgeschichte* (1950) is worth consulting. It publishes many articles on the history of both western and nonwestern ideas as well as valuable research reports. The *Archiv für Begriffsgeschichte* (1955) publishes thematic studies of key words and ideas in the history of western thought and is also worth consulting.

The *Dictionary of the History of Ideas: Studies of Selected Pivotal Ideas* produced under Philip Wiener's general editorship is a five-volume fund of superb articles by many of the most important scholars in the field. Articles cover ideas and themes distinctive to the history of ideas and are indexed according to seven rubrics:

The History of Ideas about the External Order of Nature
The History of Ideas in Literature and the Arts, in Aesthetical Theory
    and Literary Criticism

This work is an invaluable guide to the history of ideas.

The History of Ideas and the Classical World

The ancient Greeks are rightly credited with devising the fields, the
ideas, and even many of the terms which still dominate the intellectual
life of the modern world. The Greeks chiefly during the classical period
from about 600 to 300 B.C. raised most of the questions and proffered
many of the answers which governed the development of western thought
for more than two thousand years. Their contribution is surpassed in
brilliance only by the scientific explosion of the nineteenth and twentieth
centuries. Despite the immediate relevance and familiarity of much of
Greek thought, the reader will find it necessary to give up many modern
habits of thought and adopt a radically different attitude toward intellectual life in that milieu in order to appreciate the history of ideas in antiquity.

The most important difference between the modern and ancient
worlds of thought is the different roles played by science in the two civilizations. Science is the central and controlling force in intellectual development in the modern world. Even those intellectuals who disdain science
and technology orbit around a scientific epicenter. The exploration and
comprehension of the universe has largely been left to scientists who
describe reality in terms of mathematics and repeatable experiments.
Philosophers and theologians may regret this dominance, but they accept
it. When scientists speak, philosophers and theologians may groan, but
in the end they obey. In the ancient world this relationship was normally
reversed. Before and after the great period of Greek advance, and even
during that enlightenment, scientific theory was commonly dominated
by religious and philosophic ideas and presuppositions. Science did
advance and geniuses like Archimedes were heroes in the Greek world,
but science did not determine the world view accepted by educated
people. Philosophy and religion formed the general world view and
science normally worked within that scheme toward ends consistent
with the prejudices of that age. As a result ancient science never became
a discipline based on mathematical analysis of observation. Nor was
experiment matured to the point where it could either sponsor an indus-
trial revolution or provide reason a secure haven against the impact of
the religious superstition typical of the late ancient period.

Ancient intellectuals also differed in their ideas concerning the practical application of knowledge. They were aware that rational discussion might lead to social reform, and during the brief bloom of the Greek polis, or city-state, political debate and philosophical skepticism became important public forces. Most intellectuals, however, during much of the ancient classical period considered philosophy and science to be unimportant as formulas for the reconstruction of society. Certainly the ancient intellectual did not hope that the rational control and direction of society could give the average person an appreciably higher standard of living.

Finally, the reader should be aware that rhetoric was crucially important in the ancient world. The rapidly disintegrating standards and habits of good writing today may make this ancient emphasis on proper expression seem a wasteful and even bizarre preoccupation, but much of the intellectual history of Greece and Rome can be understood only if the central importance of good expression is kept in mind. Rhetoric emphasized good style and gave it an importance lacking in the twentieth century. It also produced the habits of careful linguistic ability characteristic of the ancient period. Rhetoric, however, was also partly responsible for the persistence of tradition and the deadly imitative spirit which helped destroy the Greek enlightenment.

The Organization of This Bibliography

This bibliography surveys the most important bibliographical guides and writings on the history of philosophy, science, aesthetics, and religious thought in antiquity. This scope is consistent with the definition of the history of ideas outlined earlier and pays special attention to ideas and themes which migrated from one field to another. The summary of sources for each field is intended to provide the fundamental knowledge of its separate development necessary for the study of its interactions with other fields. This volume does not pretend to be a complete résumé of writings in these four fields. It is intended, however, to be a guide to the most important surveys, scholarly achievements, and bibliographical resources which hopefully will enable readers to extend their knowledge.

Part II of this introduction briefly outlines two classes of bibliographical guides: first, those used by graduate students in any area of history, and second, those used by students and scholars interested in the full range of ancient classical history. Both types of guides include nonserial and serial bibliographies and those periodicals, handbooks, and encyclopedias considered most valuable because of their bibliographical emphasis. Periodical listings are followed by the publication date of the first issue or the inclusive dates for defunct periodicals. The introduction concludes with brief résumés of some of the most useful surveys and cultural cross sections of ancient Greek and Roman civilization. The later specialized chapters of the bibliography occasionally crossreference these general sources. Students will, however, need to develop the habit of regularly consulting them.

The chapters devoted to the history of ancient philosophy, science, aesthetics, and religion will follow the same general pattern adopted in the introduction by listing the most important bibliographical resources first and then listing some of the important scholarly writings in each area. The listing and discussion of the writings follow certain general and flexibly interpreted principles. The discussions normally move from the most general to the more specialized works, and they crossreference relevant material discussed under other headings. Works in English have been preferred to those in other languages, yet many of the most important works are available only in French or German. Unfortunately, the citation of works in Italian is limited to the most obvious reference works and major studies, so the user will find it necessary to consult the recommended bibliographical guides to overcome this deficiency. In general the works listed are positively recommended as worthwhile contributions to the history of ideas. Works not recommended are listed only when they are well known and therefore require comment or to illustrate a faulty approach to the history of ideas.

Part II: General Bibliographical Resources

The Most General Bibliographical Guides

THE MOST POPULAR American reference guide is undoubtedly Constance Winchell's *Guide to Reference Books*, which surveys the important reference and bibliographical guides in all fields of scholarship and provides good annotations and cross references. Winchell is regularly updated. Albert J. Walford, *Guide to Reference Materials* (3 vols.), is more detailed than Winchell but concentrates on British materials, which are somewhat harder to find in American libraries. Volume 2 covers the social and historical sciences, philosophy, and religion; volume 3, literature and the arts. Robert J. Collison, *Bibliographies, Subject and National: A*

Guide to Their Contents, Arrangement, and Use, is less detailed than either Winchell or Walford, but it is a concise and well-written summary. These English-language sources are usually sufficient to meet the reader's most general bibliographical needs, but there are additional valuable guides to continental European sources. L. N. Maclès, *Les Sources du travail bibliographique* (3 vols. in 4), and her *Manuel de bibliographie* are important guides especially to French material. Wilhelm Totok, Rolf Weitzel, and Karl-Heinz Weimann, *Handbuch der bibliographischen Nachschlagewerke,* is a standard German guide. In addition to these guides every student should become acquainted with Theodore Bestermann, *A World Bibliography of Bibliographies* (5 vols.), which is one of the monuments in the development of the science of bibliography. Bestermann surveys the bibliographical resources available in all areas of the history of ideas and lists defunct and active bibliographical sources—thereby presenting a general history of bibliography. Bestermann's survey needs continual reediting and serial updating and that service is provided by the Wilson Company, *Bibliographical Index: A Cumulative Bibliography of Bibliographies* (1938), published quarterly with annual cumulations covering bibliographical books and articles. *The Bibliographical Index* also lists bibliographies included in new books.

GUIDES TO PERIODICAL LITERATURE

Scholars devote a major part of their time to journal literature in their field. The history of ideas, being the broadest and most complex of all disciplines, requires the scholar in that field to devote even more time to journals. *Ulrich's International Periodical Directory* lists the major serials in all fields. There is, however, no entirely satisfactory general index to scholarly articles in English. The best available indexes include the *Social Science and Humanities Index* (1907), a Wilson Company quarterly previously entitled the *International Index,* and the *British Humanities Index* (1915), a Library Association publication formerly entitled the *Subject Index to Periodicals.* Unfortunately neither publication covers non-English language journals and the *Social Science and Humanities Index* gives meager citations in the field of art criticism and history. These guides can be supplemented with the French *Bulletin signalétique* and the German *Internationale Bibliographie.* The *Bulletin signalétique* (1961), issued eight times a year under the sponsorship of the Centre national de la recherche scientifique, testifies to the excellence of French bibliographical work. It surveys journal literature in all major languages and in all areas of the history of ideas. It also lists book reviews and also provides a check on new books. It contains short but useful annotations. The *Bulletin* is divided into separate numbered sections (or manuals) by field. The most important fields of interest in the history of ideas are: psychology (390), philosophy (519), sociology (521), the history of science (522), literature and art (523), and religion (527). The German *Internationale Bibliographie der Zeitschriften-*

literatur aus allen Gebiete des Wissens (1964–1965) is a semiannual publication previously entitled the *Bibliographie der fremdsprachigen Zeitschriftenliteratur* (1911). It lists citations by author and subject but is not annotated.

BOOK REVIEWS

There is no ideal guide to scholarly book reviews. The best known index is the *Book Review Digest* (1905), a Wilson publication which excerpts selected reviews. The *Book Review Digest* coverage of works of general interest is better than its coverage of scholarly studies. The *Book Review Index* (1965) and the *Index to Book Reviews in the Humanities* (1960) provide somewhat greater coverage of scholarly publications. The *Book Review Index* covers only English-language journals; the *Index to Book Reviews in the Humanities* indexes some reviews published in foreign-language journals. The defects of English-language indexes are partially compensated by the publication of a German serial, the *Internationale Bibliographie der Rezensionen* (1971), which appears annually in three parts with lists of authors, reviewers, book titles, and topics. This service indexes scholarly works but usually lists only one review for each book. For further information on available book review resources see Richard A. Gray, *A Guide to Book Review Citations: A Bibliography of Sources.*

Most American libraries shelve a number of publications which provide students and lay readers quick summaries and reviews of new books. The quality of reviews and the reliability of coverage vary widely, but together these sources provide a valuable check on new work in the history of ideas.

The *New York Times Book Review* and the *Times Literary Supplement* (the book review section of the *London Times*) are both worth reading. The *New York Times Book Review* is uneven in quality and tends to have literary critics review works in history, philosophy, and religion as well as in fiction and literary history. As a result reviews are often impressionistic and sometimes ill-formed. The *Times Literary Supplement* provides better reviews prepared by anonymous reviewers. American book reviews have been greatly improved by the *New York Review of Books* despite its overconcentration on contemporary politics and current intellectual fads. It publishes reviews of important new books in the history of ideas, usually prepared by highly competent scholars. The book review section of the monthly *Library Journal* contains synopses of new books in all fields. The reviews are cumulated annually and the cumulative lists can be found in most libraries. The *Library Journal* summaries are almost always accurate, but the evaluative comments tend to be unreliable since they are sometimes solicited from unqualified sources. British books are similarly summarized in the *British Book News*. Résumés of new French publications can be found in the topically organized *Bulletin critique du livre française,* a monthly publication. The German series *German Studies —German Language Research Contributions: A Current Survey in English* provides even better summaries translated into English. The series appears in separate issues, e.g., Philosophy and History; Modern Law and Society; Literature, Music, and the Fine Arts; and "Mundus."

General Bibliographical Guides for Ancient History

Bibliographies are either nonserial or serial. Nonserial bibliographies are complete when printed and are brought up to date by issuing a new edition. Serial bibliographies, however, are continuing. They are issued at regular intervals like any periodical and thus cite recently appearing literature. The following lists of nonserial and serial bibliographies on ancient history are by no means exhaustive but will serve as guides to the most important resources for the student of the history of ideas.

Nonserial Bibliographies

The American Historical Association published a *Guide to Historical Literature* which is available in most libraries and which competently lists citations in every area of history. The ancient classical world is covered on pages 120–169. Students of ancient history and the history of ancient ideas may find the 1931 edition of the *Guide* (reprinted 1949) most valuable. The 1931 edition concentrates on European and American history while the 1961 edition more broadly attends to the nonwestern world. The 1931 edition has excellent chapters: "Ancient Greece and the Hellenistic World" by D. McFayden (pp. 138–180); "Rome: The Republic and the Empire" by Arthur E. R. Boak (pp. 180–233); and "History of Christianity" by W. H. Allison (pp. 233–276). These surveys include fairly lengthy and generally good annotations and cite many works directly relevant to the history of ideas. Gilbert Varet, *Manuel de bibliographie philosophique* (2 vols.), is another general work with important references to the ancient world. Varet's work, in fact, is close to being the only bibliographical survey of the entire history of ideas. It covers all the component areas in the history of ideas and includes many references to the ancient world in volume 1. Volume 2 includes references to the ancient period and a discussion of the literature on various specialized areas of western thought. The broadest bibliographical coverage of works devoted solely to the ancient period is still found in the *Cambridge Ancient History* (12 vols., with 5 supplemental vols. of maps and plates). It devotes a fairly high proportion of chapters to themes relevant to the history of ancient ideas, with valuable bibliographies organized by chapter headings at the end of each volume. Martin R. P. McGuire, *Introduction to Classical Scholarship*, is somewhat narrower but still useful. The first three parts deal with classical scholarship in a narrow and more philological sense; part 4 deals with the institutional and cultural worlds of antiquity. McGuire's work is an excellent guide to the literary history of the ancient world, but

its citations in religious and philosophical-scientific history are spotty.
McGuire can be supplemented by Maurice Plautnauer, ed., *Fifty Years
(and Twelve) of Classical Scholarship,* a compilation of résumés on the history of classical literature and thought prepared by eminent British scholars. The selections are heavily oriented toward literary themes, but include
valuable chapters such as "The Greek Philosophers" by W. David Ross,
"The Greek Historians" by G. T. Griffith, and "The Roman Historians"
by A. H. McDonald. See also T. Gwiney and F. Dickinson, *Greek and
Roman Authors: A Checklist of Criticism,* which has good citations of journal
articles.

SERIAL BIBLIOGRAPHIES AND PERIODICALS

The continuing serial guides are far more valuable than the completed or nonserial bibliographies. Some of these periodicals are devoted
only to bibliographies, while others carry articles and publish substantial
bibliographical reviews.

Two French sources provide the best systematic listing of new works
relevant to the history of ideas in antiquity. The *L'Année philologique:
bibliographie critique et analytique de l'antiquité gréco-latine* (1924) is an annual
publication. Part 1 covers individual authors and textual investigations
and part 2 covers the history of literature, philosophy, the sciences, and
religion in antiquity. This is a list of publications which includes short
annotations rather than a guide to the contents or quality of the sources
referenced. *L'Année philologique* can be supplemented by the *Revue d'histoire ecclésiastique* (1900) that is technically a journal in church history but
which includes fine coverage of new publications in all areas of western
thought. These French-language publications are book lists rather than
book reviews and even the reader with meager French can use them effectively; however, the reader will normally need English-language sources
for detailed comments on publications. The best sources for reviews
ranging over the entire field of ancient classical history are the *Journal
of Hellenic Studies* (1880) and the *Journal of Roman Studies* (1911), both published in Great Britain. Their articles are usually on institutional, archaeological, or philological subjects rather than on the history of ideas; the
reviews are by the most eminent scholars. Neither devotes much space
to publications in the fields of the history of Judaism or Christianity.

Other English-language periodicals with good bibliographical coverage include *Greece and Rome* (1931) and *Phoenix* (1946). Both publish reviews and critical notes on new publications. *Classical World* (1907) carries
articles summarizing scholarly work in various areas of ancient history.
To find evaluations of publications before 1947 the student should also
use *The Year's Work in Classical Studies* (1906–1947), an excellent British
publication organized as a series of essays on new work in various areas
of ancient history. Less important guides include the *International Bibliography of the Historical Sciences* (1927), which is divided into Section E,

Greek; Section F, Roman; and Section G, Christian history. The American Bibliographical Service publications, the *Quarterly Checklist of Classical Studies* (1959) and the *International Guide to Classical Studies* (1961), which reference periodical literature, should also be consulted.

The scholar must use French and German sources for more complete bibliographical coverage. The *Revue des études anciennes* (1899), the *Revue des études grecques* (1888) and, above all, the *Revue des études latines* (1923) give lengthy book lists and excellent reviews. The most important German publication is *Lustrum: Internationale Forschungsberichte aus dem Bereich des klassischen Altertums* (1956), an annual successor to the famous *Jahresbericht über die Fortschritte der klassischen Altertumswissenschaft* (1873–1943). *Lustrum* carries essay reviews of the literature in different areas of ancient culture, many in English. It may be supplemented by referring to the shorter and wider ranging articles to be found in the *Anzeiger für Altertumswissenschaft* (1948) and *Gnomon: kritische Zeitschrift für die gesamte klassische Altertumswissenschaft* (1925).

HANDBOOKS AND ENCYCLOPEDIAS

There are several good general guides and encyclopedias in ancient history. Hermann Bengston, *Introduction to Ancient History*, is a good starting point. The work is somewhat outdated and it suffers from changes made by the translators in the bibliography, but it is still a good introduction to the field. See pages 7–23 for an interesting history of the study of the ancient world. Two French introductory guides are not yet translated into English. The best is Paul Petit, *Guide de l'étudiant en histoire ancienne*, but Pierre Grimal, *Guide de l'étudiant latiniste*, is also useful.

The *Oxford Classical Dictionary*, a fine work with succinct articles by experts on all aspects of classical history and good bibliographical suggestions, is an indispensable one-volume encyclopedia. Its German counterpart, *Lexikon der alten Welt*, edited by Carl Andresen et al., is also excellent. *A Companion to Greek Studies*, first published in 1905 and edited by Leonard Whibley, and *A Companion to Latin Studies*, first published in 1910 and edited by John E. Sandys, are rather outdated but still valuable because they provide fuller treatment of many subjects than either the *Oxford Classical Dictionary* or the *Lexikon der alten Welt*. They are collections of expert articles on various topics which appear commonly in classical literature. The famous *Pauly's Real-Encyclopädie der classischen Altertumswissenschaft*, inaugurated by A. Pauly in 1839 and revised since 1894 by a series of editors beginning with G. Wissowa, is an invaluable German work compiled for over 100 years. The *Real-Encyclopädie* comprises more than 60 regular and some 12 supplementary volumes and it is an almost complete mine of brilliant articles and excellent bibliographical notes on every aspect of classical life. The student should also examine the condensed five-volume version soon to be completed, *Der Kleiner Pauly: Lexikon der Antike auf Grundlage von Paulys Real-Encyclopädie*.

The best general collection of available English translations of ancient writings is the Loeb Classical Library, published by the Harvard University Press, which will comprise 456 volumes. It includes Greek and Latin texts with rather literal English translations on the facing pages. Other translations can be found in George B. Parks and Ruth Z. Temple, *The Greek and Latin Literatures*, volume 1 of the "Literature of the World in English Translation."

Surveys of Classical Culture

THE GREEKS

Easily the most popular sketch of Greek civilization is Edith Hamilton, *The Greek Way to Western Civilization*. Since Hamilton was a lifelong teacher of Greek literature, she was inclined to idealize her subject and slight the treatment given philosophy and science. Nonetheless, her work is an exciting introduction to Greek literature and art. Her introduction should be compared with Samuel H. Butcher, *Some Aspects of the Greek Genius*, which gives much greater attention to the religious dimension of Greek thought and to the darker side of the Greek character; for example, see Butcher's brilliant chapter on "The Melancholy of the Greeks" (pp. 13–165). Cecil Maurice Bowra is also an expert on the history of Greek literature, and his *The Greek Experience* is a topically organized study with special emphasis on the Greek aesthetical experience. Goldsworthy L. Dickinson, *The Greek View of Life*, is an exceptional sketch of the Greek political character. H. D. F. Kitto, an expert on Greek drama, surveys Greek political history and summarizes Greek cultural developments in *The Greeks*. Kitto tends to underrate the achievements of Greek philosophy and science. One of the best surveys of the Greek character and achievements is André Bonnard, *Greek Civilization* (3 vols.). Bonnard surveys the development of Greek culture from Homer to Epicurus—whom Bonnard considers one of the great figures of Greek life and thought—in a personal and sometimes flamboyant writing style. John H. Finley, *Four Stages of Greek Thought*, focuses on the development of Greek thought. Finley describes the evolution of Greek thought in four stages, beginning with the "heroic" stage in which objects, events, and personalities were grasped individually through poetic imagination and extending to the "visionary," "theoretical," and "rational" stages, which subsumed experience under general laws and categories constructed by reason. Finley's approach somewhat oversimplifies and tends to force Greek culture into his categories, but he makes interesting points concerning the Greek approach to understanding life. George Boas, *Rationalism in Greek Philosophy*, is a well-written and perceptive study of Greek rationalism with its rigorous use of the principle of noncontradiction to derive general laws about the universe which could make coherent sense of experience and give some power of predicting the future. His descriptions of the breakdown of belief in rationalism and the reliance of intellectuals on revelation and other irrational sources of authority are especially interesting. His study encompasses the entire evolution of ancient philosophy and theology but does not discuss particular thinkers in the late ancient world in detail. A different and valuable approach to Greek thought can be found in Thorleif Boman, *Hebrew Thought Compared with Greek*. Boman argues that Greek thought was concerned with the logical discovery of a clearly conceived objective truth about the world, while Hebrew thought focused on gaining personal certainty about God, history, and especially moral decisions. Hence he argues that Greek thought is oriented toward logic while Hebrew thought is based on psychological factors. He compares the two modes of thought in terms of linguistic forms and basic rubrics, such as "dynamic and static, time and space, impression and appearance." His argument is weakened, however, by the assumption that Plato typified the essential principles of all Greek thought.

Many of the most important works on the history of ancient ideas are not systematic nor are they general histories of the period. Nonetheless, they deal with broad themes so they cannot be assigned to any single area of the history of ideas. Depending on their particular emphasis, they may be more relevant to one area than to others, but scholars in every aspect of ancient thought continually consult them. Some of the most important and broadly relevant studies attempt to establish the original meaning of words in Greek (less often in Latin) and to trace the changing meanings of those terms in ancient history. Such studies at first glance seem to be more pedantic and narrow than other classical studies, yet when the terms they examine are part of the basic lexicon of society or thought, their etymology is an essential addition to the history of ancient thought. Werner Jaeger's great *Paideia: The Ideals of Greek Culture* (3 vols.) is a prime example. Jaeger traces the meaning and significance of *paideia* (education) from the Homeric to the Hellenistic eras and does more than provide a history of education in the modern sense of the word. He shows that *paideia* had a broad meaning to the Greeks encompassing the entire process of converting the child into a fully civilized human being and citizen. Jaeger thus leads the reader into virtually every nook and cranny of Greek civilization. Despite Jaeger's tendency to exaggerate Plato's role as the exemplar of Greek thought, his study is a basic mine of information for every student of the ancient world. Richard B. Onians, *The Origins of European Thought about the Body, the Individual, the Soul, the World, Time, and Fate: New Interpretations of Greek, Roman, and Kindred Evidence, Also of Some Basic Jewish and Christian Beliefs*, is far less generally admired than Jaeger's masterpiece. Onians tries to show that Greek ideas important in the development of later western thinking evolved from primitive concrete meanings to the basically abstract ideas of the classical era by tracing the etymology of such words as *psyche*. Onians's immense erudition makes the effort of reading his work worthwhile, but see also the review of Herbert J. Rose in the *Journal of Hellenic Studies* 73–74 (1953–1956):175–176. Arthur W. H. Adkins, *Merit and Responsibility: A Study in Greek Value,* like volume 1 of Jaeger's *Paideia,* examines the meaning of *arete,* the idea of excellence, in Greek literature and thought. Adkins argues that the Homeric Greeks identified excellence chiefly with military or quasi-military success and had little interest in "quiet," nonmilitary virtues or good intentions in moral decisions. He writes that in time the life of the polis weakened the military virtues and elevated the quiet virtues without overcoming standards of success by inculcating a strong sense of inner and individual moral responsibility. Chapter 7 is an especially interesting discussion of the idea of moral stain or pollution. Adkins, *From the Many to the One: A Study of Personality and Views of Human Nature in the Context of Ancient Greek Society, Values, and Beliefs,* argues that individuals had no genuine separate existence in Homeric society since they were merged in the family-tribal structure. He suggests that the competitive commercial and political life of the polis fragmented the Greeks' life habits and weakened the power of the family and that the family and the polis were sufficiently weakened to allow the development of a real idea of individual personality in the imperial period.

William C. Greene, *Moira: Fate, Good, and Evil in Greek Thought,* is less oriented to the study of the history of key terms. Greene's survey is nominally a study of why there is unwarranted evil in the world, but it actually ranges over the entire development of Greek thought to the post-Aristotelian schools. The result is a fine cross section of the Greek mind which focuses on one of the most difficult problems in constructing a rational explanation of the world. His appendices (pp. 401–428) contain valuable notes on the meaning of key terms and concepts. Bruno Snell, *The Discovery of the Mind: The Greek Origins of European Thought,* is a generally unsuccessful effort to analyze the origins and character of some elements of European thought. It is ponderously vague in the German manner and inclined to include dubious explanations, such as the claim (see chap. 10) that the structure of the Greek language was essential to the Greeks' discovery of science. The work is, however, a valuable source of information on a wide range of topics including, for example, interesting chapters on "Art and Play in Callimachus" (chap. 12) and "Arcadia: The Discovery of a Spiritual Landscape" (chap. 13).

Another group of studies deals with ancient ideas concerning the beginnings of the world and the overall history of humanity, i.e., whether these ideas represent the degeneration of the golden age or a progressive development. William K. C. Guthrie, *In the Beginning: Some Greek Views on the Origins of Life and the Early State of Man,* is a short and interesting account of the beginnings of human life and the relationship of the ideas of the golden age and the progressive evolution of humanity from the beast to civilized society (chaps. 4 and 5). A different approach can be found in Arnold Ehrhardt, *The Beginning: A Study in the Greek Philosophical Approach to the Concept of Creation from Anaximander to St. John,* which compares the Greek and Christian attitudes toward creation and summarizes Greek attitudes toward the eternity and evolution of the world (see part 1). The idea that human societies were once happier because of a simpler and more natural life style is discussed by Arthur O. Lovejoy and George Boas in *Primitivism and Related Ideas in Antiquity.* Their survey (through the Stoics) is chiefly composed of excerpts from classical literature with comments by the authors, and there is an excellent appendix on "Some Meanings of Nature." George Boas continues the same theme in his *Essays on Primitivism and Related Ideas in the Middle Ages.* Chapter 1 is on Philo and chapter 2 on "The Original Condition of Man: The Patristic Period." Obversely, the idea that humanity has risen from a brutish to a civilized state of existence and that it is capable of great improvement in the future is the subject of Ludwig Edelstein, *The Idea of Progress in Classical Antiquity.* Unfortunately, Edelstein died before completing his manuscript, but his incomplete work demonstrates that the ideas of evolutionary progress in the past and important progress in the future were known to ancient intellectuals. Compare Eric R. Dodds, *The Ancient Concept of Progress and Other Essays on Greek Literature and Belief* (pp. 1–26), which critically reviews Edelstein's argument. Dodds argues that an ancient idea of progress did exist but that it enjoyed broad support only in the fifth century B.C. The chief proponents of the idea were scientists or those philosophers most impressed with the progress of science and technology.

During the eighteenth and nineteenth centuries the Greeks were generally credited with an austere rationalism and scientific attitude toward life which they certainly did not have. The Greeks invented rationalism and were unsurpassed until recent times in the keenness and the persistence of their thinking about life. They were, however, neither unaware of irrational powers nor untouched by them. Twentieth-century scholarship has largely redressed the image of the unnaturally rational Greeks—in fact it has sometimes excessively minimized the influence of Greek rationalism. One of the best reconsiderations of Greek thought is Eric R. Dodds, *The Greeks and the Irrational.* Dodds shows that educated Greeks were always impressed by the powers of the irrational. He argues that the Greeks were influenced by the archaic notion that passions are independent powers which often force people to commit acts which they would not freely choose and that irrational states of mind (e.g., those exhibited by shamans) reveal truths about the universe not otherwise available. According to Dodds, by the fifth and fourth centuries B.C. Greek civilization shared an "inherited conglomerate" (an expression contributed by Gilbert Murray), which was an illogical and contradictory collection of traditions and superstitions that generally sanctioned social life and the established religions and relieved the normal fears of life. The rationalist sophists attacked and weakened this view among the educated but did not destroy it. By the end of the classical period rationalism was in turn weakened and irrationalism regained control of the Greeks' world view. Chapter 7 (pp. 207–236) is not of the same high quality that distinguishes the rest of Dodds's book since it introduces a specious analogy involving Plato's doctrine of the soul, his ideal state, and the institution of the shaman in primitive Greece. In sum Dodds is "must" reading for those interested in Greek civilization.

THE HELLENISTIC ERA

The Hellenistic era, between the death of Alexander (323 B.C.) and the consolidation of Roman power throughout the Mediterranean basin, now receives more sympathetic attention from scholars, but it still has not attracted as many good general studies as the classical period of Greek development.

William W. Tarn, *Hellenistic Civilization*, is an older introduction to the Hellenistic era. It is topically organized and summarizes the basic information. John Ferguson, *The Heritage of Hellenism: The Greek World from 323–31 B.C.*, is a better guide for the beginner which focuses on the period's key cultural elements. Moses Hadas, *Hellenistic Culture: Fusion and Diffusion*, is especially good on the interaction between the Greek and Judaic cultures, with an excellent review (chap. 6) of the status of education. George Sarton, *A History of Science: Hellenistic Science and Culture in the Last Three Centuries B.C.*, is another work in English which emphasizes the close relationship of science and the humanities during the Hellenistic era. Carl Schneider, *Kulturgeschichte des Hellenismus* (2 vols.), is an encyclopedic history of the social and cultural developments of the age as yet not available in English. It has a superb bibliography (pp. 989–1106).

THE ROMANS

Edith Hamilton was not as enthusiastic about the Romans as she was about the Greeks, so it is not surprising that *The Roman Way to Western Civilization* is inferior to *The Greek Way*. *The Roman Way*, however, is a good introduction for the student interested in Roman civilization despite Hamilton's use of hero worship to interest the reader. Her treatment of Cicero does not adversely affect either the historical facts or the reader, but her exaggerated view of Julius Caesar needs correcting. Martin L. Clarke, *The Roman Mind: Studies in the History of Thought from Cicero to Marcus Aurelius*, is also useful. Clarke's discussion of *humanitas* is most interesting. *Humanitas* refers to the cultivated and genteel love of humanity represented by Cicero. After Cicero the concept was eroded by a philosophic and religious disdain for literature, which was thought to distract from moral improvement. Two older works by Samuel Dill are still invaluable to beginners for their comments on Roman intellectual history and because they set intellectual life in a social and political context. These are *Roman Society from Nero to Marcus Aurelius* and *Roman Society in the Last Century of the Western Empire*.

Chester G. Starr's *Civilization and the Caesars: The Intellectual Revolution in the Roman Empire* is a study of the changes which occurred between the time of Cicero and Marcus Aurelius and the consequent effect on the intellectual life of the late ancient period. According to Starr the philosophy of the earlier Greek period was characterized by a weak concept of individual existence and thought in which the individual was dominated by the family and the state (especially the polis). Starr explains that the bonds between individuals and social institutions were largely dissolved by the political work of the Romans in building the Empire and by the skeptical sophists. The individualism which emerged was expressed in all areas of Roman life and thought, often with destructive consequences. Christianity eventually provided a way to retain the benefits of individualism while curing its defects. Under Christian influence individuals escaped the old social ties and formed links with a transcendent divine power and with other human beings in new social orders, especially that of the church. In addition nature came to be viewed as a positive good since it was governed by the same divine power. Certainly, intellectual and artistic life during the period of the early and middle Empire was more individualistic than previous ages, but it is doubtful that later developments, especially Christianity, represented an improvement in this situation. Starr fails to consider the increasing importance of irrational and magical forces in late antiquity, a tendency directly promoted by ancient Christianity. A similar tendency to ignore the relationship between ancient Christianity and irrationalism is evident in Charles M. Cochrane's *Christianity and Classical Culture: A Study of Thought and Action from Augustus to Augustine*. Cochrane considers classicism to be one expression of human pride or *hubris*, i.e., an unwillingness to recognize the limits of human power. *Hubris* was evident in the development of such ideas as that humanity could build a world "safe for civilization" (e.g., the Augustan Pax Romana) and that reason alone could fathom the universe. Roman classicism tended to consider the universe to be simply a mass of impersonal forces in perpetual conflict. Cochrane interprets Christianity as an intellectual and social antidote for classical *hubris* and the errors that flowed from it. He believed that Christianity recognized the limits and defects of human power and human reason and called to humanity's assistance the light of divine revelation. The Christian synthesis, best exemplified by Augustine, gave both humanity and nature a proper place in the scheme of the universe and summoned divinity to integrate the principles of action and thought. Cochrane's work is richly informative and his particular comments are valuable, but his bias in favor of Christian thought tends to spoil its scholarly merits. Throughout his work Christianity is represented as a means of solving the riddles which vexed the classical thinkers and as a way of building an image of the world based on the importance of personality and the possibility of progress. He even cites the doctrines of the Trinity and the Incarnation as evidence of the Christians' superior understanding of life and nature. The irrational elements in Christian thought are neither considered nor compared with classical efforts.

The history of ancient education is, strictly speaking, part of the institutional history of the ancient world rather than part of its intellectual development, yet it is essential for a full understanding of the distinctive character of classical thought. The Greek foundations of ancient education are surveyed in Frederick A. B. Beck, *Greek Education: 450–350*. Beck interprets the development of classical education as a process which replaced aristocratic ideas (i.e., excellence through birth and education in myth and poetry) with the notion that excellence is the result of both birth and environment and education through "prose" devoted to rhetoric or philosophy. The full sweep of education in the ancient world from Homer to the fall of the Roman Empire in the West is chronicled in Henri I. Marrou, *A History of Education in Antiquity*. Marrou envisions the development of ancient education as a transformation from the ideal of the "noble warrior" to that taught by the "scribe." Greek education mixed the two ideas as shown by their attention to physical excellence through athletic competition combined with mental training. In the later ancient world the scribal attitude was predominant. Marrou describes all levels of education but emphasizes higher education.

Martin L. Clarke, *Higher Education in the Ancient World*, is a recent and interesting study which is topically organized and describes education above the preparatory level. Chapter 3 on "Philosophical Teaching" is an especially interesting and important account of the character of later ancient philosophy. W. Barclay, *Educational Ideals in the Ancient World*, is narrower in scope but still well worth reading. Barclay describes ancient Christian attitudes toward education and the Christian acceptance of the idea that learning might be adapted by the church to achieve Christian ends. He also summarizes the educational attitudes of the Jews, Spartans, Athenians, and Romans. Max L. W. Laistner, *Christian and Pagan Culture in the Later Roman Empire*, is largely devoted to education in the late ancient period. Laistner describes the uniform pagan system of education, which was based chiefly on rhetoric and textual criticism, the differences between the Jewish and Christian systems, and the eventual absorption of the pagan system by the Christians.

Chapter 2: *Ancient Philosophy*

Introduction

DURING THE HIGH classical period (generally from 600 to 300 B.C.), the Greeks invented philosophy and determined most of its lasting categories and terms. After a period of rapid advance dominated by Plato and Aristotle, the field progressed and continued to be important to the educated classes. Later, however, philosophy was increasingly influenced by an imitative spirit, and the practice of learning the ideas of the great masters rather than breaking new ground became habitual. Later ancient philosophy was also increasingly influenced by the growing power of religious thought. The rapid advance of philosophy during the classical period and the limitations of space occasion this chapter's relative concentration on that period. The philosophies of Plato and Aristotle are more completely covered since they are absolutely essential to an understanding of ancient thought, but the more derivative philosophies of the post-Aristotelian period are covered in general terms. This draconian economy is necessary to keep this chapter within reasonable limits—admittedly at the expense of the later antique schools.

General Bibliographical Resources

The best nonserial guides to classical history suited to study in the history of classical philosophy were first cited on pages 11–12. See Gilbert

Varet, *Manuel de bibliographie philosophique* which amply covers ancient philosophy in its two volumes. *Fifty Years (and Twelve) of Classical Scholarship* is less detailed but has more contemporary citations. In that work W. David Ross and D. J. Allan write on "The Greek Philosophers" (chap. 5), G. T. Griffith writes on "The Greek Historians" (chap. 6), and A. H. McDonald contributes an essay on "The Roman Historians" (chap. 13). The most important general serial bibliographies (see pp. 12–13) for the study of ancient philosophy include *L'Année philologique*, which has separate sections on Plato and Aristotle, *Gnomon*, the *Anzeiger für Altertumswissenschaft*, and *Lustrum*, which publishes outstanding periodic reviews of literature on ancient philosophy. *Classical World* should also be consulted.

Bibliographies on the history of philosophy are also published in serial and nonserial form. The most useful nonserial bibliography on the history of philosophy is certainly Wilhelm Totok, *Handbuch der Geschichte der Philosophie I: Altertum*, which has an excellent introduction to the entire history of philosophy (pp. 1–11) and a thorough survey of classical philosophy (pp. 68–355). Unfortunately, the *Handbuch* is not annotated and so can only be used as a reference to the important literature. German scholarship also produced a standard and often revised history of philosophy which is so rich in bibliography that it is more a guide to literature than a standard history—see Friedrich Ueberweg and Karl Praechter, *Grundriss der Geschichte der Philosophie*, a work first published in 1862 and now in its twelfth revised edition with a new and completely revised eight-volume edition planned.

Several valuable serial bibliographies are available to students of the history of philosophy. The *Bibliography of Philosophy* (1937) and the *Répertoire bibliographique de la philosophie* (1949) are used continually. Between them these guides include everything important in the history of philosophy. The *Bibliography of Philosophy* is a multilingual review of new books with a separate section on the history of philosophy. It gives short and very helpful résumés in English, French, German, and occasionally in Italian. The *Répertoire* (whose ancestor was the *Sommaire idéologique* [1895]) covers books and periodical articles and is organized topically and chronologically. The last issue each year contains an index of book reviews. These two guides were not published during World War II (1939–1945), but that gap is well covered by C. A. de Brie, *Bibliographica Philosophica* (2 vols.). The *Répertoire*'s coverage of periodical literature can be supplemented by consulting section 519 of the *Bulletin signalétique* and *The Philosopher's Index: An International Index to Philosophical Periodicals* (1967), a quarterly with annual cumulations and good abstracts by the authors of articles.

A general summary and suggestions on available bibliographical resources can be found in Paul G. Kuntz, "Progress in Philosophical Bibliography," *International Philosophical Quarterly* 10 (1964):291–310.

Periodicals

The general periodicals in ancient history carry many articles and reviews relevant to the history of philosophy, and the *Journal of the History of Ideas* is indispensable for articles on antiquity. General periodicals can be supplemented by many specialized journals. One of the best is the relatively new *Journal of the History of Philosophy* (1963), which publishes many articles and reviews on the ancient world, especially on Plato and Aristotle. The British journal *Philosophical Books* (1960) is entirely devoted to reviews, many of them by the most eminent scholars in the field. The *Review of Metaphysics* (1947) is somewhat less acute in its reviews but still invaluable for its abstracts of new books and articles, and it publishes many articles on the history of ancient ideas. *Mind* (1876) and *Philosophical Review* (1892) also carry good critical reviews and many articles on ancient thought. *History and Theory* (1960) is somewhat less valuable for the study of the ancient period since it concentrates on the philosophy of history in its regular issues and the periodic "Beihefte" (supplements devoted largely to bibliographies). Two journals (chiefly in English) are devoted solely to ancient thought: *Phronesis: A Journal for Ancient History* (1955), which unfortunately has no reviews, and θπ *Theta-Pi: A Journal for Greek and Early Christian Philosophy* (1972), published under the general editorship of Cornelia J. de Vogel. Other journals carry occasional bibliographical résumés; e.g., Leo Sweeney's "Foreign Books on Greek Philosophers" in the *Modern Schoolman* 50 (1972):76–86 and 219–232.

Among foreign-language periodicals two French journals have excellent bibliographical reports: *Les Études philosophiques* (1926) and *Archives de philosophie: recherches et documentation* (1923). The latter devotes each issue to a particular figure or theme in the history of philosophy. The Belgian *Revue internationale de philosophie* (1938) is nearly as good; it carries some articles in English and is available in a Johnson Reprint Corporation reprint. The German periodicals with the most valuable bibliographies include *Philosophische Rundschau* (1957), *Philosophischer Literaturanzeiger* (1949), *Philosophisches Jahrbuch* (1888–1942; n.s. 1948), and the *Archiv für die Geschichte der Philosophie* (1888–1924; 1931–1932; n.s. 1959).

Handbooks and Encyclopedias

The best English-language encyclopedia covering the entire range of philosophy is undoubtedly *The Encyclopedia of Philosophy* (8 vols.), under the general editorship of Paul Edwards. It contains well-written articles on every important topic in the history and contemporary status of philosophy with unusually good bibliographical end notes accompanying each article. J. O. Ormson, *The Concise Encyclopedia of Western*

Philosophy and Philosophers, is a useful shorter guide. F. E. Peters, *Greek Philosophical Terms,* defines and cites the chief usages of key Greek terms. The best foreign-language encyclopedia is the Italian *Enciclopedia filosofica* (6 vols.). The German *Historisches Wörterbuch der Philosophie,* edited by Joachim Ritter, now includes two volumes (to "F") of good articles with excellent bibliographical notes.

Several good handbooks on research in philosophy have recently appeared. Probably the best is Richard T. de George, *A Guide to Philosophical Bibliography and Research,* but Henry J. Koren, *Research in Philosophy: A Bibliographical Introduction to Philosophy,* and D. H. Borchardt, *How to Find Out in Philosophy and Psychology,* are also valuable.

General Surveys

Several fine surveys of classical philosophy are now published in English. Introductions include Arthur H. Armstrong, *Introduction to Ancient Philosophy,* and Joseph Owens, *A History of Ancient Western Philosophy.* Armstrong is an expert on the philosophy of Plotinus; hence his survey is unusually strong on the late ancient period. Owens pays little attention to the late ancient period, but his accounts of the development of the pre-Socratics, Plato, and Aristotle, are succinct and interesting. The older survey by the German master Wilhelm Windelband, *A History of Ancient Philosophy,* is also excellent.

From these simple introductions to the entire range of ancient philosophical development, the student should progress to the use of a standard work published in the nineteenth century which is still one of the best ever written on ancient philosophy: Eduard Zeller, *Die Philosophie der Griechen in ihrer geschichtlichen Entwicklung.* The volumes translated into English include *Presocratic Philosophy* (2 vols.), *Socrates and the Socratic Schools, Plato and the Older Academy, Aristotle and the Earlier Peripatetics* (2 vols.), *Stoics, Epicureans, and Sceptics,* and *A History of Eclecticism.* Zeller was inclined to exaggerate the rationalism of Greek philosophy and did not discuss several issues concerning Plato and Aristotle which have busied modern scholars. His work is still full of information and provocative ideas. Another less provocative, but accurate and judicious account of the development of philosophy in the ancient world can be found in volume 1 of Frederick Copleston's *A History of Philosophy* (8 vols.). Copleston's preference for Christian principle is often evident in his writings on pagan philosophers, but his summaries are nonetheless clear and critical and they are recommended as introductions to several aspects of ancient philosophy. Volume 1, part 1, covers through Plato; volume 1, part 2, covers the rest of the ancient world, except for patristic thought.

Other valuable general works restrict themselves essentially to the classical period—generally to the death of Aristotle. The beginner can use William K. C. Guthrie, *The Greek Philosophers from Thales to Aristotle,* which includes a competent introduction, and Robert S. Brumbaugh, *The Philosophers of Greece.* Brumbaugh communicates a generous and beneficial enthusiasm for Greek thought to the reader and supplements his generally clear text with illustrative charts showing relationships between various thinkers and their ideas. One of the most famous general studies of Greek thought, John Burnet, *Greek Philosophy I: Thales to Plato,* is still valuable for beginning students. Burnet represents the pre-Socratics as being more secular than they were, and he argues that the early dialogues of Plato give an accurate historical picture of Socrates' opinions. However, his thorough knowledge of the sources and clear, forceful style make *Greek Philosophy* indispensable reading for any student. Theodor Gomperz, *Greek Thinkers: A History of Ancient Philosophy* (4 vols.), is less brilliant than Burnet but eminently readable throughout and especially good in its treatment of Aristotle. Volume 1 covers the pre-Socratics; volume 2, Socrates and Early Plato; volume 3, Plato; and volume 4, Aristotle and his successors. Benjamin A. G. Fuller, *History of Greek Philosophy* (3 vols.), is unoriginal but still a fine survey based on the theories of Zeller and Burnet. The volumes are divided to cover "Thales to Democritus," "The Sophists, Socrates, Plato," and "Aristotle." Volume 2 is probably the most successful; it has an excellent résumé of Plato's thought. More recently, William K. C. Guthrie has begun to issue a survey of Greek philosophy in five volumes. The three volumes completed to date are *The Earlier Presocratics and the Pythagoreans: The Presocratic Tradition from Parmenides to Democritus* and *The Fifth Century Enlightenment.* Guthrie's survey is too complex for the average student, but his command of recent scholarship, excellent bibliographies, and judicious discussion of every important problem in the development of Greek thought make it indispensable for the scholar.

Good general surveys of philosophy in later antiquity are harder to find, although general studies of the Christian Fathers often cover the chief elements of pagan thought. Arthur H. Armstrong edited *The Cambridge History of Later Greek and Early Medieval Philosophy.* Part 1 by Philip Merlan is an especially fine summary of the transition from classical to later ancient philosophy. The *Cambridge History* includes chapters by Henry Chadwick on Philo, Armstrong on Plotinus, A. C. Lloyd on "The Later Neoplatonists," and good summaries of the chief ideas of the patristic writers.

A collection of articles by John P. Anton and George L. Kustas, *Essays in Ancient Greek Philosophy,* has selections of good quality on the pre-Socratics, Plato, Aristotle, and the post-Aristotelians. *Studies in Intellectual History,* edited by George Boas, has an excellent essay by Harold Cherniss, "The History of Ideas and Ancient Greek Philosophy," which argues that Greek philosophers did not interest themselves in the history of ideas. They generally conceived of philosophy as the study of a universal and objective truth to which individual thinkers had access without an important knowledge of prior varieties of philosophic opinion.

Other surveys which deal with only one branch of the history of philosophy shed light on Greek and Roman philosophic development. The best introduction to the history of ethical thought is Alasdair MacIntyre, *A Short History of Ethics: A History of Moral Philosophy from the Homeric Age to the Twentieth Century.* MacIntyre writes plainly and well, with clear résumés of the ethical theories of all major thinkers. Chapters 1–9 cover the ancient world. Vernon Bourke, *History of Ethics,* is a more detailed reference style survey. Bourke covers secondary as well as primary thinkers in the history of ethics, so his survey is more difficult for the student to use. He is, however, accurate and his work includes a fine bibliography (pp. 353–419).

The studies of ethical thought confined to the ancient world include John Ferguson, *Moral Values in the Ancient World,* which is informative but weakened by Ferguson's argument that Christianity alone provided a sound basis for integrating moral values into one system through the concepts of God and *agape* (i.e., divine love). Ferguson underrates the integrative quality of much Greek and Roman ethical thought and nowhere does he apply the same critical standards to Christian ethics as he applies to non-Christian thought. He does not, for example, treat the charges of impracticality and superstition frequently attributed to Christian thought. Ferguson's attitude toward classical ethics should be compared with Eduard Schwartz, *Ethik der Griechen,* which is an interesting study of the evolution of Greek ethics. The study encompasses Greek ethics from its archaic and aristocratic beginning, the interweaving of ethics and the polis, the end of the age of an independent polis, and the ethics of individual autarchy and freedom. His appreciation of the positive side of the ethic of autarchy distinguishes his work from Ferguson's. Consult Felix Heinimann, *Nomos und Physis: Herkunft und Bedeutung einer Antithese in griechischen Denken des 5. Jahrhunderts,* on the early development of ethical theory. Several histories of the development of logic are also important. E. Kapp, *Greek Foundations of Traditional Logic,* provides an introductory survey. Innocenty Bochenski, *History of Formal Logic,* is more difficult to use but more complete. Part 1, chapters 6–8, cover the period to Aristotle; part 2, Aristotle; part 3, the Megarian-Stoic school; and part 4, the "Close of Antiquity." The recent work of William and Martha Kneale, *The Development of Logic,* devotes chapters 1–3 to the ancient world and has an excellent summary of the theories of Aristotle. Geoffrey E. R. Lloyd, *Polarity and Analogy: Two Types of Argumentation in Early Greek Thought,* is indispensable to the study of the development of logic in the ancient world. This is a masterful analysis of the early Greek concept of polarity (i.e., apparently opposite qualities: hot-cold, wet-dry), and the use of analogy to identify logically important similarities between objects and functions. Lloyd analyzes the use of these techniques of logical discourse by the pre-Socratics, Plato, and Aristotle. The result is one of the best recent books in any area of ancient philosophy.

The history of ancient psychology is treated by George B. Brett, *A History of Psychology: Ancient and Patristic.* This is a clearly written and accurate review solidly based on an analysis of relevant texts. Also see Anthelme E. Chaignet, *Histoire de la psychologie des Grecs* (5 vols.), a detailed study remarkable for its extensive survey of the post-Aristotelian period (vols. 2–5). The classic study of John I. Beare, *Greek Theories of Elementary Cognition from Alcmaean to Aristotle,* is also basic to the study of Greek psychology. Beare is especially interesting in his discussion of the idea of the five senses and the development of the idea of the *sensus communis,* i.e., the faculty for synthesizing the information conveyed from the senses to the mind. The work is topically divided and ends the discussion of each topic with comments on Aristotle's contributions.

The Loeb Classical Library has been recommended as a source of key writings in every area of the history of ancient ideas. More specialized sources will be recommended below in particular areas. There is, however, one basic tool useful at all levels of scholarship, Cornelia J. de Vogel, *Greek Philosophy: A Collection of Texts Selected and Supplemented with Some Notes and Explanations* (3 vols.). Volume 1 covers through Plato; volume 2, Aristotle and the earlier post-Aristotelians; and volume 3, the later ancient period. De Vogel cites crucial selections from philosophical texts and comments on both the texts and the contents. The texts themselves are not translated.

The Pre-Socratics

Bibliographical Guides

The pre-Socratics are well covered in the nonserial bibliographies listed above, especially in Totok, *Handbuch der Geschichte der Philosophie* 1:103–129; Varet, *Manuel de bibliographie philosophique* (vol. 1, chap. 2); and in Ueberweg-Praechter, *Grundriss der Geschichte der Philosophie* (vol. 1). Other good guides are available. John M. Robinson, *An Introduction to Early Greek Philosophy*, has a short and well-annotated bibliography which lists the most important works. There are extensive (unannotated) bibliographies in the first three volumes of William K. C. Guthrie, *A History of Greek Philosophy*. The journals listed above contain occasional résumés of work on the pre-Socratics. See for instance Edwin L. Minar's report in *Classical World* 47 (1953–1954):161 ff.; G. B. Kerferd, "Recent Works on Presocratic Philosophy," in the *American Philosophical Quarterly* 2 (1965):1–11; and Leo Sweeney, "Foreign Books on Greek Philosophers," in *The Modern Schoolman* 50 (1972): 76–86, which has some citations relevant to the pre-Socratics. Excellent articles on the pre-Socratics are also gathered in two German collections: *Archiv für Begriffsgeschichte* 9 (1964):47–185, a report on the 1961 Deutsche Forschungsgemeinschaft conference on the pre-Socratics, and in volume 9 of the Wege der Forschung series, edited by Hans Georg Gadamer, *Um die Begriffswelt der Vorsokratiker*. By far the best collection of scholarly material is David J. Furley and Reginald E. Allen, *Studies in the Presocratic Philosophy I: The Beginnings of Philosophy*. Articles published in this work will be individually cited below.

Source Collections

Only fragments of the writings of the pre-Socratics remain extant, so it is actually possible to read the source evidence left from these first philosophers and theoretical scientists. The standard collection for scholars is Hermann Diels (later with Walther Kranz), *Die Fragmente der Vorsokratiker* (3 vols). This collection was first published in 1903 with the Greek text, a German translation, and the testimonia about the pre-Socratics written by later ancients. Diels was translated into English by Kathleen Freeman, *Ancilla to the Pre-Socratic Philosophers: A Complete Translation of the Fragments in Diels' "Fragmente der Vorsokratiker,"* and *The Pre-Socratic Philosophers: A Companion to Diels' "Fragmente der Vorsokratiker."* The latter is essentially a handbook of basic information about the pre-Socratics and the ancient sources of information on each thinker. Volume 1 of Cornelia J. de Vogel, *Greek Philosophy*, is strictly for the advanced scholar. It covers the period from Thales to Plato, including the Greek texts of extant evidence supplemented by notes and commentaries. Geoffrey S. Kirk and John E. Raven, *The Presocratic Philosophers*, is also designed chiefly for the scholar. It combines a judicious selection of texts with detailed notes on the integrity of the fragments and their place in the development of Greek philosophy. Philip Wheelwright, *The Presocratics*, is a collection designed primarily for less advanced students with a good exposition and criticism.

John M. Robinson, *An Introduction to Early Greek Philosophy*, and Reginald E. Allen, *Greek Philosophy: Thales to Aristotle*, also contain valuable translations of source materials. A recent collection of translations from Diels-Kranz of the remains of the sophists is also available in an edition by Rosamund K. Sprague, *The Older Sophists*.

General Surveys

The best older and general histories of the pre-Socratics cited above are Eduard Zeller, *A History of Greek Philosophy from the Earliest Period to the Time of Socrates* (vols. 1 and 2), and John Burnet, *Greek Philosophy I: Thales to Plato*. Burnet more fully develops his thesis that the pre-Socratics were protoscientists, generally rational, and antimythological in their world views in *Early Greek Philosophy*. Burnet summarizes the major pre-Socratic ideas and writes in excellent Victorian prose. More recent sketches are found in John M. Robinson, *An Introduction to Early Greek Philosophy*, a collection of translated texts accompanied by judicious comments, and Edward Hussey, *The Presocratics*. Hussey's clear and careful account focuses on the question of Near Eastern and mythological influence and has an especially good treatment of Parmenides. Felix M. Cleve, *The Giants of Pre-Sophistic Greek Philosophy* (2 vols.), is more difficult to evaluate. Cleve makes many interesting and provocative observations and his treatment of Anaxagoras is especially good, but his work is marred by vitriolic attacks on philosophers and ideas he dislikes. For example, Cleve alleges that Parmenides was a "glossomorph" (II, 524 ff.) who philosophized about words with no referents (e.g., *Einai* or "To be"), thus fostering a tradition of philosophical confusion which has plagued western philosophy ever since.

One of the fascinating problems in the history of philosophy is the continuing search for an answer to the question of why the Greeks invented philosophy and theoretical science. Several theories have been advanced, including the notion that the pre-Socratics were inspired by the advance of technology and middle class attitudes, by the wisdom of Near Eastern thought (this merely recasts the question), and by the religious ideas and mythology of sixth century B.C. Greece. The role of technology and middle class interests in promoting philosophy and science is referenced in chapter 3. John Burnet denies that there was any significant Near Eastern influence in *Greek Philosophy* (pp. 1–13) and in *Early Greek Philosophy* (pp. 1–30), as does William K. C. Guthrie, *History of Greek Philosophy* (vol. 1, chap. 2, pp. 26–39). A cautious case which suggests there was some Near Eastern influence is advanced by M. L. West, *Early Greek Philosophy and the Orient*. For example, West argues that the Persian magi influenced the Greeks' acceptance of the ideas that there is a pure being beyond the senses and that the material world is composed of a few simple elements. West, however, established nothing more than that there were certain parallels between pre-Socratic and magi thought.

The greatest scholarly interest in the sources and original character of pre-Socratic philosophy probably involves the question of whether the first Greek philosophy, born in Miletus in Asia Minor, was essentially secular and irreligious or whether it inherited the religious and mythological categories of the sixth and fifth centuries B.C. The argument that the Milesians were essentially secular and disinterested in religion despite their occasional use of religious words and phrases is well summarized by John Burnet in "Science and Religion," chapter 2 (pp. 80–129) of *Early Greek Philosophy*. The principal opposition to Burnet's interpretation is especially associated with the British scholar Francis Cornford. Cornford first presented his argument in *From Religion to Philosophy: A Study of the Origins of Western Speculation*. Cornford applies the social theories of Emile Durkheim and argues that Milesian philosophy, like Greek religion, was a mental projection of the collective consciousness of Greek society. He suggests that Milesian categories were far from being completely novel, that they did not repudiate religion and myth, that they were prefigured in religious thought, and that the Milesians translated the collective consciousness into philosophical terms but did not repudiate the prior world view. According to Cornford the Milesians' belief in *hylozoism* retained the older idea that humanity and nature are both alive or animistically related; their belief in the regular operation of the universe was a projection of the lawful government of human society. Eventually these concepts were converted into a fully secular philosophy by the branch of pre-Socratic philosophy that led to the atomism of Democritus. The Pythagoreans represented another branch which remained essentially mystical and religious in character. Cornford's *Principium Sapientiae: The Origins of Greek Philosophical Thought* argues that the first philosophers were part of an archaic system of thought which combined seer, poet, and sage. He thus believes that Milesian thought was not scientific in the modern sense but rather poetic and inspirational in character. A genuinely scientific and empirical point of view was first developed by the practitioners of medicine. For an acute critique of Cornford's theories, see Gregory Vlastos, "Review of F. M. Cornford's *Principium Sapientiae*," in Furley and Allen, *Studies in Presocratic Philosophy* 1:42–56.

Werner Jaeger, *The Theology of the Early Greek Philosophers*, is a much more cautious approach to the problem, especially in avoiding the use of anthropological ideas in the analysis of early Greek thought. Jaeger rejects Burnet's thesis that the protoscientific pre-Socratics were uninterested in religion and he argues that they founded natural religion and theology and used reason to construct an acceptable idea of God and to purge superstition from religious thought. Jaeger's argument is critically reviewed by Gregory Vlastos, "Theology and Philosophy in Early Greek

Thought," in Furley and Allen (pp. 92–130). Vlastos agrees that the Milesians may have been interested in reforming religion but insists that Jaeger drastically underestimates the gap which divided them from any established religion. According to Vlastos, the Milesians were not the moral purifiers of traditional religion; they were the first to place religion into a completely natural sphere, within a conceptual system of uniform laws governing nature without miracles or cults. The Milesians did more than reform religion; they revolutionized it.

Roy K. Hack, *God in Greek Philosophy to the Time of Socrates,* is less well known than either Cornford or Jaeger. Hack considers that pre-Socratic philosophy combined the traditional idea of the gods as powers in the universe (with one god or power supreme) and the cosmogenetic force which created and shaped the universe. The pre-Socratics combined these traditional ideas in their *arche* (i.e., causing principle of the universe). The notion of an abstract and impersonal *arche* with the divine quality of immutability was original with them. Olof Gigon, *Der Ursprung der griechischen Philosophie von Hesiod bis Parmenides,* is less interested in the question of religious influence but emphasizes the importance of mythological systems (e.g., Hesiod) on the pre-Socratics. Michael Stokes, "Hesiodic and Milesian Cosmologies," in *Phronesis* 7 (1962):1–36 and 8 (1963):1–35, judiciously reviews the literary evidence on this subject.

The great scholarly interest in the relationship of pre-Socratic thought to the religious environment and the theory that religious ideas and motives may have inspired the pre-Socratics have modified, but not destroyed, the Burnet thesis. Burnet's general position is still represented in Leon Robin, *Greek Thought and the Origins of the Scientific Spirit.* Robin denies that there was any important Near Eastern influence on the pre-Socratics. He identifies the roots of their thought as being two philosophical motives—the development of an adequate picture of reality and the adequate justification of moral rules. More recently William K. C. Guthrie, *History of Greek Philosophy* (vol. 1, chap. 2, pp. 26–39), provided a balanced judgment on the entire issue. According to Guthrie neither religion nor technical motives but ideology, the natural Greek sense of wonder, and the leisure enjoyed by the nonpriestly types in Greek society promoted the development of philosophy and science.

Harold Cherniss, *Aristotle's Criticism of Presocratic Philosophy,* is of basic importance to the study of pre-Socratic philosophy. Cherniss argues that Aristotle distorted the ideas of the pre-Socratics either out of ignorance of their exact views or as part of an effort to promote his own metaphysics. Aristotle's references to the pre-Socratics are analyzed in detail, but the Cherniss thesis has been criticized for never deciding exactly what the pre-Socratics did believe—a necessary proof of Aristotle's alleged distortion. Alfred E. Taylor respectfully and critically reviews the subject in *Mind* 46 (1937):247–250, and so does William K. C.

Guthrie, "Aristotle as Historian," in Furley and Allen, *Studies in Presocratic Philosophy* I:239–255.

ANAXIMANDER

There are several good studies on Anaximander, the most influential Ionian. Charles Kahn, *Anaximander and the Origins of Greek Cosmology*, is a recent and much debated study. Kahn views Anaximander as the father of a scientific cosmology because of his concept of geometric organization in the universe, the balance of the elements, and cosmic periodicity. Kahn includes an interesting discussion of the *apeiron* (i.e., the unlimited), which he believes was Anaximander's *arche*, and argues for the basic unity of pre-Socratic thought about the cosmos. He supports his argument with unusually good use of evidence on the Greek medical tradition. Kahn's claim that Anaximander was a fairly sophisticated scientist has been controverted; for example, see D. R. Dicks, "Solstices, Equinoxes, and the Presocratics," in the *Journal of Hellenic Studies* 86 (1966):26–40. Dicks argues that the pre-Socratics in general cannot be considered to have been scientists and that Anaximander in particular lacked the mathematically advanced notion of the universe credited to him by Kahn. Dicks concedes that Anaximander may have understood the relatively simple idea of the solstice but argues that the mathematics he needed to comprehend the more advanced idea of the equinoxes were not developed until Philolaus in the fifth century. Paul Seligman, *The Apeiron of Anaximander: A Study of the Origin and Function of Metaphysics*, is a good review of the various meanings of *apeiron* which concludes that it was meant to be a living source of nature which presided over the cycle of development and destruction in the world. Seligman further argues that Hesiodic cosmology contributed to Anaximander's thought—and that he transposed those elements into philosophic terms. Theo G. Sinnige, *Matter and Infinity in the Presocratic Schools and Plato*, is less valuable, but it is an interesting study of the development of ideas relating to matter which descended from ancient myths and inclined philosophers to monism and those concerning infinity as it evolved from a positive *arche* to become a Pythagorean indeterminate. The most recent book-length study is Leo Sweeney, *Infinity in the Presocratics: A Bibliographical and Philosophical Study*, an excellent review of the primary evidence and secondary literature on the problem—with special attention to the writings of Anaximander. Sweeney traces the idea of the infinite from Anaximander (who thought it was a transcendent *arche*) through the Pythagoreans (who combined it with the idea of limit) and Parmenides (who opposed the idea of infinity and kept that of strict limit or determination) and the post-Parmenideans, including the atomists. The work is the first in a series of studies by Sweeney on the idea of the infinite in western thought. On a related theme Michael C. Stokes, *One and Many in Presocratic Philosophy*, is a complex, philologically oriented study on the idea that there was unity in origin and common substrate or substance. The study concludes that the Milesians were not monistic materialists, and it includes thoughtful comments concerning the analyses of Parmenides and Aristotle on the same problem.

The important articles on Anaximander include Geoffrey S. Kirk, "Some Problems in Anaximander," in the *Classic Quarterly* n.s. 5 (1955):21–38, writing on the extent of the available fragments and indirect evidence and on the question of whether Anaximander believed that the *apeiron* was an *arche*, i.e., an intermediate substance and source of innumerable worlds. Gregory Vlastos, "Equality and Justice in Early Greek Cosmologies," in *Classical Philology* 42 (1947):156–178, uses Greek medical writings to support his view that Anaximander's idea of justice and retribution did not involve a conflict between the *apeiron* and the elements but that there was only conflict between the elements themselves and that the reabsorption of the elements by the *apeiron* achieves rebalance and justice between the elements. The article is reprinted in Furley and Allen, *Studies in the Presocratic Philosophy* (pp. 56–92). The same collection (pp. 281–323) has a translation of Uvo Holscher, "Anaximander and the Beginnings of Greek Philosophy," which argues that the *apeiron* descended from Near Eastern myths about the origin of the cosmos and not from Hesiod.

THE PYTHAGOREANS

In addition to the relevant sections of the general histories (especially volume 1 of Guthrie's *History of Greek Philosophy*), there are several good recent studies of Pythagoreanism. All of them face the question of the authenticity and reliability of traditions about Pythagoras. Pythagoras left no written teachings, so the problem of reconstructing his ideas is as difficult as reconstructing the teachings of Jesus. A skeptical view of the reliability of the earliest fragments, attributed to Philolaus (fifth century B.C.), appears in Geoffrey S. Kirk and John Raven, *The Presocratic Philosophers: A Critical History with a Selection of Texts* (pp. 308–311). The authenticity of the fragments is defended by Giorgio de Santillana and W. Pitts, "Philolaus in Limbo: Or What Happened to the Pythagoreans?", in *Isis* (1951):112–120. Walter Burkert, *Lore and Science in Ancient Pythagoreanism*, is also skeptical about reestablishing the opinions of Pythagoras, but his work has useful arguments on the Pythagorean tradition, especially its religious ideas. Cornelia J. de Vogel, *Pythagoras and Early Pythagoreanism: An Interpretation of Neglected Evidence on the Philosopher Pythagoras*, critically reviews the evidence concerning Pythagoras and concludes that the evidence suffices to reconstruct the opinions of Pythagoras. De Vogel believes that he was at once a philosopher, a religious figure, and a preacher of moral reform to the people of Croton. J. A. Philip, *Pythagoras and Early Pythagoreanism*, also argues that Pythagoras had important moral and philosophical aims, but this study is hampered by inconsistent use of historical evidence. Philip uses Aristotle's remarks as the primary evidence, yet he draws conclusions about Pythagoras—a problematic procedure since Aristotle talked of the Pythagorean tradition but gave no information on Pythagoras himself. Philip also has excellent criticisms of Burkert, especially on his association of the Pythagoreans with a "shamanistic" tradition. For a critical review of Philip, see de Vogel in the *Journal of Hellenic Studies* 89 (1969):163–165. On the conflict between the two most important fifth-century schools, see John E. Raven, *Pythagoreans and Eleatics*.

HERACLITUS

The study of Heraclitus is facilitated by collections of relevant fragments with useful commentaries. Philip Wheelwright, *Heraclitus*, translates the fragments and adds comments, an introduction, and bibliographical notes. Geoffrey S. Kirk, *Heraclitus: The Cosmic Fragments*, is a more complex analysis of the texts. See also M. Marcovich, "Heracleitos," in supplementary volume 10 of the *Real-Encyclopädie* (pp. 246–320), which reviews in detail scholarship on the fragments. Abel Jeannière, *La Pensée d'Héraclite d'Éphèse et la vision présocratique du monde*, is a topical study with translations of the fragments.

PARMENIDES

Parmenides' work is analyzed by Leonardo Tarán, *Parmenides: A Text with Translation, Commentary, and Critical Essays*. Tarán also includes good comments on recent scholarship in the field. General studies include K. Reinhardt, *Parmenides und die Geschichte der griechischen Philosophie*, and W. J. Verdenius, *Parmenides: Some Comments on His Poem*, which includes a judicious consideration of various interpretations of Parmenides. Alexander P. D. Mourelatos, *The Route of Parmenides: A Study of Word, Image, and Argument in the Fragments*, argues for Parmenides' debt to the epic tradition of writing descended from Homer. Because he was part of the epic tradition of writing, Parmenides presented the search for truth in poetic terms such as "the journey" and viewed error as "wandering."

The continual stream of periodical literature on Parmenides includes the interesting articles by G. E. L. Owen, "Eleatic Questions," in the *Classical Quarterly* 54 (1960):84–102, which argues that Parmenides must be understood as a philosopher addressing philosophical questions rather than as a cosmologist; and that by Charles H. Kahn, "The Thesis of Parmenides," *Review of Metaphysics* 22 (1969), which follows Burnet's view that Parmenides was vitally interested in criticizing the physical theories of his predecessors. Kahn responds to criticisms of his argument in volume 23 (1969) of the same journal: "More on Parmenides."

EMPEDOCLES

The current state of scholarship concerning Empedocles is well summarized in Robinson, *An Introduction to Early Greek Philosophy* (chap. 8), and Guthrie, *A History of Greek Philosophy* (vol. 2, chap. 3). A fine bibliographical review of publications on this subject from 1805–1965 is included in D. O'Brien, *Empedocles' Cosmic Cycle: A Reconstruction from the Fragments and Secondary Sources*. O'Brien analyzes the Empedoclean themes of rest, movement, and the elements and concludes that strife was the only principle of movement, love the only principle of rest; the analysis of these themes initiated by Empedocles introduced the problem of the "one and the many." The first three volumes of a detailed and complex study of the fragments by Jean Bollack, *Empédocle*, are complete. Volume 1, *Introduction à l'ancienne physique*, analyzes the available evidence on Empedocles and summarizes his system; volume 2 (1969) lists and translates the texts; volumes 3 and 4 will comment on those texts in detail.

One of several important scholarly articles on Empedocles was written by Friedrich Solmsen, "Love and Strife in Empedocles' Cosmology," and appears in volume 1 (pp. 274–314) of his *Kleine Schriften* (2 vols.). Solmsen convincingly argues that Empedocles did not believe in a dual cosmos, but rather that strife built the physical cosmos while love built the living elements of the cosmos. Edwin Minar, "Cosmic Periods in the Philosophy of Empedocles" (pp. 39–58), in Anton and Kustas's *Essays in Ancient Greek Philosophy*, is also interesting. See in the same collection where Charles H. Kahn, "Religion and Natural Philosophy in Empedocles' Doctrine of the Soul" (pp. 3–39) introduces the argument that Empedocles' scientific *On Nature* and his religious *Purifications* are not necessarily contradictory. Kahn holds that Empedocles regarded the universe (hence nature) as divine just as Plato did and that both elements of his thought were eventually controlled by growing spiritual interests.

ANAXAGORAS

An excellent guide to this literature can be found in Daniel Gershenson and Daniel A. Greenberg, *Anaxagoras and the Birth of Physics*. Part 2 summarizes the ancient testimonia and part 3 reviews modern interpretations. The philosophy of Anaxagoras is well summarized in the general histories already recommended, especially in Guthrie, but there is only one book-length study in English, Felix Cleve, *The Philosophy of Anaxagoras: An Attempt at Reconstruction*, which is difficult to evaluate. Cleve covers all of the relevant material and makes many interesting suggestions concerning particular problems, but his treatment has major defects. He rejects nearly all of Aristotle's testimony as unreliable and insists on making certain points without introducing any definitive evidence. For example, Cleve believes that Anaxagoras held a theory of cosmic periodicity and denies that Anaxagoras thought the world rested on a layer of air.

A good study by Gregory Vlastos, "The Physical Theory of Anaxagoras," appeared in the *American Philosophical Review* 59 (1950):31–57. Vlastos suggests that Anaxagoras thought the universe was composed of "seeds" constituted of a mixture of "energies" in different ratios and so the universe allotted "being" to all its parts, not just to the "one," as in Parmenides' system. John Raven, "The Basis of Anaxagoras's Cosmology," in the *Classical Quarterly* 48 (1954):123–137, describes how Anaxagoras divided the world into "spheres of mind" and the "seeds and things" and how he pictured the construction of seeds (*spermata*) from the "portions" (*moira*). D. Bargrave-Weaver, "The Cosmology of Anaxagoras," *Phronesis* 4 (1959):77–79, concentrates on the mixture of causes governing the development of the cosmos to its present state and not on the basic elements. See also Margaret E. Reesor, "The Problem of Anaxagoras" (pp. 81–87), in Anton and Kustas's *Essays in Ancient Greek Philosophy*, for a discussion of how Anaxagoras attempted to show that sense impressions could provide reliable knowledge about the world.

THE ATOMISTS

The general histories' comments on atomism should be supplemented by Cyril Bailey, *Greek Atomists and Epicurus*, which focuses on Epicurus and devotes the first three chapters to the antecedents of atomism. David J. Furley, *Two Studies in the Greek Atomists*, concentrates on Epicurus and the conflict between his philosophy and Aristotle's. Furley's "Study I" concerns the atomism of the pre-Socratics and the question of infinite divisibility. Thomas Cole, *Democritus and the Sources of Greek Anthropology*, is an interesting special study which attempts to reconstruct the anthropology of Democritus on the basis of later writings. Cole argues that Democritus believed in the evolution of humanity from a bestial to a civilized level and considered the development of philosophy and technology to be important to that evolution. This argument is inconclusive because of the paucity of the available evidence, but Cole contributes to the theory that the ancient Greeks thought in terms of progressive evolution. The same general theme is emphasized by Eric Havelock (see p. 82). Also compare Cole with Gregory Vlastos, "Ethics and Physics in Democritus," in the *Philosophical Review* 54 (1945):578–592 and 55 (1946):53–64. Vlastos argues that Democritus developed a coherent ethical theory based on his physics and rejected romantic notions of love and strife as governors of the universe in seeking an objective standard of balance and justice. This in turn gave Democritus an effective answer to Protagoras, who charged that human opinion alone determines justice.

The best study of the sophists is Maria Untersteiner, *The Sophists*, a summary and interpretation of the life, writings, and doctrines of each sophist. Untersteiner has been criticized for underestimating the critical skeptical propensities of the sophists and for exaggerating their interest in cosmology. Her work is still a provocative and informative introduction to the field. Untersteiner can be supplemented by William K. C. Guthrie, "The World of the Sophists," in volume 3, part 1, of *A History of Greek Philosophy*, available in paperback.

Socrates

Nearly all studies of Plato deal with Socrates and the development of his philosophy. The real Socrates is difficult to separate from idealized impressions of him as they appear in the dialogues of Plato. The literature recommended for the study of Plato is therefore helpful in studying Socrates. A few general works which concentrate on Socrates are also helpful. Alfred E. Taylor, *Socrates,* briefly reviews his life and opinions. Gregory Vlastos has edited *The Philosophy of Socrates: A Collection of Critical Essays,* a fine collection of scholarly articles. The first three essays by Vlastos, A. R. Lacy, and K. J. Dover reconstruct the real opinions of Socrates and the remaining articles describe his philosophical work and influence on Plato. The best recent account of Socratic philosophy is Norman Gulley, *The Philosophy of Socrates,* which treats the Socratic *elenchus,* the unity of the virtues, and the paradox inherent in equating knowledge and virtue. Gulley judiciously weighs the evidence in Plato's dialogues and the writings of Aristotle. Finally, a review of later interpretations of Socrates in western philosophy is found in M. A. Raschini, *Interpretazioni socratiche.*

Plato

Bibliographical Resources

All of the general bibliographies, nonserial and serial, on the history of the ancient world and the history of ancient philosophy have separate sections devoted to Plato. The Plato section in *L' Année philologique* (part 1) and Wilhelm Totok, *Handbuch der Geschichte der Philosophie* 1:146–212, are worth special reference. There are other bibliographies devoted solely to the study of Plato. One of the Bibliographische Einfuhrungen in das Studium der Philosophie series, Olof Gigon, *Platon,* is useful but somewhat out of date. The best introductory bibliography on Plato for English-reading students is the annotated guide in Robert S. Brumbaugh, *Plato for the Modern Age* (pp. 237–252). There is a reasonably good bibliography classified according to general areas of Plato's philosophical interest in *Plato: A Collection of Critical Essays,* edited by Gregory Vlastos (vol. 1, pp.

305–312, and vol. 2, pp. 274–278). In addition Paul Friedländer, *Introduction to Plato* (vols. 2 and 3), has bibliographies devoted to each of the dialogues.

The more complex studies of Plato include the magnificent surveys of recent Platonic scholarship by Harold Cherniss, *Lustrum* 4 (1959) and 5 (1960), and T. B. Rosenmeyer, "Platonic Scholarship: 1945–1955," in the *Classical Weekly* 50 (1957):173 ff. E. Manasse, *Bucher über Platon* (2 vols.), first appeared as supplements to the journal *Philosophische Rundschau*. Joseph Owens, "Recent Footnotes to Plato," in the *Review of Metaphysics* 20(1967):648–661), chiefly reviews the works of Crombie and Ryle (see p. 40 below) and makes some general remarks on the present state of Plato scholarship.

The history of scholarship devoted to the study of Plato is a complex and fascinating field. There is a good résumé in J. Geffchen, *Griechische Literaturgeschichte* 2:137–144, in the collected notes for the volume. See also Pierre Schuhl, "Vingt années d'études platoniciennes: 1938–1958," in *Études platoniciennes*.

Critical Editions and Translations

There are numerous anthologies, selections, and complete editions, translated and untranslated, which include the writings of Plato. Scholars who wish to consult Greek texts can use the five-volume Oxford Classical Texts edition of John Burnet, *Platonis Opera*, or the Loeb Classical Library edition by H. N. Fowler, W. R. M. Lamb, R. B. Bury, and Paul Shorey in 12 volumes. Less advanced students may consult several convenient collections. One of the most popular collections is that of Edith Hamilton and Huntington Cairns, *The Collected Dialogues Including the Letters*, which compiles scholarly translations of the various dialogues. One of the older standard collections is Benjamin Jowett, *The Dialogues of Plato* (4 vols.), first published in 1871 and recently reprinted. Jowett's English usage is somewhat out of date, but his translation has introductory comments of generally high quality. The Clarendon Press reprint was reedited to bring Jowett up to date. The Library of Liberal Arts reprints and sponsors translations and commentaries on the important dialogues by eminent scholars which are cited below under each special area of Platonic thought.

General Introductions

All of the general histories of philosophy, ancient philosophy, and Greek thought give major attention to Plato as the founder of western philosophical speculation. The most general histories include Copleston,

A History of Philosophy, which devotes volume 1, part 1, chapters 17–26, to an accurate and balanced résumé of Plato's writings and ideas. Surveys of ancient philosophy include Armstrong's *Introduction to Ancient Philosophy* (chaps. 4, 5, and 6) and Owens's *A History of Ancient Western Philosophy* (chaps. 10–12). These are succinct studies, but there is no reason to use them in place of Copleston's fuller treatment. Students should, however, read Windelband's account of Plato's thought in his *History of Ancient Philosophy* (chap. 5): "Materialism and Idealism—Democritus and Plato." John Burnet, one of the greatest modern Plato scholars, devotes chapters 12–17, part 3, of his *Greek Philosophy I: Thales to Plato* to Plato. The student should, however, remember that Burnet argues that the earlier dialogues are historically accurate accounts of Socrates' real opinions, a position no longer supported by many scholars. Several chapters of the topically organized *Plato and the Older Academy* by Eduard Zeller will be recommended below under each special area of Plato's thought. Theodor Gomperz, *Greek Thinkers* (vol. 2, book 5, and vol. 3), largely organized according to the dialogues, and Benjamin A. G. Fuller, *A History of Greek Philosophy* (vol. 2), are less essential but worth consulting for their clear and detailed accounts.

It is not feasible to cite more than a few selected general studies on the career and philosophy of Plato. The following references cover Plato's intellectual development and represent a full range of general scholarly interpretation. Alexander Koyré, *Discovering Plato*, is a good starting point for students because it explains Plato's use of the dialogue to guide his readers to the discovery of knowledge while avoiding the dissemination of dogma. Alfred E. Taylor, *The Mind of Plato*, is an older and able reference for beginners. Taylor's most significant attempt to reconstruct the probable order of composition of Plato's dialogues is found in *Plato, the Man and His Work*. Paul Shorey, *What Plato Said*, synthesizes the contents of the dialogues and has invaluable cross references for each major idea plus excellent bibliographical notes. Shorey's *The Unity of Plato's Thought* is a clear synopsis. The latter title indicates that Shorey is a proponent of the idea that there was an essential unity in Plato's philosophy throughout his career. Rupert C. Lodge, *The Philosophy of Plato*, is not clearly written; nonetheless, it is valuable because it systematically compares the opinions of Plato and his predecessors on each important topic and it has an appendix which responds to some of the recent scholarly criticisms of Plato. Guy C. Field also treats the connection between Plato and his contemporaries in *Plato and His Contemporaries: A Study in Fourth Century Life and Thought* and *The Philosophy of Plato*. The latter work is brought up to date with an appendix by R. C. Cross. Two recent surveys are especially suitable for beginners. Robert S. Brumbaugh, *Plato for the Modern Age*, is an exceptionally clear presentation with unusual emphasis on Plato's and the Academy's interest in mathematics and the sciences. Raphael Demos,

The Philosophy of Plato, is a more advanced, topically organized survey; part 1 is on Plato's idea of "reality"; part 2, on "appearance"; and part 3, on "man." This survey is thus based on the crucial issues of Plato's epistemology and metaphysics. The best of the less advanced introductions to Plato is G. M. Grube, *Plato's Thought.* Grube introduces the chief themes of Plato's philosophy in delightfully clear prose style. His treatments of pleasure and *eros* (chaps. 2 and 3), the gods (chap. 5), and education (chap. 7) are best.

Paul Friedländer, *Plato: An Introduction,* is a multivolume survey of the career, writings, and ideas of Plato. Volumes 2 and 3 treat the individual dialogues. The work is well documented and it includes interesting comments on modern philosophers such as Heidegger and Jaspers. There is a valuable addendum to volume 1 by Huntington Cairns, "Plato as a Jurist" (pp. 286–314).

One of the best of the multivolume studies of Plato is Ian M. Crombie, *An Examination of Plato's Doctrines* (2 vols.). Volume 1 of this detailed and carefully written study covers "Man and Society"; volume 2, "Knowledge and Reality." According to Crombie Plato's dialogues are not an exposition of a finished system of thought, but rather they demonstrate an appropriate methodology for inquiry and provide tentative solutions to philosophical problems. Crombie's position is well argued and he uses recent philosophy and linguistic studies to explicate Plato's meanings and his problems. A shortened and simplified version of his work is found in *Plato: The Midwife's Apprentice.*

Two older works on Platonic scholarship have been largely superseded by more recent studies but are still monuments of erudition and progress in the study of ancient thought. George Grote, *Plato and the Other Companions of Sokrates* (4 vols.), devotes volume 1 to Plato's life and predecessors and the remaining volumes to detailed studies of each dialogue. Ulrich von Wilamowitz-Moellendorff made important contributions to nearly all areas of the study of ancient Greek culture; see *Platon* (2 vols.). Volume 1 covers the life and works of Plato; volume 2 has textual criticisms and commentaries on the dialogues.

Two other major scholars, Gilbert Ryle and John Herman Randall, have done interesting and provocative studies of Plato, but they must be used with caution by the beginner because they introduce highly controversial theories about Plato's ideas and development. Ryle, *Plato's Progress,* plausibly and skeptically argues that the purported letters of Plato, including the famous "Seventh Letter," are not authentic and contain little legitimate information on the life of Plato. He departs from the generally accepted interpretations and reconstructs the life of Plato and develops a highly controversial theory of the course of Plato's career and thought. Ryle suggests that Plato's philosophy had little direct influence on the development of Aristotle's thought. He argues that the Academy was not founded until late in Plato's career and he attributes its procedures to Aristotle rather than to Plato. Ryle further argues that Plato's original philosophic method was not dialectic but merely a recitation of dialogues in which Plato played the part of Socrates. This style of recitation (which was used at various festivals) apparently ended in some kind of legal action against Plato. Subsequently Plato and his disciples (probably including Aristotle) made several important trips to Sicily. Ryle's overall argument tends to deny the fixed character of Plato's philosophy, declares that Aristotle was essentially independent of Plato, and makes reconstruction of Plato's career and philosophical intent a fair procedure for any scholar (see A. Wasserstein's review in *Philosophical Books* 8 (1967):23–27). Partly inspired by Ryle's procedure and conclusions, John Herman Randall also devised an interpretation of Plato's philosophy in *Plato: Dramatist of the Life of Reason*. Randall is also skeptical about traditional sources for the life of Plato and argues that Plato had no system of metaphysics or at least did not expound such a system in his dialogues. He concludes that the world of forms was really an artistic and dramatic representation of Plato's perfect life toward which all people ought to strive; thus, Plato's ideal was not another world but rather a process of perfecting human character and one's own life. Randall understood the Greek ideal to mean that life is a work of art requiring the greatest skill and self-discipline. Chapter 16 treats immortality by arguing that Plato believed it is achieved in human thought and art and not in an eternity of "twanging harps." This idea of immortality is an appealing one, but Randall is probably wrong in believing that Plato conceived of immortality in this way.

Eric A. Havelock, *Preface to Plato*, is stimulating. Havelock argues that Plato devised written, abstract categories for intellectual discourse in place of the primarily oral tradition—thus he credits Plato with completing the process begun by the pre-Socratics. The oral tradition was voiced in poetic expressions of particular and concrete concepts and was used to teach by example. Plato's "prose" method sought to communicate in terms of abstract categories and relied on the force of undeniable reason in teaching. Plato's strictures on the role of poets in the actual as well as the ideal society can be understood only in terms of this process in the history of Greek society. Robert E. Cushman, *Therapeia: Plato's Concept of Philosophy*, suggests that moral conversion was a precursor to the achievement of understanding in Plato's system—i.e., to Plato, metaphysical knowledge was not only logical, it was decisional. He believed, according to Cushman, that the promise and example of philosophical knowledge could inspire the moral conversion and commitment needed to achieve understanding; thus philosophy was considered therapy to redress the inverted values of the average person. Cushman's study largely reverses Plato's feeling that knowledge caused virtue and was coeval with it, yet it illuminates virtually every aspect of Plato's ideas and focuses attention on Plato's undoubted interest in morality.

The *Republic* is a clear and complete résumé of the middle period of Plato's philosophical development, so several commentaries are recommended as introductions to Plato's entire philosophy. Richard L. Nettleship, *Lectures on the "Republic" of Plato*, is still valuable. Francis M. Cornford's translation of the *Republic*, a magnificent work with excellent explanatory notes, and Robert C. Cross and A. D. Woozley, *Plato's Republic": A Philosophical Commentary*, which carefully and judiciously discusses every major issue, are better references for student use.

One persisting problem in Platonic studies involves Aristotle's accounts of Plato's doctrines, which sometimes differ from the doctrines presented in the dialogues. Harold Cherniss, an American scholar, has exhaustively studied Aristotle's comments on Plato and the Academy and his now classic study concludes that Aristotle is an unreliable source of information about Plato and for the pre-Socratics as well (see p. 31 above). His argument appears in *Aristotle's Criticism of Plato and the Academy* (vol. 1), reviewed critically in *Mind* 55 (1946):263–272. Also see *The Riddle of the Early Academy*. In the latter work Cherniss comments on the tendency of scholarly interpretations of Plato's "Lecture on the Good" to believe that Plato developed a different set of doctrines in lecture than he did in the dialogues. Scholars thus try to explain the discrepancies between Aristotle's and the dialogues' accounts of Plato's teachings, i.e., they argue that Aristotle referred to the real teachings developed in the lectures. Cherniss, however, denies that Plato taught by lectures to the Academy or taught any esoteric doctrine. The arguments he develops are frequently qualified and disputed by other scholars, but the two books are invariably considered to be indispensable for the study of Plato. The question of whether there was a "Lecture on the Good" and an esoteric doctrine persists and a recent reconsideration appears in Hans J. Krämer, *Arete bei Platon und Aristoteles: zum Wesen und zur Geschichte der Platonischen Ontologie*. Krämer's wide-ranging and complex argument asserts there was a "Lecture on the Good" and that it was a verbal teaching behind all of the dialogues. Krämer also argues that Plato's philosophy was unified with the Parmenidean tradition of the "one" from the start. He saw the universe as a conflict of the "one"—i.e., unity—and the forces of disunity. The forms were devised later by Plato to mediate between them. Krämer includes an excellent review of the scholarly controversy surrounding the "Lecture on the Good." Krämer has by no means persuaded a majority of scholars that there was a body of esoteric teachings behind the dialogues, but he has reopened the question and presented a most sophisticated argument.

Collections of Critical Essays

The most recent collection in English was edited by Gregory Vlastos, *Plato: A Collection of Critical Essays* (2 vols.). Volume 1 is devoted to

"Metaphysics and Epistemology," volume 2 to "Ethics, Politics, and the Philosophy of Art and Religion." An older, still useful, collection is that edited by Ingemar Düring and G. E. L. Owen, *Aristotle and Plato in the Mid-Fourth Century*. The articles in this work deal with the evolution of Aristotle's thought and nearly all of them are valuable sources of information on Plato.

Epistemology and Metaphysics

The general histories of ancient philosophy and introductions to the philosophy of Plato all devote considerable attention to Plato's epistemology (i.e., his theory of how knowledge is gained) and to his metaphysics, especially to the crucial issue of his theory of the forms. Frederich Copleston typically provides a sound introduction in his *A History of Philosophy* (vol. 1, part 1); chapter 19, "The Theory of Knowledge," and chapter 20, "The Doctrine of Forms," are especially useful. Windelband's *A History of Ancient Philosophy* (chap. 5) places the epistemological and metaphysical issues within a broader context of alternative theories, and Zeller's *Plato and the Older Academy* (chap. 6) is a magnificent summary of Plato's *"Dialectic or the Doctrine of Ideas."* An introduction to Plato with a detailed and judicious analysis of his epistemology and metaphysics is Ian Crombie, *An Examination of Plato's Doctrines;* see volume 2, part 1, "Theory of Knowledge," and parts 3 and 4, "Metaphysics and Logic." The treatment of this general subject in Robert C. Cross and A. D. Woozley, *Plato's Republic": A Philosophic Commentary,* is also valuable.

Perhaps the best introduction to Plato's epistemology is Norman Gulley, *Plato's Theory of Knowledge*. Gulley argues that Plato's epistemology evolved from a theory of recollection outlined in the *Meno,* became a more critical questioning of the effects of sensible objects on the process of understanding, and finally focused on mathematics as the most reliable form of knowledge. The consistent theme in Plato's writings is his evident distrust of the senses and material reality; however, the antidotes he suggested to overcome the baleful influence of matter varied throughout his career. Walter G. Runciman, *Plato's Later Epistemology,* also argues that Plato's epistemology evolved. He considers the *Theaetetus* and the *Sophist* to be Plato's most sophisticated and serious efforts to solve the problem of the best sources of knowledge. The *Theaetetus* and the *Sophist* are also the center of interest in Francis M. Cornford's argument that there was an essential continuity in Plato's theory of knowledge. See the excellent notes and commentary in Cornford's *Plato's Theory of Knowledge: The "Theaetetus" and the "Sophist" of Plato Translated with a Running Commentary.*

The question of logic and Plato's method of thinking about experience is discussed in a general study by Kenneth M. Sayre, *Plato's Analytic Method*. Sayre reviews the methods used in all of the dialogues and he finds Plato's most mature method (that of "collection and division") in the *Sophist*. Sayre makes extensive use of modern logical analysis in his explanation of Plato's method. Richard Robinson, *Plato's Earlier Dialectic*, is an argument that in the *Republic* Plato believed hypothetical reasoning would help the philosopher to overcome the distorting effects of sense data and lead him to further provisional inferences about reality; by the time Plato wrote the *Parmenides*, however, he believed hypotheses were inadequate means to the truth. In later dialogues he preferred the logical method of "division." Robinson's argument is criticized in Thomas Rosenmeyer's article, "Plato's Hypothesis and the Upward Path," in John P. Anton and George L. Kustas, *Essays in Ancient Greek Philosophy* (pp. 354–367). A valuable older work by a masterful scholar, Wincenty Lutoslawski, *The Origin and Growth of Plato's Logic*, is a source of information on all relevant citations from the dialogues. Many excellent references to Plato's logic appear in the general surveys recommended above, especially see Kneale, Bochenski, Kapp, and Lloyd, *Polarity and Analogy* (see p. 26).

John Raven, *Plato's Thought in the Making: A Study of the Development of His Metaphysics*, is the best introduction to Plato's metaphysics. Raven suggests that Plato's metaphysics developed away from the starting place provided by Socrates to become a mature—but never completely satisfactory—doctrine of the ideas or forms. Raven emphasizes the middle dialogues (part 2) in an interesting discussion of Plato's three allegories, i.e., the sun, the divided line, and the cave. Raven interprets the allegories to be a discussion of the contents of the intelligible world, the world of the forms which transcend the material world, rather than a discussion of the intelligible and material worlds together. W. David Ross, *Plato's Theory of Ideas*, argues that Plato's thought evolved from an original belief inherited from Socrates that the forms are immanent (i.e., confined to the material or sensible world) to a belief that the forms are transcendent. Ross believes that this theory never completely satisfied Plato. Julius Stenzel, *Plato's Method of Dialectic*, also argues for an evolution in Plato's thought about the forms. Stenzel believes that Plato (following Socrates) first regarded the theory of the forms as a hypothesis. In the later dialogues, however, he regarded the forms as existing independently and capable of being comprehended by the logical method of division into classes. William F. R. Hardie, *A Study in Plato*, convincingly argues that Plato meant that the forms were separable and transcendent. Hardie also asserts that the neo-Platonist interpretation of the highest good as transcending all descriptions and particular forms of existence correctly represented Plato's position. John A. Stewart, *Plato's Doctrine of Ideas*, takes a fundamentally different position. Stewart interprets Plato in Kantian terms. He suggests that the forms or ideas are significant in the dialogues because they are first "points of view," that is, methods of discourse useful in organizing changing human experience under general categories or rules. The forms are elements of human understanding and aspiration rather than self-existing archetypes above the flux of the material world. The forms are also aesthetically useful since they are idealized versions of experience.

Other studies concentrate on the *Parmenides*, which is perhaps the most important of the metaphysical dialogues. Francis M. Cornford, *Plato and Parmenides*, has an excellent translation and commentary on the dialogue (and on Parmenides' "Way of Truth"). Robert S. Brumbaugh, *Plato on the One*, reproduces the text with a translation and excellent comments focused on the central problems of the dialogue. Brumbaugh is more difficult to read than Cornford, but his careful organization and sympathetic evaluation of Plato make this a valuable book. W. F. Lynch, *An Approach to the Metaphysics of Plato through the Parmenides*, is an informative study centered on alternative hypotheses in the dialogue. Lynch covers the major issues involved in interpreting the *Parmenides* and his extensive footnotes provide a general idea of the scholarly dispute in the field. He emphasizes Plato's thoughts on "participation" as a mediating element between being and nonbeing. Unfortunately Lynch's work is not always clear since he tends to employ jargon at important points. Volume 1 of Gregory Vlastos, *Plato, A Collection of Critical Essays* (2 vols.), is a valuable collection of articles on Plato's epistemology and metaphysics with many comments on the *Parmenides*. The chief scholarly interpretations of the dialogue are reviewed by Walter G. Runciman, "Plato's *Parmenides*" (pp. 149–185), in Reginald B. Allen, *Studies in Plato's Metaphysics*. Also see Harold F. Cherniss, "The Philosophical Economy of the Theory of Ideas" (pp. 1–13), in Reginald E. Allen, *Studies in Plato's Metaphysics*, which visualizes the theory of the forms as an attempt to "save the phenomena" and provide a stable standard for the judgment of sensations about physical objects. This standard parallels similar attempts in ethics and epistemology.

Cosmology and Mathematics: Plato and Science

A continuing scholarly dispute exists in evaluating Plato's attitude toward science, specifically his role in helping or hindering its development. Most historians in the field believe that he hindered the development of science. The strongest indictment is expressed in all of Benjamin Farrington's writings but most succinctly in *Greek Science* (chap. 7) (see below, p. 91–92, on Farrington and the following histories of science). According to Farrington, Plato was the spokesman for certain elements in Greek society which opposed the development of technology and considered manual labor degrading. An equally strong condemnation of Plato's influence in retarding the development of science is expressed by

George Sarton, *A History of Science* 1:395–431 (see the critical review by J. Haden, "The Challenge of the History of Science, I," in the *Review of Metaphysics* 7 [1953]:74–88). Less critical comments are found in René Taton, *History of Science* 1:217–227, "Plato and the Sophists," and in Marshall Clagett, *Greek Science in Antiquity* (part 1).

Some valiant—and ultimately unsuccessful—efforts have been made to save Plato from the charge of being antiscientific or even unscientific. These works emphasize Plato's great interest in mathematics and its value in his effort to describe reality. They also cite his injunction in the *Timaeus* to use astronomy to find the philosophically best statements about the heavens consistent with observed facts. Robert S. Brumbaugh, who is personally interested in Plato's mathematics, makes a case in defense of Plato in his "Plato and the History of Science," *Studium Generale* 9 (1961):520–529, and in *Plato for the Modern Age*, part 3, especially chapter 6, "Science in the Academy." Another defense of Plato centered on his use of mathematics is Paul Shorey, "Platonism and the History of Science," in the *Proceedings of the American Philosophical Society* 66 (1927):159–182. See also Guy C. Field, "Plato and Natural Science," in *Philosophy* 8 (1933):131–141, and Ludwig Edelstein, "Platonism or Aristotelianism," in the *Bulletin of the History of Medicine* 8 (1940):757–769. The best balanced view of the question is perhaps found in Geoffrey E. R. Lloyd, "Plato as a Natural Scientist," in the *Journal of Hellenic Studies* 88 (1968):78–93. Lloyd agrees that Plato contributed to science and that he accepted the study of nature as part of a study of reason in the material world. Nor did Plato's preference for reason over observation lack compensating benefits for science (as the later theories of Galileo and other scientists amply prove). It is true, however, that Plato considered the material world, whether judged by reason or by observation, to be inferior and thus unlikely to justify the development of science in the full sense of the term.

Plato discussed the character and importance of mathematical knowledge in several dialogues, but the *Timaeus* comes closest to being a treatise on science. Alfred E. Taylor, *A Commentary on Plato's "Timaeus,"* is an exegesis of immense erudition which suggests that Plato meant the *Timaeus* as a metaphor rather than a literal description of the universe and that Plato's science combined Pythagorean religion and mathematics wth the biology of Empedocles. Taylor's interpretation is criticized as an attempt to convert Plato into a modern scientist in the introduction to Francis M. Cornford, *Plato's Cosmology. The "Timaeus" of Plato Translated with a Running Commentary.*

Plato's mathematical thought can be plausibly regarded either as part of his metaphysics or part of his science and cosmology. Robert S. Brumbaugh, *Plato's Mathematical Imagination: The Mathematical Passages in the Dialogues and Their Interpretation*, is a clear introduction to the subject which illustrates the use of mathematics throughout Plato's philosophical system. Anders Wedberg, *Plato's Philosophy of Mathematics*, is an even better short résumé emphasizing the connection between Plato's mathematics and his theory of ideas (see the fine summary in chap. 3). Wedberg considers that Plato probably believed in mathematical ideas as intermediate objects between the forms and the sensible world. Edward A. Maziarz and Thomas Greenwood, *Greek Mathematical Philosophy*, devote part 2 to the "Mathematical Ontology of Plato." François Lasserre, *The Birth of Mathematics in the Age of Plato*, is strongest in its discussion of Eudoxus (d. 338 B.C.), but chapter 3 has much information on Plato's theory of geometry.

Psychology and Ethics

The general surveys of ancient philosophy and introductions to the philosophy of Plato all deal with his psychology and ethics, but they treat his ethics better than they deal with his psychology. Copleston, *A History of Philosophy* (vol. 1, part 1), is an exception which treats the psychology of Plato and his ethical theories in chapters 21 and 22, respectively. Paul Shorey, *The Unity of Plato's Thought*, surveys the two fields in section 3 (pp. 40–49) on psychology and section 1 (pp. 9–27) on ethics. Eduard Zeller, *Plato and the Older Academy* (chaps. 10 and 11), emphasizes the link between Plato's ideas of individual virtue and the good state. Rupert C. Lodge, *The Philosophy of Plato* (chaps. 4 and 5), summarizes Plato's ethics using Lodge's excellent technique which juxtaposes the opinions of Plato and his predecessors. Ian Crombie, *An Examination of Plato's Doctrines* (vol. 1, chaps. 6 and 7), and Alasdair MacIntyre, *A Short History of Ethics* (chaps. 4, 5, and 6), concentrate on Plato's ethical ideas expressed in the *Gorgias* and the *Republic*.

Further information on Plato's psychology is available in George Brett, *A History of Psychology: Ancient and Patristic* (chaps. 7, 8, and 9), and Anthelme Chaignet, *Histoire de la psychologie des Grecs* (vol. 1, chap. 22). Also see T. M. Robinson, *Plato's Psychology*, for a sound, systematic survey of Plato's references to the soul (including valuable comments on the world soul mentioned in the *Timaeus*). Robinson contributes little to an understanding of cognition or moral decisions since he does not deal at length with the functions of the soul or the related psychological elements.

An effective study by Rupert C. Lodge, *Plato's Theory of Ethics*, is devoted solely to Plato's theory of ethics. Lodge reviews the objects of Plato's ethical interest and his criteria for determining ethical values, then considers which of 24 concepts expressed in the dialogues represented Plato's highest ethical good. He concludes that behavior which promotes an ideal by harmonizing the elements in concrete situations into organic wholes is Plato's ideal—Plato meant that the highest potential of each person should be realized in unison with others. Scholars criticize Lodge's choice and suggest that he underrates the degree to which Plato's ethical thought evolved throughout his career. John Gould, *The Development of Plato's Ethics*, treats the importance of the idea of the morally good as it evolved from the individual to the community as a unit of moral discourse and as it developed from relative optimism to relative pessimism concerning the power of moral choice. Gould emphasizes an analysis of the *Meno* and the *Republic*. See also Gould, *Platonic Love*, which argues that Plato considered love to be an emotional means of apprehending the good and a necessary concomitant of reason in a search for truth—indeed Plato defined reason as the most intense of desires. Gould uses that combination of emotion and logic to seek an explanation of the Socratic paradoxes and an identification of knowledge and virtue. Plato's idea of love is compared with the Christian, Romantic, and Freudian ideas. Michael J. O'Brien, *The Socratic Paradoxes and the Greek Mind*, reviews the general background of the development of Plato's ethics and then turns to an argument directed against such scholars as Eric R. Dodds. Dodds and other scholars argue that Plato's ethics developed first the belief that virtue is knowledge and then a gloomier view that human nature permits perverse actions. Following Shorey and others, O'Brien denies that there was a basic evolution in the development of Plato's ethics. According to O'Brien the *Republic* represented Plato's mature position, and it made self-control induced by both character and education a prerequisite to an enlightened morality. O'Brien argues that Plato maintained this position throughout his later career.

Plato's ethics are discussed in commentaries on the *Republic*. See especially H. W. B. Joseph, *The Form of the Good in Plato's "Republic,"* and Neville R. Murphy, *The Interpretation of Plato's "Republic."* Murphy's interpretation of Plato's metaphysics has been criticized, but his treatment of Plato's "real interest" as an internal link between moral life, individual happiness, and freedom is excellent. John A. Stewart, *Plato's Doctrine of Ideas*, is an important treatment of the study of Plato's ethics. Stewart argues that the forms were meant to galvanize moral action rather than to literally describe reality. The closely related theme of educational theory is treated in Rupert C. Lodge, *Plato's Theory of Education;* especially see the appendix by S. Frank on the "Education of Women according to Plato." Richard L. Nettleship, *The Theory of Education in the "Republic" of Plato*, is an outstanding study of the topic by one of the great teachers of Plato's doctrines. John E. Adamson, *The Theory of Education in Plato's "Republic,"* is an older but valuable survey of the same material. Eric Havelock, *Preface to Plato*, has a valuable, interesting, and informative albeit unconvincing argument that Plato's work represented a new approach to education based on written and abstract reasoning as compared to the oral, poetic, and concrete "education" provided in older Greek traditions.

Political Theory

The philosophy of Plato involved political ideals and practice, so all of the general surveys of ancient philosophy discuss his political ideas. The student would be well advised, however, to forego reading the general sources and consult surveys directly focused on Plato's political theory. Two exceptions are Copleston, *A History of Philosophy* (vol. 1, part 1, chap. 23), which accurately summarizes Plato's political theory and emphasizes the close relationship of his political ideas to his ethical ideas, and Ian Crombie, *An Examination of Plato's Doctrines* (vol. 1, chaps. 3 and 4), on *The Republic, The Stateman,* and *The Laws.*

Similarly, it is not necessary to spend much time consulting the general histories of political theory in the West and in the ancient world (see p. 158 ff. below). T. A. Sinclair, *A History of Greek Political Thought* (chaps. 7–10), is a useful summary of the development of Plato's chief ideas, but students will find more fruitful the masterful survey by Ernest Barker, *Greek Political Theory: Plato and His Predecessors,* (chaps. 6–17). Chapters 8–11 are an excellent summary and critique of the *Republic* and the thin appendix on the "Later History of Plato's Political Theory" is interesting. There is an exceptionally detailed examination of relevant sources in Erik Wolf, *Griechische Rechtsdenken;* see volume 3, part 1, chapter 1, on Socrates and volume 4, parts 1 and 3, on Plato.

Two works dealing with Plato's attitude toward the individual have recently appeared. This issue is important to a general understanding of Plato and because Plato's political theory is the subject of consistent charges that he scorned the ordinary individual and was only concerned with the welfare of the elite. The two studies are Robert W. Hall, *Plato and the Individual,* and H. D. Rankin, *Plato and the Individual.* Hall's work is an erudite study of the dialogues which concludes that Plato began with an aristocratic ideal of the individual based on *arete* (the sum of good qualities that produce character) which became a relatively democratic or "demotic" theory. Hall suggests that in the end Plato's idea of special philosophic virtue became moribund and that he took a position compatible with modern individualism. Hall does not sustain his argument, but the work is nonetheless a most interesting and informative study of the dialogues, especially the *Republic.* Rankin's work comments on Plato and Greek society in general, with provocative chapters on "Man, Woman, and Eros" and "Old Age, Thanatos, and Last Things" plus a wide range of anthropological and psychological data from outside classical Greece. He argues that Plato was interested not only in the structure of the ideal state but also in the renewal of the individual in the imperfect state.

In addition to the general works a number of studies are devoted solely to Plato's political theory. Jean Luccioni, *La Pensée politique de Platon*, is a competent general study with an excellent bibliography (pp. 323–331). Luccioni considers the personal, historical, philosophical, and religious factors which influenced Plato's political philosophy. Many recent discussions of Plato's political theory charge that he was an authoritarian and thus a precursor of the totalitarian movements that have plagued the modern world. Plato allegedly did not advocate the dignity and rights of the individual as nineteenth-century historians assumed but instead opposed the basic principles of liberalism. One of the first works to accuse Plato of these political faults was Richard H. S. Crossman, *Plato Today*, but the chief exponent of the charge is undoubtedly Karl Popper, who developed his argument in volume 1 of *The Open Society and Its Enemies* (2 vols.). Popper argues that Plato's political theory was an attempt to protect the privileges of the Greek elite, who elevated the rights of noble birth and wealth and opposed social change. Popper suggests that there was a direct, logical, and causal link between Plato's philosophy and such movements as Naziism. Such attacks on Plato have produced heated controversy. The arguments are collected in an anthology by Thomas L. Thorsen, *Plato: Totalitarian or Democrat?* The best collection, edited by Remford Bambrough, *Popper and Politics: Some Contributions to a Modern Controversy*, has especially good articles: Popper's apologia, directed chiefly against Levinson (pp. 323–343); H. B. Acton, "The Alleged Fascism of Plato" (pp. 38–49), an excellent defense of Plato; Guy C. Field, "On Misunderstanding Plato" (pp. 71–85); and the review of Popper's *Open Society* by John Plamenatz (pp. 136–146). The controversy is also reviewed by V. Goldschmidt, *Platonism et pensée contemporaine*, "Les Querelles sur le Platonisme" (pp. 135–265), and Popper's theory is attacked by William C. Greene, "Platonism and Its Critics," in *Harvard Studies in Classical Philology* 61 (1953):39–71. A criticism of Plato which differs with Popper can be found in Alban D. Winspear, *The Genesis of Plato's Thought*. Winspear argues that Plato represented the middle classes, not the aristocracy. His work is an excellent treatment of the general and Greek background to Plato's political theory, with discussions of "The Conservative Philosophy" (pp. 75–111), which links Plato to Pythagoreanism, and "The Progressive Philosophy" (pp. 112–160). Other attacks on Plato's social views can also be found in the work of critics interested in the retarding effect Plato had on the development of ancient science (see pp. 88–90 above).

Plato's critics, especially Popper, have prompted several spirited defenses. The best of them may be Ronald B. Levinson, *In Defense of Plato*, which reviews and criticizes all of the attacks on Plato. Levinson chiefly defends Plato against specific charges and does not attempt to demonstrate the positive value of his political philosophy. John Wild's *Plato's*

Theory of Man: An Introduction to the Realistic Philosophy of Culture and *Plato's Modern Enemies and the Theory of Nature Law* attempt to prove there is a positive connection between Plato and modern liberalism. Wild suggests that the metaphysical realism of Plato and Aristotle provided an ontological foundation for the subsequent development of natural law theories which constituted a rational system logically opposed to the "will-worship" and subjectivity typical of the German idealism that was the nursery of modern totalitarianism. In defense of Plato see also Francis M. Cornford, "The Marxist View of Ancient Philosophy," in *The Unwritten Philosophy and Other Essays* (1942):117–138, and Lazlo G. Versenyi, "Plato and His Liberal Opponents," in *Philosophy* 46 (1971):222–236. According to Versenyi Plato preferred a system of constitutional government basically similar to those of modern liberal democracies, aside from his discussion of an ideal state under a philosopher king. Versenyi notes that Plato's willingness to argue the merits of alternative systems is, in any case, more consistent with the principles of liberalism than the blind faith of its opponents.

The works which focus on Plato's *Laws* include an excellent study by Glen R. Morrow, *Plato's Cretan City: A Historical Interpretation of the "Laws."* Morrow demonstrates that the state Plato recommended for the real world was based on a mixed polity similar to that recommended by Aristotle. Morrow's "Plato and the Rule of Law," volume 2 (pp. 144–166) in Gregory Vlastos, *Plato: A Collection of Critical Essays,* also argues that Plato clearly understood the importance of judicial procedures to protect individuals from abuses by the state. Also see Maurice Vanhoutte, *La Philosophie politique de Platon dans les "Lois,"* which systematically surveys the text and the ideas expressed in the *Laws* and includes an especially good treatment of the elements which led Plato to compose the work and the arguments he advanced.

Theology

An introduction to Plato's religious thought and its place in the context of his philosophy and Greek culture in general is found in Edward Caird, *The Evolution of Theology in the Greek Philosophers* (2 vols.). Paul E. More, *The Religion of Plato,* is also a good source. More cites the relevant passages from the writings of Plato—chiefly from the *Laws* and the *Timaeus*—and comments on the passages. Another excellent older work is Friedrich Solmsen, *Plato's Theology.* Solmsen believes Plato was a self-conscious reformer of theology who argued for an immanent divinity expressed in a "world soul" and in the heavenly bodies. Following Plato the Stoics adopted the theme of an immanent divinity in the universe, whereas Aristotle promoted an opposing interpretation—i.e., that divinity was necessarily transcendent.

James K. Feibleman, *Religious Platonism: The Influence of Religion on Plato and the Influence of Plato on Religion,* connects Plato's theology with later ancient theology. Feibleman's treatment of the later period, however, is better than his work on Plato. His argument concerning Plato (pp. 15–85) is seriously weakened by his most unconvincing supposition that there was a division between the idealistic and realistic strains in Plato's thought. Feibleman considers that Orphism influenced Plato. Arthur O. Lovejoy, *The Great Chain of Being* (chap. 3), brilliantly discusses Plato's idea of the totally self-sufficient Good and the "Self-Transcending Fecundity" which necessarily sustains the range of all possible creatures. Recent contributions to this subject include V. Goldschmidt, "La Religion de Platon," in *Platonisme et pensée contemporaine* (pp. 17–129), and J. B. McMinn, "Plato as Philosophical Theologian," in *Phronesis* 5 (1960):23–31.

Aesthetics

The general surveys of the history of aesthetics (see chap. 4 below) devote attention to Plato. Monroe C. Beardsley, *Aesthetics from Classical Greece to the Present* (see chap. 2), has a well-organized and easy to use summary with a helpful bibliography. Katherine Gilbert and Helmut Kuhn, *A History of Esthetics* (chap. 2), is a more complex résumé. The best source, however, is certainly J. G. Warry, *Greek Aesthetical Theory* (chaps. 1–4). It is a clear and succinct explanation of the diverse elements in Plato's attitude toward beauty and the arts. The general histories of philosophy and introductions to Plato's philosophy include Copleston's *A History of Philosophy* (vol. 1, part 1, chap. 25), with a typically judicious and accurate summary, and Zeller's *Plato and the Older Academy,* which groups Plato's opinions on beauty and art with those on religion (chap. 12). Raphael Demos, *The Philosophy of Plato* (chaps. 11–13), Lodge, *The Philosophy of Plato* (chaps. 6–7), and above all G. M. Grube, *Plato's Thought* (chap. 6), are also strongly recommended.

Specialized studies of Plato's aesthetics include Rupert C. Lodge's systematic and informative *Plato's Theory of Art* and a brief study by Whitney J. Oates, *Plato's View of Art.* Oates discusses the role of the artist ist in Plato's thought—i.e., artists, by representing the ideal in visible form, personally transcended human limitations and inspired others to live in accordance with the perfect pattern of the forms. William C. Greene, "Plato's View of Poetry," in *Harvard Studies in Classical Philology* (1928):1–75, suggests that Plato thought that although artists represent eternal verities in sensible form and thus cooperate with philosophy, they also revel in the sensible world; thus art stands opposed to philosophy.

Aristotle

Bibliographical Resources

The best general guide to literature on Aristotle is Wilhelm Totok, *Handbuch der Geschichte der Philosophie* (pp. 214–264). Totok covers all the important general works to 1964 and follows with a list of specialized works under subheadings which classify Aristotelian philosophy. Also see Gilbert Varet, *Manuel de bibliographie philosophique* 1:120–130, and volume 1 of Ueberweg-Praechter's *Grundriss der Geschichte der Philosophie*. All of the serial bibliographies on ancient history and the history of philosophy carry citations of Aristotelian scholarship. The best resource is probably *L' Année philologique* (part 1), which has a separate section on Aristotle.

These standard sources can be supplemented by the short and somewhat outdated bibliography by Maria-Dominique Philippe, *Aristoteles*, and several good reviews which cite journal literature, including H. S. Long, "A Bibliographical Survey of Recent Work on Aristotle," in *Classical World* 51 (1958):47 ff.; Anton-Hermann Chroust, "The First Thirty Years of Modern Aristotle Scholarship," in *Classica et Mediaevalia* 24 (1963) 27–57; and Franz Dirlmeier, "Zum Gegenwartigen Stand der Aristotelesforschung," in *Wiener Studien* 76 (1963):54–67. Also see the bibliographical comments in Ingemar Düring, *Aristoteles: Darstellung und Interpretation seines Denkens* (pp. 623–640), and in Paul Moraux, *Aristoteles in der neueren Forschung*, which includes Chroust's survey of the impact of the Jaeger thesis on Aristotelian scholarship and a fine survey of the Aristotelian tradition (pp. 250–420). Many important articles on Aristotle are published in the *Proceeding of the Aristotle Society* (1887; now in a 1964 Johnson reprint), indexed by J. W. Scott, *A Synoptic Index to the Proceedings of the Aristotelian Society: 1900–1949*.

The beginning student can find brief bibliographies in several introductions to Aristotle's thought: D. J. Allan, *The Philosophy of Aristotle* (pp. 166–169), Marjorie Grene, *A Portrait of Aristotle* (pp. 253–264), and Geoffrey E. R. Lloyd, *Aristotle: The Growth and Structure of His Thought* (pp. 316–318).

Critical Editions and Translations

The standard translation of the Aristotelian corpus is by J. A. Smith and W. David Ross, *The Works of Aristotle Translated into English* (12 vols.).

In addition J. L. Ackrill is editing the Clarendon Aristotle, a series of translations with commentaries on important parts of the literature. The critical and untranslated *Aristotelis Opera* in five volumes edited by I. Bekker is for the advanced scholar. There are new editions of volumes 1, 2, 4, and 5. Volume 5, by H. Bonitz, the *Index Aristotelicus,* coordinates the key terms in Aristotle's text. English-language indices include Thomas Kiernan, *Aristotle Dictionary,* and Troy W. Organ, *An Index to Aristotle in English Translation.*

General Introductions

Copleston, *A History of Philosophy,* is a sound summary; see volume 1, part 2, chapters 27–34. Also see Arthur H. Armstrong, *An Introduction to Ancient Philosophy,* (chaps. 7–10), and Joseph Owens, *A History of Ancient Western Philosophy* (chaps. 13–15). Wilhelm Windelband, *History of Ancient Philosophy* (chap. 6), is a topically organized review of the essentials of Aristotle's system. The most important multivolume history is Eduard Zeller, *Aristotle and the Earlier Peripatetics* (2 vols.). Gomperz devotes volume 4 of *Greek Thinkers* and Fuller, volume 3 of *History of Greek Philosophy* to Aristotle. Neither is very original, but both have succinct and clear expositions of this difficult phase in the development of western thought.

In recent years a number of one-volume introductions to the complex world of Aristotle's philosophy have become available. Perhaps the best starting point is with two surveys which include criticisms of the Jaeger thesis. Geoffrey E. R. Lloyd, *Aristotle: The Growth and Structure of His Thought,* is a fine and accurate survey of the major elements in Aristotle's thought. Lloyd admits that Aristotle's philosophy evolved yet argues that he was essentially consistent. Marjorie Grene, *A Portrait of Aristotle,* has an excellent critique of Jaeger (pp. 13–38) and an interesting argument favoring the fundamental importance of Aristotle's biological theories. John Ferguson, *Aristotle,* is unreliable in its interpretation of the significance of the historical roots of Aristotle's thought, but it has a clear résumé of the chief topics with bibliographic notes and references.

More detailed surveys include D. J. Allan, *The Philosophy of Aristotle,* and a work best suited for reference, W. David Ross, *Aristotle.* Allan's treatment of the physical theories of Aristotle is excellent and he includes bibliographical suggestions. His treatment of Aristotle's biology is weak. Ross's treatment is even and thorough. The best scholarly synthesis of studies on Aristotle's philosophy is probably Ingemar Düring, *Aristoteles: Darstellung und Interpretation seines Denkens,* already cited for its excellent bibliography (pp. 623–640). Düring, one of the leading Aristotelian scholars, includes a detailed and up-to-date résumé of the problems associated with Aristotle's philosophy and begins each chapter by reviewing Aristotle's writings on the topic. Valuable, though narrower, studies include Frederick J. E. Woodbridge, *Aristotle's Vision of Nature,* and John Herman Randall, *Aristotle.* Woodbridge's essays were actually lectures delivered in 1930 which were edited for publication by his student, Randall. Woodbridge insists that it is important to interpret Aristotle's metaphysics in terms of energy and process rather than as fixed and static forms—the latter was the view of Aristotle inherited from medieval scholasticism. Randall's work emphasizes the same point, that is, the need for understanding Aristotle's universe as a collection of processes rather than as static substances. Randall makes too much of the similarities between Aristotle's system as he understands it and modern physics. Ingemar Düring, *Aristotle in the Ancient Biographical Tradition,* is a searching analysis of the ancient tradition about Aristotle's life, writings, and his reaction to Plato. The history of interpretations of Aristotle's philosophy is covered in J. Moreau, *Aristote et son école* (pp. 259–297).

Collections of articles which cover the full spectrum of Aristotelian thought include J. M. E. Moravcsik, *Aristotle: A Collection of Critical Essays,* with a fine bibliography; Ingemar Düring and G. E. L. Owen, *Aristotle and Plato in the Mid-Fourth Century;* and *Autour d'Aristote,* a *festschrift* honoring Auguste Mansion.

Special Studies

The theories of Werner Jaeger and Harold Cherniss are basic to modern scholarship on Aristotle. Jaeger's seminal *Aristotle: Fundamentals of the History of His Development* shattered the commonly accepted idea that Aristotle's corpus contained a system of thought lacking any important development. Jaeger's analysis of that development, however, is often disputed. Jaeger argues that Aristotle began his philosophic career as a distinct Platonist who shared the basic principles of his master. Jaeger theorizes that Aristotle gradually freed himself from Plato's domination and developed in his later years a distinctive, even anti-Platonic philosophy chiefly devoted to biology. Jaeger's thesis is especially important— and controversial—in analyzing the order and meaning of Aristotle's *Metaphysics.* Cherniss wrote two studies of Aristotle's remarks concerning his philosophic predecessors: *Aristotle's Criticism of Presocratic Philosophy* and *Aristotle's Criticism of Plato and the Academy.* Cherniss argues that Aristotle was unreliable as a historian because he distorted the ideas of his predecessors through ignorance of details and because he used the past to defend and explicate his own philosophy.

Virtually every work on Aristotle deals with the Jaeger thesis, and there is a great body of literature devoted to the problem. Scholarly discussions are briefly summarized in *Autour d'Aristote* (p. 18 ff.) by G. Verbeke; articles written by eminent scholars are to be found in Düring and

Owen, *Aristotle and Plato in the Mid-Fourth Century*. W. David Ross, "The Development of Aristotle's Thought" (pp. 1–19), agrees that Aristotle's thought evolved but argues that it did not occur "so far or so fast" as Jaeger supposed. For instance, Aristotle always retained the idea of the prime unmoved-mover. An essay by Cornelia J. de Vogel, "The Legend of the Platonizing Aristotle" (pp. 248–259), argues that the young Aristotle tentatively supported Platonism, dropped that belief very early to support a system based on concrete substances, and moved closer to Platonic metaphysics in his later years. De Vogel also develops her interpretation in "Did Aristotle Ever Accept Plato's Theory of Transcendent Ideas?" in her *Philosophia I: Studies in Greek Philosophy* (pp. 295–331). See the monumental study by Enrico Berti, *La Filosofia del primo Aristotele*, which argues that there was an essential continuity between the later doctrines of Plato and the early Aristotle, a stage which mediated Plato's views and the mature doctrines of Aristotle. Berti, however, does not believe that Aristotle ever accepted the transcendent forms.

Metaphysics and Theology

Theology can be considered a logical part of Aristotle's metaphysics, unlike Plato's, but some scholars have argued that Aristotle contains no real theology. Short résumés of this central interpretation of the philosophy of Aristotle are in Frederick Copleston, *History of Philosophy* (vol. 1, part 2, chaps. 28 and 29); Eduard Zeller, *Aristotle and the Earlier Peripatetics* (see vol. 1, chaps. 6 and 7 on metaphysics and chap. 16 on theology); and Theodor Gomperz, *Greek Thinkers* (vol. 4, chaps. 7, 9, 10, 18, and 19). The noteworthy general introductions to the philosophy of Aristotle include D. J. Allan, *The Philosophy of Aristotle* (part 4 and part 2; chaps. 3 and 4 are exceptional), and W. David Ross, *Aristotle* (chaps. 2 and 6). See Geoffrey E. R. Lloyd, *Aristotle: The Growth and Structure of His Thought*, chapter 6, "Logic and Metaphysics," for a much simpler discussion. But Ingemar Düring's *Aristoteles: Darstellung und Interpretation seines Denkens* is the best general discussion of Aristotle's metaphysics, especially concerning the methods and categories related to his biological theories.

Aristotle discusses his metaphysics and theology in *Metaphysics*, one of the most complex compendiums of philosophical argument in the history of western thought. Virtually every discussion of the subject inevitably becomes an exegesis of that text. The critical edition most used in Britain and North America is W. David Ross, *Metaphysics* (2 vols.). Ross includes a cautious and thoughtful introduction and a commentary on Aristotle's text. The best text for students, however, may well be Hippocrates A. Apostle, *Aristotle's Metaphysics*, a translation with excellent notes explaining the text. Leo Elders, *Aristotle's Theology: A Commentary on Book Λ of the Metaphysics,* also has a long and useful introduction.

METAPHYSICS

The collection of articles on Aristotle's metaphysics in Fritz Peter Hager, *Metaphysik und Theologie von Aristoteles,* includes an informative discussion of the general problem by Hans Wagner in the review "Zum Problem der Aristotelischen Metaphysik Begriffes" from *Philosophische Rundschau* 7 (1959):511-521. There is an interesting response by Philip Merlan.

Probably the best detailed study of Aristotle's metaphysics is Joseph Owens, *The Doctrine of Being in the Aristotelian Metaphysics: A Study in the Greek Background of Medieval Thought.* Owens studies Aristotle's confusing ideas and his terminology associated with being in the *Metaphysics.* Basically Owens argues that Aristotle's *Metaphysics* is a consistent and sensible account of being and that it explains the apparent contradiction in Aristotle's argument between being, *ens commune* (i.e., that quality all things have in common), and being, *ens perfectissimum* (i.e., the purest or most perfect being). The key to the problem, Owens believes, is that Aristotle's key terms (e.g., "entity") are equivocal and refer to that which establishes a distinctive being in all things while the distinguishing entities themselves are ontologically derived from a separate and perfect entity—"As entity extends to all beings, so the primary entity extends to all entities." Owens has been criticized for making Aristotle more consistent (and more "scholastic") than he was. See Alan Gewirth in the *Philosophical Review* 62 (1953):577-589 for a detailed critical review. On a closely related question see Owens, "The Grounds of Universality in Aristotle," in the *American Philosophical Quarterly* 3 (1966):162-169, for an argument that Aristotle conceived that the mind abstracts forms from objects during perception and remains in contact with them and actualizes the potentiality of the objects through abstraction. A less complex study of the *Metaphysics* is found in Emerson Buchanan, *Aristotle's Theory of Being,* which considers all the possible meanings of *ousia* ("being" in the broadest sense) in the text. The author concludes that *ousia* meant the concrete individual, matter, form, and action, unified by participation in the actualization of being. Pierre Aubenque, *Le Problème de l'être chez Aristote,* is as yet untranslated. Aubenque thoroughly and eruditely analyzes the *Metaphysics,* but his conclusions are not generally accepted. Contrary to Jaeger, who divides the *Metaphysics* chronologically, Aubenque divides it into sections dealing with ontology (the study of being in general) and theology (the study of the highest or most perfect being). He thinks the *Metaphysics* posed the problems of the subject and should not be regarded as a systematic exposition—thus Aubenque is not surprised that Aristotle did not fully explain how the movable universe is derived from the unmovable. Enrico Berti, *L'Unita del sapere in Aristotele*, is another work untranslated from the Italian. Berti's views are also contained in "Physique et métaphysique selon Aristote" (pp. 18–31) in Ingemar Düring, *Naturphilosophie bei Aristoteles und Theophrast*. He comments on the distinction between metaphysics and physics (the science of the movable). John P. Anton, *Aristotle's Theory of Contrariety*, is a more specialized work which studies Aristotle's probable ideas concerning the relationship between contraries or opposite qualities: how they operate and how their interaction influences substances and knowledge.

THEOLOGY

The studies recommended for the study of Aristotle's metaphysics are also informative about his theology because god (or the gods) was a logical construct necessary to his metaphysical (and physical) universe. In addition to these sources, consult Hans von Arnim, "Die Entwicklung der Aristotelischen Gotteslehre," in Fritz Peter Hager, *Metaphysik und Theologie von Aristoteles* (pp. 1–74), which suggests that the idea of god was a culmination of Aristotle's philosophical development, and William K. C. Guthrie, "The Development of Aristotle's Theology," in *Classical Quarterly* 27 (1933):162–171 and (1934):90–98. Guthrie partially opposes the views of Jaeger and von Arnim. He perceives development in Aristotle's theological thinking accompanied by an abiding unity with Plato represented by Aristotle's assumption that matter is controlled by a higher and purer being—hence the notion of an unmoved mover, i.e., god. W. J. Verdenius, "Traditional and Personal Elements in Aristotle's Religion," *Phronesis* 5 (1960):56–70, is very interesting because it argues convincingly that Aristotle regarded tradition to be a "natural" and hence informative source of human experience. Aristotle's acceptance of tradition, according to Verdenius, made him accept ideas such as divine providence without being able to synthesize them with his transcendent god. Harry A. Wolfson, "The Knowability of and Describability of God in Plato and Aristotle," in *Harvard Studies in Classical Philology* 56–57 (1947):233–249, is an excellent contribution to the study of Aristotle and the study of all Greek thought. Wolfson explains that Greeks, like Aristotle, assumed that human reason was capable of comprehending the character of God, whereas Jewish and Christian thought normally considered God beyond human understanding.

Logic

No one denies that the development of logical processes was important in Greek philosophy before Aristotle, but it is generally agreed that Aristotle was the founder of formal logic. Aristotle first systematized the rules for proper argument and considered the relationship of that system to other areas of his philosophy. The general histories of ancient philosophy and the introductions to Aristotle all deal with his logic, but except for Copleston's simple summary in the *History of Philosophy* (vol. 1, part 2, chap. 28) and Düring's summary in *Aristoteles* (pp. 183–291), it is best to turn directly to the histories of logic. All of them devote major attention to Aristotle. Kapp, *The Greek Foundations of Traditional Logic*, and Lloyd, *Polarity and Analogy*, discuss Aristotle as the culmination of Greek logical thought. Bochenski, *The History of Formal Logic* (part 2), and Kneale, *The Development of Logic* (chap. 2), are excellent résumés. Chaignet, *Histoire de la psychologie des Grecs* (vol. 1, part 2), contains relevant material and an analysis of Aristotle's concept of the process of cognition and thinking by synthesis.

The important writings of Aristotle on logic include *The Categories, On Interpretation, Prior Analytics, Posterior Analytics*, and the *Topics*. Invaluable comments are included in the critical edition by Ross on the *Prior and Posterior Analytics* and in a contribution to the Clarendon Aristotle series by J. L. Ackrill which translates and comments on the *Categories* and *De Interpretatione*.

General studies of Aristotle's logic include James W. Miller, *The Structure of Aristotle's Logic*, which has an effective short introduction to major problems and interpretations, and J. M. Le Blond, *Logique et méthode chez Aristote*, which examines the relationship between Aristotle's principles of knowledge in the sciences and his actual use of logic in the scientific treatises. Aristotle's presuppositions and method of analysis are also discussed in *Aristote et les problèmes de méthode*, edited by Suzanne Mansion from the papers of the Aristotelian Symposium (1960). The most general periodical articles include G. E. L. Owen, "Logic and Metaphysics in Some Earlier Works of Aristotle," in *Aristotle and Plato in the Mid-Fourth Century*, edited by Ingemar Düring (pp. 163–190); C. M. Gillespie, "The Aristotelian Categories," in *Classical Quarterly* 19 (1925):75–84; and E. Weil, "La Place de la logique dans la pensée aristotelicienne," in the *Revue de métaphysique et morale* 56 (1951):283–315.

The syllogism, the central method of Aristotle's logical analysis, is discussed in the seminal work of Jan Lukasiewicz, *Aristotle's Syllogism from the Standpoint of Modern Formal Logic*. (Also see the excellent critical review of Lukasiewicz's first edition by J. L. Austin in *Mind* 61 (1952): 395–404 and Gunther Patzig, *Aristotle's Theory of the Syllogism: A Logico-Philological Study of Book A of the "Prior Analytics."*) Patzig argues that Aristotle's logic was a formal system which should not be regarded as derived from his metaphysical system but as an independent analysis of relations. The idea that Aristotle's logic was based on the Greek subject-predicate formula was, Patzig thinks, later conceived by the scholastics.

The origins of Aristotle's logic and especially its relationship to Plato's dialectic are discussed in Friedrich Solmsen, "Aristotle's Syllogism and Its Platonic Background," in *Philosophical Review* 60 (1951):563–571, a review of Rooss's edition of *The Prior and the Posterior Analytics;* and Paul Shorey, "The Origins of the Syllogism," in *Classical Philology* 19 (1924): 1–25, which argues that the syllogism was born of the dialectic.

The Philosophy of Nature

Aristotle's study of nature, or science as the modern world understands it, involved his concepts of the "separate," the "moving," and the "temporal" as opposed to metaphysics, which was ultimately the study of the "eternal." Aristotle's thinking did not make a distinction between physics and biology as in modern thought nor was it a commitment to modern methods of experiment and mathematized quantification that make science and metaphysics independent of each other. (See Richard McKeon, "Aristotle's Conception of the Development and the Nature of Scientific Method," in the *Journal of the History of Ideas* 8 (1947):3–45.) Aristotle shared these attitudes with Plato, yet Aristotle is much better regarded by recent historians of science. This is partly because Aristotle made his universals inherent in the material world and hence did not exhibit Plato's evident disdain for the material world. Aristotle is also better regarded because he was a practicing scientist. The records of his biological observations demonstrate that he was an acute observer, capable of critically evaluating evidence—despite his philosophical prejudice and plain foolishness, which are sufficient to counter the notion that he was practically a modern biologist in his observation.

The general histories of science and the histories of both the physical and the biological sciences in antiquity devote attention to Aristotle and deal with him more sympathetically than they do Plato. One survey, however, has an especially excellent summary of Aristotle's cosmology: Samuel Sambursky, *The Physical World of the Greeks* (chap. 3). (For details on Sambursky and related writings, see below, chapter 3, p. 96). The general histories of philosophy are uneven in their treatment of Aristotle's philosophy of nature. Zeller, *Aristotle and the Earlier Peripatetics*, is very good on cosmology. It correctly combines treatment of the heavens, mechanics, and life under one heading, "Physics"; the discussion of Aristotle's biology, however, is weak. Most of the more recent introductions to the philosophy of Aristotle have good discussions of his philosophy of nature. D. J. Allan, *The Philosophy of Aristotle*, is a fine short synopsis (pp. 23–70), and W. David Ross, *Aristotle*, discusses "The Philosophy of Nature" (chap. 3) and "Biology" (chap. 4). Geoffrey E. R. Lloyd, *Aristotle: The Growth and Structure of His Thought*, emphasizes physics (chaps. 7 and 8); and Marjorie Grene, *A Portrait of Aristotle*, focuses on biology. The best discussion is in Düring, *Aristoteles* (pp. 506–554 and 291–400).

There is a wide-ranging collection of articles in Ingemar Düring, *Natur-philosophie bei Aristoteles und Theophrast*.

The important texts on physics, i.e., the nonbiological dimension of Aristotle's philosophy of nature, are the *Physics* and *De Caelo* (or *On the Heavens)*. On the *Physics* see W. David Ross, *Aristotle's Physics*, especially the excellent introduction (pp. 1–119), and Hippocrates P. Apostle's translation with extensive commentaries and a glossary. On the *De Caelo* see Leo Elder, *Aristotle's Cosmology: A Commentary on the "De Caelo."*

English-language surveys include the older standard by Friedrich Solmsen, *Aristotle's System of the Physical World*, which supports the basic coherence and logic of Aristotle's cosmology and includes an excellent study of Aristotle's use of pre-Socratic and Platonic themes. Solmsen argues that Plato and the Academy, because of their interest in the problem of change, prepared the way for many distinctively Aristotelian principles of physics. Melbourne G. Evans, *The Physical Philosophy of Aristotle*, is a recent work which has a sound review of basic facts but which tends to isolate Aristotle's principles of physics from his principles of biology. Thus Evans interprets Aristotle's *kinesis* as a purely physical type of change similar to that recognized in modern physics without recognizing how the same principle of change equally applied to Aristotle's biological thought. Evans continually compares Aristotle's physics to modern science.

Another excellent survey, Auguste Mansion, *Introduction à la physique aristotelicienne*, is also helpful, but the best source for the study of Aristotle's physics is Wolfgang Wieland, *Die Aristotelische Physik*. Wieland focuses on Aristotle's presuppositions and method in the physical sciences. Part 3 is a useful résumé of the system.

Aristotle was disinterested in mathematics compared to Plato; however, he did have mathematical opinions important in fully understanding his science. Thomas Heath, *Mathematics in Aristotle*, is a short presentation and analysis of the important mathematical references in Aristotle's writings. The best account of the meaning of mathematics to Aristotle is found in Hippocrates G. Apostle, *Aristotle's Philosophy of Mathematics*. There is also an interesting argument that Aristotle was aware of non-Euclidean approaches to geometry in I. Toth, "Non-Euclidean Geometry before Euclid," in *Scientific American* 221:5 (1969):87–102.

Biology

The extant biological writings of Aristotle indicate that he was chiefly interested in zoology rather than botany. His student Theophrastus is rightly remembered as the founder of botany. There is a general overview of Aristotle's speculations about animals within the general context of his philosophy and cultural environment in D. M. Balme, "Aristotle and the Beginnings of Zoology," in the *Journal of the Society for the Bibliography of Natural History* 5:4 (1970):272–285. Balme has a good short account of the *pneuma* (i.e., the vital heat of animal existence). See Thomas E. Lones, *Aristotle's Researches in Natural Science*, for a useful survey of Aristotle's biological writings and his citation of the observations of animal life. On the important writings themselves, see Ingemar Düring, *Aristotle's "De Partibus Animalium": Critical and Literary Commentaries*, and the commentaries on the *De Generatione Animalium* in the standard editions, especially Smith and Ross (vol. 6). The *Historia Animalium* appears in an excellent German translation with commentary by H. Aubert and F. Wimmer (2 vols.) and in Smith and Ross, (vol. 4). Consult the general histories of ancient science, especially those on biology in Chapter 3, for further comments on the biological theories of Aristotle and his school.

There is much recent interest in the place of Aristotle's biological ideas in his system of thought. Several scholars note (1) that biology was a more important part of Aristotle's thinking than usually supposed and (2) that he was a better biologist than commonly thought. The first proposition is increasingly accepted and it was championed by D'Arcy Thompson, "Aristotle the Naturalist" (pp. 37–78), in *Science and the Classics*, and by J. M. Le Blond in both "The Biological Bias of Aristotle," in *The Modern Schoolman* 12 (1935):82–84, and in his *Aristote, philosophe de la vie*. It is supported more recently by Marjorie Grene, *A Portrait of Aristotle*, which argues that the relationship of the concrete individual to a species or class was an idea probably suggested to Aristotle as a result of his work in biological classification rather than as a result of his thinking in physics or metaphysics. Grene is also interested in the second proposition—alternatively stated, that Aristotle had some advantages over modern biologists in developing a theory of life. Grene argues the point in a recent article, "Aristotle and Modern Biology," in the *Journal of the History of Ideas* 33 (1972):395–424. She suggests that Aristotle's idea of a pluralistic and realistic science is superior to the "orthodox" uniformity and phenomenalism characteristic of modern biologists and that his investigation of particular subjects in their environmental context is superior to modern methods (i.e., the adoption of common subjects and methods and the rejection of claims which pretend to penetrate reality). Grene further suggests that Aristotle's teleology, normally considered a completely unscientific element in his thought, is compatible with modern science. She suggests that *telos* refers to the adult form into which a subject is growing rather than a cosmic purpose; *telos* thus is a regulative idea useful in guiding scientific exploration of life processes.

Another view of purpose in Aristotle's biology is discussed by A. Preus, "Science and Philosophy in Aristotle's Generation of Animals," in the *Journal of History of Biology* 3 (1970):1–52. Preus emphasizes that purpose in biological processes is defined by function rather than by the form of the object or consciousness of goal, i.e., it is the *pneuma* not metaphysical goals or forms which structures an infant. See George K. Plochmann, "Nature and the Living Thing in Aristotle's Biology," in the *Journal of the History of Ideas* 14 (1953):167–191, for another view of purpose or finality in Aristotle's biology. E. Joly, "La Biologie d'Aristote," in the *Revue philosophique* 158 (1968):219–253, reviews the opinions of other scholars and suggests that Aristotle was not a good biologist.

Psychology, Ethics, and Politics

The general histories of philosophy and the general introductions to Aristotle's philosophy typically cover these integrally related topics. Copleston's *History of Philosophy* (vol. 1, part 2, chaps. 30, 31, and 32) covers psychology, ethics, and politics, respectively. Zeller's *Aristotle and the Earlier Peripatetics* (vol. 1, chap. 11) covers psychology; volume 2, chapters 12 and 13, cover ethics and politics. Gomperz, *Greek Thinkers* (vol. 4), is worth special consultation. Chapters 15–17 are on psychology, chapters 20–25 on ethics. Ross's *Aristotle* (chaps. 5, 7, and 8) is one of the better general introductions which focuses closely on Aristotle's writings in these areas. Lloyd's *Aristotle: The Growth and Structure of His Thought* has good résumés in chapters 9, 10, and 11. Düring produces useful treatments of Aristotle's psychology (pp. 554–586) and his ethics and society (pp. 434–506) in *Aristoteles*.

PSYCHOLOGY

See W. W. Fortenbaugh, "Recent Scholarship on the Psychology of Aristotle," in *Classical World* 60 (1966-1967):316 ff., which is a useful guide to recent works. The general histories of psychology in antiquity are also valuable, including Brett, *A History of Psychology, Ancient and Patristic* (chaps. 10, 11, 12, and 13), Chaignet, *Histoire de la psychologie des Grecs* (vol. 1, part 2), and Beare, *Theories of Elementary Cognition*, which concludes each section with comments on Aristotle's use of his predecessors' ideas.

Aristotle's most important work on psychology is the *De Anima*. There is an excellent translation with commentary by Robert D. Hicks and a critical edition with introduction and comments by W. David Ross. Ross prepared the standard edition with added comments on the *Parva Naturalia*. Arthur K. Griffin, *Aristotle's Psychology of Conduct*, compiles comments from Aristotle's ethical and political writings which illuminate his ideas concerning the nature of the soul as it is involved in human conduct. Other older general studies include Clarence W. Shute, *The Psychology of Aristotle: An Analysis of the Living Being*, and E. E. Spicer, *Aristotle's Conception of the Soul*. The most important study is Franciscus J. C. Nuyens, *L'Évolution de la psychologie d'Aristote*. Nuyens, a proponent of the Jaeger thesis, divides the evolution of Aristotle's ideas on the soul into three stages: (1) the Platonic, (2) the "mechanistic-instrumentalist," in which the soul is no longer hostile to the body, and (3) the final or mature stage, where he evolves the doctrine that the soul is the form of the body. Although Nuyens's thesis is criticized for being too rigid, his work is nonetheless indispensable (especially for his comments concerning the *De Anima*).

ETHICS

Chapter 7 of Alasdair MacIntyre, *A Short History of Ethics*, is an adequate introduction to Aristotle's ethics. Thereafter the student should go directly to Aristotle's ethical writings and the excellent commentaries on them. Thomas Marshall, *Aristotle's Theory of Conduct*, provides lengthy excerpts from Aristotle's writings, paraphrases his arguments, and then adds the author's comments. The texts are available in several translations including the Smith and Ross edition and the Loeb Classical Library. The most important commentaries are on *The Nicomachean Ethics*. Harold H. Joachim's interesting but rather difficult to read lectures, edited after his death by D. A. Rees, are in English, but the best sources are in French and German. See René-Antoine Gauthier and Jean Yves Jolif, *L'Éthique à Nicomaque* (2 vols. in 3). Volume 1 contains the introduction and translation and volume 2 is a commentary on the text. Franz Dirlmeier, *Nikomachische Ethik*, provides a translation and commentary.

Several excellent studies which have appeared in the last decade concentrate on Aristotle's attempt to explain the relationship between knowledge and virtue and voluntary and involuntary actions. The best of these is James J. Walsh, *Aristotle's Conception of Moral Weakness*, a study of wrong behavior on the part of those who suffer from moral weakness. Walsh believes that Aristotle's ethical theory is compatible with Socrates' identification of knowledge and virtue. The morally weak person fails to see the relationship between a particular moral situation and moral principles. Walsh uses an "integrative method," i.e., he uses the nonethical writings to illuminate the meaning of the ethical texts, and he includes judicious comments on other interpretations. Ronald D. Milo, *Aristotle on Practical Knowledge and Weakness of Will*, is not as important as Walsh, but it is well worth reading. Milo is critical of the idea that one can never knowingly do wrong, an error inherited by Aristotle from Socrates and Plato. Milo alleges that Aristotle confuses the ability to see what one ought to do (practical knowledge) with the ability to do it (prudence). René-Antoine Gauthier, *La Morale d'Aristote*, argues that Aristotle was an intellectual elitist who badly underestimated the effect of passion on human conduct; hence he underrated the importance of the will in his system of ethics. Gauthier's argument that Aristotle meant the idea of the mean to be a metaphor is less convincing.

Aristotle's ethical theory is more broadly treated by W. F. R. Hardie, *Aristotle's Ethical Theory*, and J. Donald Monan, *Moral Knowledge and Its*

Methodology in Aristotle. Hardie concentrates on the *Nicomachean Ethic,* with a detailed paraphrase and discussion of the text that presumes a fair degree of prior knowledge on the part of the reader. Chapter 13 summarizes Aristotle's reflections on the question of moral weakness. Monan concentrates on the successive stages in the development of Aristotle's moral theories and argues that the *Eudemian Ethics* represented his mature position. Monan's discussion of the distinction between ethics based on human rationality and that based on observed experience is very good. Whitney J. Oates, *Aristotle and the Problem of Value,* is critical of Aristotle's role in the development of ethical thought. Oates argues that Aristotle seriously weakened ethical thought by denying Plato's transcendent forms, which were a secure metaphysical foundation on which to base ethical values. Oates succeeds in showing that a metaphysical defense of ethics is difficult without resorting to transcendence, but he fails to answer the question of whether Aristotle's objections to the Platonic forms were ill-conceived and illogical. Part 7 (pp. 260–335) discusses the *Nicomachean Ethics.*

The collection by James J. Walsh and Henry L. Shapiro, *Aristotle's Ethics: Issues and Interpretations,* reproduces several good comments including a translation from Gauthier's *La Morale d'Aristote* of "On the Nature of Aristotle's Ethics" and an interesting argument by John Dewey, "The Nature of Aims." Also see D. J. Allan, "The Practical Syllogism" (pp. 327–343), in *Autour d'Aristote;* R. Jackson, "Rationalism and Intellectualism in the *Ethics* of Aristotle," in *Mind* 51 (1942):343–360; and Geoffrey E. R. Lloyd, "The Role of Medical and Biological Analogies in Aristotle's *Ethics,*" in *Phronesis* 13 (1968):68–83. Lloyd notes the use of these analogies in Aristotle's idea that man *qua* man has a distinctive function and that his notion of moral excellence, although relative to the individual, is not indeterminate when judged in terms of the species. There are absolute standards for both the physical and the moral qualities of the species, even though individual deformities might depart from those standards.

POLITICAL THEORY

The general histories of political theory essential to the student of Aristotle include Charles H. McIlwain, *The Growth of Political Thought in the West* (chap. 3), and Ernest Barker, *The Political Thought of Plato and Aristotle* (including chap. 5) (see p. 80 below).

Aristotle's political theory is elaborated in the *Politics.* There is a fine older edition with generous and interesting comments by W. L. Newman (4 vols.) and a more recent one-volume edition by Ernest Barker, *The Politics.* A translation with comments by Richard Robinson on books 3 and 4 appears in the Clarendon Aristotle series.

Most studies of Greek political theory and many which chiefly concentrate on Plato include extensive comments about Aristotle. Max Hamburger, *Morals and Laws: The Growth of Aristotle's Legal Theory,* should also be consulted. Hamburger's valuable study emphasizes the close connection between Aristotle's political theory (especially on the proper construction of constitutions) and ethical theory; he also notes Aristotle's appreciation of politics as an inexact science. Aristotle believed legal systems are imperfect and that good government is dependent on equity and civic friendship. Another basic work, unfortunately untranslated, is Ulrich von Wilamowitz-Moellendorff, *Aristoteles und Athens*, first published in 1893. Volume 1 analyzes Aristotle's writings on the politics of Athens and its history; volume 2 investigates the principles of his political analysis and polity. Finally, there are good articles on Aristotle's political theory in the Foundation Hardt collection, *La Politique d'Aristote*.

Aesthetics

The most general introductions to the history of philosophy deal with Aristotle's aesthetics. See Copleston's *A History of Philosophy* (vol. 1, part 2, chap. 33), Zeller's *Aristotle and the Earlier Peripatetics* (vol. 2, chaps. 14 and 15 on "Rhetoric and the Fine Arts"), and Gomperz's *Greek Thinkers* (vol. 4, chaps. 35–38). These general introductions to Aristotle's philosophy also have adequate treatments of his aesthetics. Ingemar Düring, *Aristoteles* (pp. 118–183), is especially recommended. The general histories of aesthetics (see chapter 4 below) that should be consulted on Aristotle include Monroe C. Beardsley, *Aesthetics from Classical Greece to the Present* (chap. 3), Katherine Gilbert and Helmut Kuhn, *History of Esthetics* (chap. 3), and J. G. Warry, *Greek Aesthetic Theory* (chaps. 5, 6, and 7). In addition see the surveys of the history of literary criticism cited below (p. 111), all of which have adequate chapters on Aristotle. G. M. Grube, *The Greek and Roman Critics* (chap. 3), is especially recommended for its integration of scholarship in the field.

Scholarship on Aristotle's aesthetics centers on the *Poetics*. The most important works include Lane Cooper and A. Gudeman, *A Bibliography of the "Poetics" of Aristotle*, supplemented by M. T. Herrick, in the *American Journal of Philology* 52 (1931):168–174. See also Gerald F. Else, "Survey of Works on Aristotle's *Poetics*, 1940–1954," *Classical World* 48 (1954–1955):73–82.

The meaning of Aristotle's *Poetics* is simply treated by Lane Cooper in *The "Poetics" of Aristotle: Its Meaning and Influence*, one of the Our Debt to Greece and Rome series. Other important works are commentaries on the text of the *Poetics*. Editions suitable for student use include Lane Cooper, *Aristotle on the Art of Fiction*. One of the best commentaries is Samuel H. Butcher, *Aristotle's Theory of Poetry and Fine Art*, with the Greek text, a translation, and valuable commentaries. Gerald F. Else, *Aristotle's "Poetics": The Argument*, is a critical edition for scholars with translations and comments. Else includes many interesting and provocative suggestions about the original text and its interpretation; for example, he theorizes that in drama catharsis, or the "purgation of the emotions," did not refer to the effect of a drama on an audience but to the resolution of the crisis within the plot of a drama. John Jones, *On Aristotle and Greek Tragedy*, is an interesting reinterpretation. Jones believes that the understanding of Greek drama and Aristotle's comments on it have been ruinously governed by a modern preoccupation with the development of the self. Accordingly, he suggests that modern readers presume that the tragic hero is the center of Greek drama and that Aristotle's comments refer chiefly to the role of the hero and his fall. Jones holds that Aristotle was interested in the actions of the plays and not in the development of the characters and that Aristotle consciously defended didactic poetry despite Plato's strictures. Jones's work is generally of high caliber and his comments on Sophocles are superior. An interesting study of the idea of catharsis by T. Brunius appears in volume 1 of the *Dictionary of the History of Ideas* (pp. 264–270).

Post-Aristotelian Philosophy

Bibliographical Resources

All of the serial and nonserial guides to the history of philosophy have important citations on the post-Aristotelian period. The increase in religious interest during late antiquity means that guides to the history of the ancient church and pagan religion (see chap. 5 below) are also relevant. The bibliographical notes in Arthur H. Armstrong, *The Cambridge History of Later Greek and Early Medieval Philosophy* (pp. 670–693), and in volumes 1 and 2 of Frederick Ueberweg and Karl Praechter, *Grundriss*, are specially recommended. See also Wilhelm Totok in the *Handbuch der Geschichte der Philosophie* I:268–355. The serial guides especially recommended include *L'Année philologique* and the *Revue d'histoire ecclésiastique*.

General Introductions

Frederich Copleston's *A History of Philosophy* (vol. 1, part 2, chaps. 35–47) is devoted to the post-Aristotelian period with accurate résumés of the tenets of the significant schools. The Christian Fathers, however, especially Augustine, are discussed in volume 2, part 1, chapters 2–10. Arthur H. Armstrong, an expert on late ancient philosophy in general and Plotinus in particular, has a fine discussion of the period in his *Introduction to Ancient Philosophy* (chaps. 11–19). The more recent works, however, have not diminished the value of Eduard Zeller or made his work superfluous. See his *A History of Eclecticism in Greek Philosophy*, which discusses the tendency of the various schools of late antiquity to borrow from each other and to blend together. Zeller's *Stoics, Epicureans, and Sceptics* is a fine topical résumé of the chief philosophies; part 2 is on the Stoics, part 3 on the Epicureans, and part 4 on the skepticism of Pyrrho and the Academy. The most important recent work devoted solely to late ancient philosophy is, of course, *The Cambridge History of Later Greek and Early Medieval Philosophy*, edited by Arthur H. Armstrong with contributions by outstanding historians of ancient philosophy. The relevant parts of this basic work are cited under separate headings in the following pages.

Skepticism

Excellent summaries of the development of skepticism can be found in Eduard Zeller, *Stoics, Epicureans, and Sceptics* (part 4), and in Edwyn Bevan, *Stoics and Sceptics* (pp. 121–152). Good general studies include Philip P. Hallie, *Scepticism, Man, and God: Selections from the Writings of Sextus Empiricus* (pp. 3–31), with an annotated bibliography (pp. 217–222); and M. M. Patrick, *The Greek Sceptics*, which includes the basic information and an interesting argument that ancient skepticism was influenced by medical theories. Also available in English is an older survey, N. MacColl, *The Greek Sceptics, Pyrrho to Sextus*, and Charlotte L. Stough, *Greek Skepticism: A Study in Epistemology*, which argues that the roots of skepticism are to be found in the philosophy of the classical period. The skeptics proceeded from the Aristotelian idea that knowledge begins with sense data and the Greek distinction between appearance and reality —which was a nascent skepticism. The movement was divided concerning the uncertainty of appearance: the Pyrronists urged the suspension of all conclusions while the academic skeptics searched for criteria to establish probable truths as guides to conduct. These surveys should be supplemented by the excellent general French work, V. Brochard, *Les Sceptiques grecs*.

Epicurus (d. 270 B.C.)

The recent literature is reviewed by P. de Lacy, "Some Recent Publications on Epicurus and Epicureanism," in *Classical World* 48 (1954–1955):169 ff. The original sources appear in a collection by Cyril Bailey,

Epicurus: The Extant Remains with Short Critical Apparatus, Translations, and Notes, and another by G. K. Strodach, *The Philosophy of Epicurus: Letters, Doctrines, and Parallel Passages from Lucretius*, which contains an introduction with a résumé of Epicurus's thought.

John Rist, one of the best and most prolific students of late ancient philosophy, has recently published a topically organized introduction to the career and opinions of Epicurus: *Epicurus: An Introduction*. Rist comments on scholarly opinions about Epicurus and his philosophy. An older and still interesting account in Alfred E. Taylor, *Epicurus*, argues that Epicurus's chief interests were morality and the achievement of happiness rather than scientific questions. Thus Epicurus constructed a rational theory of hedonism which applied to all people rather than to an intellectual few, contrary to other classical theories of ethics. Benjamin Farrington, *The Faith of Epicurus*, is a rather different approach. Farrington suggests that Epicurus championed science against superstition, ignorance, and the antiscientific theories of Plato and Aristotle. Epicurus's advice to avoid public life was, according to Farrington, based on the belief that friendship has been replaced by naked interest and power as the basis for social interaction. Farrington acknowledges that his interpretation of Epicurus's attitude toward Plato and Aristotle is indebted to the seminal works of the Italian E. Bignone, *Epicuro: fragmenti, testimonianze* and *L'Aristotele perduto e la formazione filosofica de Epicuro* (2 vols.). Bignone argues that Epicurus wished to return to pre-Socratic themes in reaction against the philosophic corruption of Plato and the early Aristotle. Bignone is one of the few writers on Epicurus who are approved by Norman W. de Witt. In *Epicurus and His Philosophy* de Witt disputes most previous interpretations of Epicurus, especially Zeller's, and presents his own. He argues that Epicurus returned to Ionian philosophy to counter Platonism, that he opposed nature to reason as the chief source of truth, but that he did not suggest that sensation was the sole and infallible source of truth. He pictures Epicurus as a moral reformer and suggests that his followers' missionary fervor made Epicureanism a factor in preparing the way for the spread of Christianity. André-Jean Festugière, *Epicurus and His Gods*, argues that Epicurus did not intend to destroy belief in the gods; rather he tried to persuade humanity that the gods were good and that they were concerned with human welfare, not with seeking revenge for humanity's lack of loyalty to them. Festugière's chapters on the superstitions of the ancient world and on the "astral religion" developed by the Platonists are especially informative.

Students of Epicurus's philosophy are invariably interested in his atomism (i.e., the idea that the universe is composed of invisible and impenetrable particles). Depending on the weight given to atomism Epicurus can either be pictured as a protoscientist or a moralist. Cyril Bailey links Epicurus to the pre-Socratic atomists in *The Greek Atomists and Epicurus*. Bailey concludes that Epicurus did not merely adopt the atomism of Democritus but modified it to fashion a coherent and consistent sensationalism—only then could atomism serve as the metaphysical and epistemological basis of his philosophy. David J. Furley, *Two Studies in the Greek Atomists*, divides the studies to examine attitudes concerning the indivisibility of matter and to compare Aristotle's and Epicurus's explanations of voluntary behavior.

There is an interesting collection of articles in *Les Études philosophiques* n.s. 22 (1967) devoted to "Questions épicuriennes." C. Diano, "Épicure: la philosophie du plaisir et la société des amis" (pp. 173–187), is especially worth reading. Other insightful articles on Epicurus and his tradition include two by Friedrich Solmsen, "Epicurus and Cosmological Heresies" and "Epicurus on the Growth and Decline of the Cosmos," both republished in volume 1 of his *Kleine Schriften*. Solmsen follows the general lead of Bignone to argue that Epicurus (and Lucretius) defended the orthodox pre-Socratic attitude (i.e., that the cosmos originated, grew, and declined) against the view of Plato and Aristotle that the cosmos is eternal and divine. According to Solmsen this defense emphasized that Epicurus believed that the cosmos is natural and subject to change rather than divine. In his argument Epicurus applied biological concepts of nutrition and growth to the cosmos to explain its life history.

Stoicism

In addition to the recommended general histories of ancient philosophy, the student can find brief but adequate summaries of Stoicism in W. L. Davidson, *The Stoic Creed*, and in R. M. Wenley, *Stoicism and Its Influence*, published in the Our Debt to Greece and Rome series. Davidson is topically arranged and Wenley has a short chronological résumé of the development of Stoicism followed by a topical study of its chief ideas and a brief sketch of its influence on later Europe. Robert D. Hicks, *Stoic and Epicurean*, is a sound summary of Stoic ideas with useful chronological tables and a bibliography of sources. Hicks argues that Stoic thought was intensely practical and that it subordinated all other areas of speculation to ethics. Donald R. Dudley, *History of Cynicism*, is another excellent introduction with the important insight that Stoicism was indebted to Cynicism and that Cynic preachers were a continuing influence in the later ancient world because they sometimes competed with the Stoics and sometimes reinforced them. Dudley brilliantly cites the career of Dio Chrysostom to evoke an image of the role of the moral missionary in the ancient world.

Edwyn Bevan, *Stoics and Sceptics*, does not systematically review Stoic thought, but it is recommended because it emphasizes that the ethical character of Stoicism from Zeno on. The chapter on Posidonius is especially well written; it argues that Posidonius redirected Stoicism toward a more religious purpose: to make humanity "feel at home in the universe." Bevan has an exceptionally clear writing style. The student is also advised to consult E. V. Arnold, *Roman Stoicism*, which has a generally topical approach to the subject. Arnold's comments on the ethical orientation of the Stoic and the concept of the soul as a refuge from the turbulence of the world (chaps. 11–15) are especially valuable. His excellent bibliography (pp. 437–451) is divided into two parts: "Ancient Writers and Philosophers" and "Modern Writers." The comments of Martin L. Clarke in *The Roman Mind*, cited above, has an excellent treatment of Cicero (chap. 2) and Stoicism (chap. 3). Best of all, see "The Stoic Way of Life" (chap. 11), which emphasizes the Stoic interest in will and moral effort and the importance of moral teachers as heroic examples.

These general histories of Stoicism should be read with caution because of recent disputes over the character and the development of Stoicism. Every student should read Ludwig Edelstein, *The Meaning of Stoicism*, because the author flatly contradicts several assumptions accepted by the introductions recommended above. Edelstein, for example, denies that the Stoic ideal involved a suppression of emotion or an indifferent attitude toward suffering. He suggests that the Stoics recommended the careful control of emotions through reason and that they believed sympathetic emotions are positively required. Edelstein's treatment of "The Stoic Concept of Nature" and "Stoic Self-Criticism," his comments on Panaetius and Posidonius, and "The Stoic Way of Life" are equally controversial.

The attempt to correct traditional opinions about the Stoics and comment on the present trends in scholarly study is continued in the valuable work of John Rist, *Stoic Philosophy*. Rist's topically organized study emphasizes the efforts of the Stoics to solve the fundamental metaphysical and ethical issues raised by Aristotle. Johnny Christensen, *An Essay on the Unity of Stoic Philosophy*, is a short and clearly written general study which argues that the unifying theme of Stoic philosophy is its rational conception of reality and its consequent conclusion that physical and moral laws are identical. Max Pohlenz, *Die Stoa: Geschichte einer geistigen Bewegung* (2 vols.) is an indispensable general study which emphasizes the importance the Stoics attached to the use of knowledge as a means of improving the moral quality of human life.

On a slightly less general level Samuel Sambursky, *Physics of the Stoics*, gives major attention to the Stoic ideas of the continuum and continuity, which they used against the atomists. Sambursky also discusses *pneuma* as a force of cohesion and sympathy in the universe. The Stoic conception of time is discussed by Victor Goldschmidt in *Le Système stoicien et l'idée de temps*. This work is a thorough summary of time, its classical background, and its role in every aspect of Stoic thought. The same topic, without a direct treatment of the Stoics, is covered by John F. Calla-han, *Four Views of Time in Ancient Philosophy*, with fairly good treatments of Plato, Aristotle, Plotinus, and Augustine, who respectively used time in a metaphorical, physical, metaphysical, and psychological sense.

Stoic psychology is covered in two general studies already cited, George Brett, *A History of Psychology, Ancient and Patristic* (chap. 15), and Anthelme Chaignet, *Histoire de la psychologie des Grecs* (vol. 2 and vols. 3–5). Stoic epistemology and logic are covered in William and Martha Kneale, *The Development of Logic*, chapter 3 on "The Megarians and the Stoics," and in a well-documented study by G. Watson, *The Stoic Theory of Knowledge*. Watson interprets much of Stoic epistemological writing as a response to attacks by the skeptics. Benson Mates, *Stoic Logic*, is worth consulting on Zeno, Cleanthes, and Chrysippus. Mates notes that the Stoics broke with Aristotle and adopted a system of logic based on proposition and inference. His concluding comments treat other schol-arly evaluations of Stoic logic. Essays on various aspects of Stoicism appear in A. A. Long, *Problems in Stoicism*. The standard scholarly collec-tion of the writings of the Stoics is Hermann von Arnim, *Stoicorum Veterum Fragmenta* (4 vols.).

Neo-Platonism

The best introduction to the development of neo-Platonic thought in the ancient world aside from the general histories already cited is still Thomas Whittaker, *The Neo-Platonists: A Study in the History of Hel-lenism*. Whittaker is deficient in his treatment of Plotinus compared to other works, but his work is valuable for its attention to Proclus and Iam-blichus (followers of Plotinus) and the general influence of neo-Platinism on western thought. Philip Merlan, *From Platonism to Neo-Platonism*, is not really an introductory survey. It is a most interesting study of the evo-lution of ancient Platonism which discusses a variety of topics. Merlan explains that the neo-Platonists continued a process of explicating the philosophy of Plato begun with Aristotle. He includes an excellent treat-ment of the pivotal figure Posidonius. R. T. Wallis, *Neoplatonism*, is an especially concise survey which emphasizes the religious aspects of the movement. The German scholar Hans J. Krämer has done two important studies of neo-Platonism. *Der Ursprung der Geistmetaphysik: Untersuchun-gen zur Geschichte des Platonismus zwischen Platon und Plotin* deals with the evolution of the neo-Platonic idea of divine intelligences (intermedi-aries between the realm of pure being and the sensible world). *Platonism und hellenistische Philosophie* studies the interpretations of Plato's phi-losophy in the late fourth-century Academy and in early Hellenistic thought. Krämer devotes special attention to the skepticism of the Acad-emy, the influence of the *Timaeus* on the Stoics and Epicureans, their theory of values, and Epicurus on "minimal parts."

PLOTINUS

The most convenient edition of *The Enneads* for student use is Stephen MacKenna's translation, first done in five volumes in 1927–30 but now available in a fourth edition with a foreword by Eric R. Dodds and an introduction by Paul Henry. A critical edition intended for advanced scholars is being prepared by Paul Henry and H. R. Schwyzer entitled *Plotini Opera*. This edition was begun in 1951 and now contains two volumes covering the first five *Enneads*. Volume 2 has been translated into English. This work also appears as part of the Oxford Classical Texts series. The text of *The Enneads* is reconstructed from the best philological and archaeological evidence available and a translation appears on each facing page. A Loeb Classical Library edition in six volumes is in preparation under the editorship of Arthur H. Armstrong. Paul Henry makes several remarkable contributions by reconstructing the thought of Plotinus and the text of *The Enneads* in *Études plotiniennes* (vol. 1), *Les États du texte de Plotin,* and *Les Manuscrits des "Ennéades."* He also treats the use of Plotinus's thought in later antiquity in *Plotin et l'occident.*

Introductions in English include an older but well-written study by William R. Inge, *The Philosophy of Plotinus* (2 vols.). Inge is especially interesting because he shares with Plotinus an intense interest in mysticism. More recent studies include Arthur H. Armstrong, *The Architecture of the Intelligible Universe in the Philosophy of Plotinus: An Analytic and Historical Study.* Armstrong focuses on Plotinus's view of the intellect in understanding the universe and the higher reality of the "one," *nous,* and the soul. See also Philippus V. Pistorius, *Plotinus and Neoplatonism: An Introductory Study.* Emile Bréhier, *The Philosophy of Plotinus,* concentrates on the intermediaries and the role of the "one" in Plotinus's system, and he notes that Plotinus was familiar with Indian mystical ideas (see chap. 7, "The Orientalism of Plotinus"). John Rist, *Plotinus: The Road to Reality,* is somewhat disjointed but is nonetheless a good study of various themes in the philosophy of Plotinus. Rist raises a central question concerning how the "one" can be the basis of all existence and at the same time transcendent. Chapter 13 notes the important originality of Plotinus. Eric Dodds, "Traditional and Personal Achievement in the Philosophy of Plotinus," in *The Ancient Concept of Progress and Other Essays on Greek Literature and Belief* (pp. 126–140), is an important essay which argues that Plotinus remained a true Hellenist in his philosophy. He attempted to solve the spiritual problems of his time within the context of rationalism. His idea of mysticism was rational: for him the comprehension of the "one" meant the use of analytic reason, not its denial. Spiritual progress was not by revelation or magic; it was by the rational exploration of the self.

One of the significant elements in the philosophy of Plotinus was his attitude toward evil and especially his attitude toward the relationship of evil to the material world. Plotinus criticized the gnostics for their insistence that matter itself was evil, yet there was a strong dualism in his own system which rather clearly suggests that the flesh is a detriment to spiritual progress. The general issue of the origins and character of evil are reviewed in Benjamin A. G. Fuller, *The Problem of Evil in Plotinus*. He discusses the distinction of metaphysical, physical, and moral evil and reviews the roles of each in earlier Greek philosophy. Fuller also examines the contradictory beliefs—the goodness of the world vs. matter as nonbeing (and thus evil)—and the consequences inherent in Plotinus. Plotinus attempted to combine these two ideas in his theory of emanations, but Fuller concludes that he failed. The problem of evil is treated within the entire context of post-Aristotelian philosophy in William C. Greene, *Moira: Fate, Good, and Evil in Greek Thought* (chap. 11), and with less focus in Edward Caird, *The Evolution of Theology in the Greek Philosophers* (vol. 2, chaps. 16–19 on the Stoics and chaps. 20–26 on the neo-Platonists).

There are innumerable journal articles which deal with Plotinus; none are more interesting than the exchange between Philip Merlan, Eric R. Dodds, and Arthur H. Armstrong on the question of whether Plotinus believed in (or even practiced) magic. Merlan argues that Plotinus actively practiced magic and that the practice was consistent with the mental world of the third century A.D.; see "Plotinus and Magic," *Isis* 44 (1953): 341–348. Dodds concedes that Plotinus believed in magic but argues that he scorned its use because he believed it exploited universal power for personal ends; see *The Greeks and the Irrational* (Appendix 2:2, p. 285). Armstrong argues that Plotinus believed in magic but that it was limited to the control of physical elements in humanity, i.e., magic could control the body of the philosopher but not the "real self," the intellect, or anything divine; see "Was Plotinus a Magician?", *Phronesis* 1:1 (1955):73–79. Additional material on Plotinus can be found in the entire issue of the *Revue internationale de philosophie* 1970 (2) and in *Les Sources de Plotin*, a series of important papers and discussions by eminent scholars. This is one of the Entretiens sur l'antiquité classique series.

Historical Writings

All of the serial and nonserial bibliographies in ancient history and the history of ancient philosophy cover major publications concerning the historians of Greece and Rome. Maurice Platnauer, *Fifty Years (and Twelve) of Classical Scholarship*, devotes chapter 6 by G. T. Griffith to "The

Greek Historians" and chapter 13 by A. D. McDonald to "The Roman Historians." The continual reviews of literature on Herodotus, Thucydides, and Tacitus in *Classical World* are also informative. Albin Lesky, *A History of Greek Literature*, has excellent bibliographical references on historical writing.

Several convenient anthologies of the writings of the Greek historians have been published. The older collection by Francis R. B. Godolphin, *The Greek Historians* (2 vols.), is still good and can now be supplemented by Moses I. Finley, *The Greek Historians*. The scholarly and critical edition of sources is F. Jacoby, *Die Fragmente der griechischen Historiker* (15 vols.).

James W. Thompson, *History of Historical Writings* (2 vols.), is a sound reference survey. Chapters 1–8 in volume 1 cover the history of the ancient world, pagan and Christian. Robin G. Collingwood, *The Idea of History*, is equally broad in scope but is basically an interpretive work which tries to define the principal characteristics of the historical method. Part 1 on the ancient world develops Collingwood's theme that Herodotus's interest in the particulars of the past rather than Thucydides' interest in the broad cycles and patterns of the past was the starting point of historical scholarship. The development of history in the ancient world is covered by James T. Shotwell, *An Introduction to the History of History*. Shotwell deals essentially with the ancient world; there are bibliographical notes at the end of each chapter and judicious criticisms of the major historians. Another old standard is John B. Bury, *The Ancient Greek Historians*. It surveys the major writers to Livy. There is little reason to refer to Shotwell or Bury if the two following works are available. Michael Grant, *The Ancient Historians*, is a survey encompassing the period from the beginning of recorded history to the conflict of Christian and pagan histories. Grant's style is urbane and eminently readable; his treatment of Thucydides (chaps. 4–7) is especially good. Stephen Usher, *The Historians of Greece and Rome*, surveys the important classical writers of history and emphasizes the mixture of rhetoric and genuine history in their writings. As noted, the ubiquity and importance of rhetoric in the classical world must be emphasized because it mixed with every field of intellectual expression.

Kurt von Fritz, *Die Griechische Geschichtsschreibung* (now 1 vol. in 2), is as yet untranslated. The period to Thucydides is covered in volumes 1 and 2: the first is an analysis; the second contains notes and invaluable comments on scholarship in the field.

Somewhat narrower studies include Arnold W. Gomme, *The Greek Attitude toward Poetry and History*. Gomme denies that the Greeks made the sharp distinction between poetry and history familiar to the modern world. Both forms were used to relate past events and they applied overlapping methods and standards. Thus Greek historians like Thucydides were sensitive to questions of evidence and they used poetic and rhetorical devices to dramatize events. Chester G. Starr, *The Awakening of the Greek Historical Spirit*, examines the Greek invention of history and correlates its development with the general advance of Greek self-consciousness and their interest in exploring every area of human experience. Starr's work encompasses the period of Herodotus. François Chatelet, *La Naissance de l'histoire*, covers to Isocrates and argues that the polis motivated a deepening sense of history in Greek thought, i.e., history developed within the deeper self-consciousness of the Greeks generated by the political life of the polis and the efforts to justify the polis's role in Greek life.

Herodotus

Herodotus is not as important as Thucydides in developing a genuine historical method or in contributing to the history of ideas, but he is well worth studying to compare his work with the historical revolution begun by Thucydides. The literature on Herodotus is reviewed by Paul MacKendrick, "Herodotus 1954–1963," in *Classical World* 56 (1962–(1963):269 ff. The best evaluation of Herodotus's place in the development of history is J. L. Myres, *Herodotus, Father of History*. Aubrey de Selincourt, *The World of Herodotus*, is also worth consulting. Selincourt's survey places Herodotus into the general context of Greek history and culture. Part 4 is an exceptionally good synopsis of the general character of Greek literature, including science and philosophy. Also see Kurt von Fritz, *Die Griechische Geschichtsschreibung* (vol. 1, chap. 5), and the scholarly collection edited by Walter Marg, *Herodot: eine Auswahl aus der Neueren Forschung*.

Thucydides

Reviews of recent scholarship on Thucydides can be found in F. M. Wassermann, "Thucydidean Scholarship: 1942–1956," in *Classical World* 55 (1956–1957:65ff., and M. Chambers, *Classical World* 58 (1963–1964):6ff.

The best introduction to Thucydides is John Finley, *Thucydides*, which effectively surveys the contents of the writings and the general background. Finley sees Thucydides as an example of the distinctive Greek ability to grasp detailed reality and also derive general ideas and laws from it. He was closely related to the sophists as well as to the medical tradition in his analysis of human nature and motivation. Other good introductions include George F. Abbott, *Thucydides: A Study in Historical Reality*, which praises Thucydides for objectivity in his analysis of the causes of the Peloponnesian Wars, and Frank E. Adcock, *Thucydides and His History*, which references several different interpretations of Thucydides. A general and more detailed survey by George B. Grundy,

Thucydides and the History of His Age (2 vols.), devotes volume 1 to the background of Thucydides' writings and a history of the manuscripts; volume 2 analyzes his description of the Peloponnesian Wars. The history of the wars is explained in detail by Arnold W. Gomme, *A Historical Commentary on Thucydides* (4 vols.). A. Andrewes and K. J. Dover assisted in the completion of volume 4, which was left incomplete at Gomme's death. H. Herter, *Thukydides*, is a useful collection of scholarly articles and Kurt von Fritz, *Die Griechische Geschichtsschreibung* (especially chap. 7), is also recommended.

The two most interesting general interpretations of Thucydides are Charles N. Cochrane, *Thucydides and the Science of History*, and Francis M. Cornford, *Thucydides Mythistoricus*. Cochrane believes that Thucydides was a genuinely scientific thinker who eschewed a mythical approach and applied the idea of human nature and the methods of investigation found in Hippocratic medicine to the study of history. Cornford, contrarily, suggests that Thucydides was very far from a scientific or modern approach to history. He organized his material according to older modes of thought represented in Greek drama, especially in Aeschylus. Thus he analyzed the Peloponnesian Wars in terms of radically simplified character strengths and weaknesses and concerned himself with human motivation rather than with the social forces that interest modern historians. Jacqueline de Romilly makes less dramatic but equally important contributions in *Thucydides and Athenian Imperialism* and *Histoire et raison chez Thucydide*. Romilly argues that imperialism was the central theme in Thucydides' writings (and therefore a key to understanding his several redactions in completing his work). According to Romilly, Thucydides took Pericles as his model and hoped for the improvement of politics through prudence and reason. In this he differed from the cosmopolitanism of Isocrates and the philosophical withdrawal of Plato. Romilly concludes that Thucydides accepted the applicability of reason to the study of history but believed that reason would provide only general rules of character and conduct—not scientific predictability.

Roman Historians

In history as in nearly all other areas of intellectual and cultural development the Roman contributions pale in comparison to those of the Greeks. Polybius, the historian most interested in the historical development of Rome, was himself Greek. Frank W. Walbank, *A Historical Commentary on Polybius* (2 vols.; to be 3 vols.), includes excellent commentaries on his writings, with the philological background and a political and social context for all of Polybius's references and ideas. Also see Walbank's *Polybius*, a topical summary with many comments on recent Polybius scholarship. Kurt von Fritz, *The Theory of the Mixed Constitution in Antiquity: A Critical Analysis of Polybius's Political Ideas*, is also essential.

Von Fritz believes that Polybius's interests as a historian and as a states-
man contributed to his theory that Roman success was influenced by
Rome's development of a balanced constitution. Three appendices
excerpt from Polybius's comments on political theory. The best systematic analysis of Polybius's thought, however, is found in P. Pedech, *La
Méthode historique de Polybe*, a topical study which also contains an excellent bibliography.

The general study by Donald R. Dudley, *The World of Tacitus;* the V.
Pöschl collection, *Tacitus;* and the reviews of recent literature in *Classical
World* 48 (1954):5 ff. and 58 (1964):5 ff. provide information on Tacitus.
See A. H. McDonald's article on Roman historiography in the *Oxford
Classical Dictionary* and Max L. W. Laistner, *The Greater Roman Historians,*
for other and more general surveys of the Roman historians.

Political Theory

General Surveys

Several general surveys of the history of political theory include sections on the classical world. The one-volume survey most familiar to
American undergraduates is undoubtedly George Sabine, *A History of
Political Theory.* Sabine's summaries are accurate and his criticisms fair;
he includes bibliographical notes. Chapters 1–7 (pp. 3–141) cover from
the Greeks to the medieval period. John Bowle, *Western Political Thought
from the Origins to Rousseau,* is less effective, but it attempts to put the
evolution of political theory into a general material and cultural context.
Pages 15–89 cover the Greeks; pages 89–145, the Romans. Christopher
Morris, *Western Political Thought I: Plato to Augustine,* is adequate. Every
student should be acquainted with Charles H. McIlwain, *The Growth of
Political Thought in the West,* although it is no longer used as a text. McIlwain was a masterful teacher and he knew the classical tradition of political ideas better than most scholars have since. This survey amply shows
his immense erudition. McIlwain's only discernible weakness as a historian of political thought was his failure to appreciate the importance
of religious motivation in the development of political ideology in his
survey of postclassical thought.

The Ancient Near East

This bibliographical survey essentially concentrates on the intellectual development of ancient Greece and Rome, but the ancient Near East cannot be ignored. Greco-Roman civilization was influenced by Near Eastern religion and to a lesser extent by Near Eastern political thought. The distinctively Greek political thought centered on the polis or city-state was unique and essentially untouched by the Near East. After the decline of the polis during the Hellenistic period, however, eastern ideas began to have an important influence, especially in the development of the idea of divine or semidivine kings as political institutions. Hence some references to the political thinking of the ancient Near East are necessary. There is a good survey of the ancient Near East in the two-volume work by Francis Dvornik, *Early Christian and Byzantine Political Philosophy: Origins and Background* (vol. 1, pp. 1–132 and 278–403). Dvornik's survey of the ancient Near East and of the Old Testament is excellent; however, his treatment of Greek and Hellenistic ideas is less valuable and his analysis of the New Testament (pp. 403–452) is weak. His treatment of Jesus completely lacks critical analysis and he even proposes that Jesus specifically attacked the Hellenistic idea of kingship (p. 432 ff.). Dvornik's review of the ancient Near East's concepts of political theory, chiefly the concept of the status of the king, are nevertheless worth reading. Occasionally, as in Egypt, kings were regarded as personally divine, but more commonly they were regarded as special stewards or servants of the gods. As stewards the kings had important ritual functions; they represented their people by petitioning the gods and they served both their gods and their people in performing certain seasonal rites. These rites commonly involved the ritual death or humiliation of the king and they may have descended from the practice of commemorating the vegetative cycle. In any case they had important magical significance. Heated arguments sometimes occur over whether the kingly ritual was adopted by the Israelites or whether their system was free of magical ceremony. The literature on this question is reviewed in "Living Issues in Biblical Scholarship: Divine Kingship and the Old Testament" in *The Expository Times* 62 (1950–1951):36–42. The argument that Israel adopted the ritual function of the king is persuasively put in Samuel H. Hooke's edition of *Myth Ritual and Kingship: Essays on the Theory and Practice of Kingship in the Ancient Near East and in Israel*. The editor's introduction (pp. 1–22), A. R. Johnson's "Hebrew Concept of Kingship" (pp. 204–236), and the critical essay by Samuel G. F. Brandon, "The Myth and Ritual Position Critically Examined" (pp. 261–293), are especially valuable. Brandon's essay, other critical comments, and an alternative theory can be found in Henri Frankfort, *Kingship and the Gods: A Study of Ancient Near Eastern Religion as the Integration of Society and Nature*.

Greek Political Theory

An appreciation of the Greek attitude toward the city-state or the polis is basic to an understanding of Greek and Roman political theory. That attitude was fundamentally different from modern attitudes toward the city and modern forms of patriotism. The Greeks of the classical period considered the polis essential to a fully civilized life—the ideas were nearly interchangeable. During the Hellenistic period and in the Roman period of antiquity, the city obviously could not maintain as exalted a station. Nonetheless, the city retained immense prestige because intellectuals continued to admire the culture of the past based on the city and because cities continued as centers of cultural activity even after they had lost political importance.

The most general survey on the role of the city in the ancient world is Mason Hammond, *The City in the Ancient World*, with an annotated bibliography of 162 pages. Victor Ehrenberg, *The Greek State*, is a fine survey of the Greek polis with a chronological summary of the Hellenic and Hellenistic states. Ehrenberg considers the polis as a distinctive element in Greek civilization which sponsored the growth of culture and the conflict of the individual with society. The conclusion (pp. 241–253) is an excellent synopsis of Ehrenberg's conception of the role of the city-state in Greek history. Mason Hammond, *City State and World State in Greek and Roman Political Theory until Augustus*, surveys the transition from Greek society and its body-politic based on the polis to the world empires of the Hellenistic-Roman era and the influence the idea of the polis had in that transition. Cicero's efforts to readapt Greek political theory for use in the Empire is emphasized. Additional information on imperial Roman attitudes toward the city as a political form ideally suited for the full development of human life is found in Lidia S. Mazzolani, *The Idea of the City in Roman Thought: From Walled City to Spiritual Commonwealth*.

Many of the most important works on Greek political theory were cited previously as contributions to the political theory of Plato and Aristotle (see above, p. 49 and p. 80). Of these the most important are the studies by Ernest Barker, *The Political Thought of Plato and Aristotle* and *Greek Political Theory: Plato and His Predecessors*. Barker's treatment of Aristotle is brilliant and he covers the full range of Greek political thought and contrasts it in an interesting way with modern political thought. Other works bearing on Greek political theory were recommended as studies of Greek civilization and Greek philosophy in general. Of the former the most important are Adkins's *Merit and Responsibility: A Study in Greek Values* and *From the Many to the One* and Jaeger's *Paideia* (see above, pp. 15–16).

The best work devoted to the history of Greek political thought suited to the beginning student is Donald Kagan, *The Great Dialogue: History of Greek Political Thought from Homer to Polybius*. Kagan emphasizes the importance of the polis in the development of Greek political ideas. His treatment of the aristocratic theories of Theognis and Pindar (chap. 3) is excellent, and he includes an interesting argument that political theory began as a dialogue between the democratic and aristocratic parties within the polis. T. A. Sinclair, *A History of Greek Political Thought*, is a competent and more detailed study of Greek political ideas to the early Roman Empire. An older work by J. L. Myres, *The Political Ideas of the Greeks: With Special Reference to Early Notions about Law, Authority, and Natural Order in Relation to Human Ordinance*, is still valuable. The best section is lecture 6 on "The Notion of Freedom *(Eleutheria)*: The Man and the Citizen." There is different and useful older work in Georg Busolt and H. Swoboda's contribution to the *Handbuch der Altertumswissenschaft, Griechische Staatskunde* (2 vols.), a reference-style treatment which covers both the institutional and theoretical development of Greek politics. See also the collection of articles by outstanding scholars, *Zur Griechischen Staatskunde*, edited by F. Gschnitzer.

Donald Kagan, *Sources in Greek Political Thought from Homer to Polybius*, and Ernest Barker, *From Alexander to Constantine: Passages and Documents Illustrating the History of Social and Political Ideas, 336 B.C.–A.D. 337*, are collections of documents.

There are a number of specialized studies on the early development of Greek political theory. Sound surveys of the general social and cultural background are included in Victor Ehrenberg, *The Greek State*, and in Werner Jaeger, *Paideia* (vol. 1), both already cited. H. Frisch, *Might and Right in Antiquity*, is a generally informative study of literary references to *dike* (justice) and other terms related to the development of ideas on individual and social rights. The multiple meanings of two further key terms are surveyed by Felix Heinimann, *Nomos und Physis: Herkunft und Bedeutung einer Antithese in griechischen Denken des 5. Jahrhunderts*. This study is equally valuable in the study of ethics and political philosophy. Martin Ostwald, *Nomos and the Beginnings of the Athenian Democracy*, provides an advanced philological study of Greek references to *thesmos* and *nomos* (custom and law). Ostwald argues that Cleisthenes deliberately instituted the use of *nomos* to designate statutes or legislation.

The idea of law was not as vital to Greek political theory as to Roman thought, but it was an important part of Greek speculation. The institutional background of law is covered in Robert J. Bonner and Gertrude E. Smith, *The Administration of Justice from Homer to Aristotle* (2 vols.). Volume 1 discusses the growth of the judiciary system; volume 2, judicial "practice and procedure." Greek legal thought is surveyed by John W. Jones, *The Law and Legal Theory of the Greeks: An Introduction*. Jones devotes chapters 1–7 to general principles and philosophical implications. Valuable summaries can also be found in two articles from the *Dictionary of the History of Ideas*: M. R. Konvitz, "Equity in Law and Ethics" (vol. 2, pp. 148–154), and Martin Ostwald, "Ancient Greek Idea of Law" (vol. 2, pp. 673–685). Erik Wolf, *Griechisches Rechtsdenken* (4 vols.), is not a study of law in the narrow sense, but it treats the general theme of the role of regulating rules in society and their relationship to justice. The volumes currently reach from the pre-Socratics to Plato.

The important theme of freedom is treated in an article by Arnaldo Momigliano, "Freedom of Speech in Antiquity," in the *Dictionary of the History of Ideas* 2:252–263, a survey which includes the ancient Near East. The best work on the ancient Greek ideal for the student is Max Pohlenz, *Freedom in Greek Life and Thought: The History of an Ideal,* which summarizes the development of the idea of freedom as political participation. Pohlenz's description of "inner freedom," integrity, and independence from externals and the separation of those themes in the Hellenistic period is excellent. His comments on differences between the Greek and Christian views of liberty, especially that of Paul the Apostle, are also useful. The differences between Greek and Christian ideas are the subject of D. Nestle's *Eleutheria: Studien zum Wesen der Freiheit bei den Griechen und im Neuen Testament.* Nestle takes a broader approach and discusses the question of free will and determinism. Unfortunately, there is no systematic study of utopian thought in the Greek or ancient worlds. The important literary references can be found in a short lecture by H. C. Baldry in his *Ancient Utopias.* There are a few interesting comments on social influences on ancient utopian thought in Moses I. Finley, "Utopianism: Ancient and Modern," in *The Critical Spirit: Essays in Honor of Herbert Marcuse* (pp. 3–21), edited by Kurt H. Wolff and Barrington Moore. Finley shows that utopian thought was influenced by social interests —thus the utopians were oriented toward fantasies rather than realizable schemes and to hierarchical structure themes.

Eric A. Havelock, *The Liberal Temper in Greek Politics,* is noteworthy because Havelock complains that the traditional admiration of Plato and Aristotle led historians, e.g., Ernest Barker, to believe their ideas were representative of Greek political thought. Havelock argues that Plato and Aristotle represented a conservative attitude toward politics and that they sought to discourage reform by insisting that human nature, hence human institutions, is fixed and immutable. They thus opposed other schools, especially the sophists, who followed Democritus in the belief that human nature is malleable and shaped by historical circumstance. According to Havelock, the sophists justified Greek efforts to promote human equality and participation in political life. Havelock's argument is based on thin evidence, but his indictment of Plato is more convincing than Karl Popper's.

Hellenistic and Roman Political Theory

The Hellenistic and Roman periods were notable for the development of ideas concerning the unity and essential equality of humanity and the notion of absolute divine rulership. The history of the former idea is covered by H. C. Baldry in his *The Unity of Mankind in Greek Thought*. Baldry argues that Greek philosophers long before Alexander had a genuine, though marginal, idea of human unity promoted by a philosophic concept of the species and a sophistic skepticism about traditional divisions between peoples. The scholarly disputes on this subject center on the role of Alexander the Great. William W. Tarn suggests that Alexander consciously adopted and was prepared to promote the idea of human unity as part of his program for political unity; see Tarn's "Alexander the Great and the Unity of Mankind" and his fuller treatment, *Alexander the Great*. Tarn's position has been vigorously attacked; see Ernst Badian, "Alexander the Great and the Unity of Mankind." Tarn's lecture and Badian's critique are both in G. T. Griffith, *Alexander the Great: The Main Problems*.

There are two good recent studies on the development of the ruler cult. See Fritz Taeger, *Charisma: Studien zur Geschichte des antiken Herrscherkultes* (2 vols.), and Lucien Cerfaux and J. Tondriau, *Un Concurrent du Christianisme: le culte des souverains dans la civilisation gréco-romain.* Taeger's use of ancient literary evidence and his appreciation (see vol. 1, chap. 1) of the religious foundations of the idea of the deified ruler are outstanding. Cerfaux and Tondriau include a detailed survey of ruler cults in the Near East, Greece, and the Roman Empire, with comments on the Christian attitude toward deified rulers and an excellent bibliography (pp. 9–73). On the Roman period see also Lily R. Taylor, *The Divinity of the Roman Emperor*, which has a good background survey in the introductory chapter and an examination of evidence concerning the divinity of Caesar and Augustus. Taylor includes an especially good list of the relevant inscriptions which have survived; however, her work has been criticized for its treatment of Near Eastern materials and for exaggerating the divinity accorded Caesar and Augustus. See the review by Arthur D. Nock in *Gnomon* 8 (1932):514–517.

Important articles include A. E. R. Boak, "The Theoretical Basis of the Deification of Rulers in Antiquity," in *Classical Journal* 11 (1916):293–297, on the relevance of the hero and Euhemerist theories of the transformation of heroes into god-figures in Greek thought; and Erwin R. Goodenough, "The Political Philosophy of Hellenistic Kingship," in *Yale Classical Studies* 1 (1928):55–102, on the ancient religious and philosophical ideas which contributed to the development of ruler cults.

Frank E. Adcock, *Roman Political Ideas and Practice*, is a convenient introduction to Roman political theory, with comments on the weakness of Roman political ideas. Francis Dvornik, *Early Christian and Byzantine Political Philosophy* (vol. 2, pp. 453–558), and volume 1 of R. W. and A. J. Carlyle's *A History of Medieval Political Theory in the West* are more complex surveys. The Carlyles' survey adopts a too liberal point of view, exaggerates the importance of Cicero and Seneca, and its treatment of imperial theory is rather thin—but their superb analysis of Christian political attitudes and Roman legal theory make their history one of the best books on Roman political thought. Two collections from the Wege der Forschung series are also recommended: R. Klein, *Prinzipät und Freiheit*, with especially good articles by C. Koch on "Roma Aeterna" and M. Fuhrmann on "Die Alleinherrschaft und das Problem der Gerechtigkeit"; and his *Das Staatsdenken der Römer*, with good articles by H. Drexler on "Die Moralische Geschichtsauffassung der Römer" and by E. Meyer on "Vom Griechischen und römischen Staatsgedanken."

The article by Gaines Post, "Ancient Roman Ideas of Law," in the *Dictionary of the History of Ideas* 2:685–690, Herbert F. Jolowicz's lucid *Historical Introduction to the Study of Roman Law*, and Fritz Schulz's *Principles of Roman Law* are excellent references on Roman law. Schulz has an especially interesting study in part 4, chapter 2, of the "Character and Tendencies of Jurisprudence in the Bureaucratic Period," which sketches the efforts of the imperial lawyers to classify the law to achieve scientific stability and simplicity of principle. Adolf Berger's *Encyclopedic Dictionary of Roman Law* explains the key terms and has an exhaustive bibliography.

Several more specialized studies on Roman political ideas focus on the history of the meaning of key terms. Donald A. Earl, *The Moral and Political Tradition of Rome*, studies the significance of such terms as *virtus* and *gloria* which emphasize that Romans thought of politics and history in moral terms. Chaim Wirszubski, *Libertas as a Political Ideal at Rome during the Late Republic and Early Principate*, traces the evolution of the idea of *libertas* through the disintegration of the late republican order. See the critical review by Arnaldo Momigliano in the *Journal of Roman Studies* 41 (1951):149–153.

Chapter 3:   ANCIENT SCIENCE

Introduction

THE CHIEF FORCE that determines the world view of educated people in the modern world is science. Philosophy and religion were more influential in the ancient world. Nonetheless, ancient science merits study because it exemplifies the brilliant achievements of the Greeks. Ancient social and intellectual forces prevented the development of a scientific method similar to that known in the modern world. Yet the Greeks were aware of the chief problems of science; they established suitable vocabularies and rubrics of thought and did basic work in developing the experimentalism and mathematical quantification which are the distinguishing characteristics of modern science. The contributions of the Greeks to mathematical and experimental methods are outlined in Israel Drabkin, "An Appraisal of Greek Science" (pp. 123–141), in volume 1 of Robert Palter, *Toward Modern Science*. Drabkin notes that the ancient Greeks used experimentation but did not write about it—thus giving the impression that they were dominated by philosophical prejudices. A similar defense can be found in William A. Heidel, *The Heroic Age of Science: The Conception, Ideals, and Methods of Science among the Ancient Greeks;* especially see part 1, "Conceptions and Ideals of Science among Greeks," and part 2, chapter 5, "Experimentation." Heidel believes that the Greeks used experimentation and that since they were aesthetically inclined, their writings did not report the dreary details of experiments. Heidel also argues that ancient scientists were amateurs, lacking standards of exactitude imposed by modern professionals.

Whatever the virtues of Greek science during the classical period, it is true that science was more thoroughly mixed with philosophic and religious ideas in the Hellenistic and Roman periods. Hence, while the influence of astrology and magic is discussed in chapter 5 below as part of the history of religious thought, it is noted that they were also instrumental in forming the world view of scientists during those periods. Progress was still being made on the level of specific and detailed investigation, but that progress never resulted in a distinctly scientific world view as a counter to the failing of philosophy and religion, nor did it encourage the practical exploitation of nature.

An understanding of ancient science requires crossreference to the development of ancient philosophy and this chapter is organized with that need in mind. It is especially important that the user consult the works recommended for the study of the scientific ideas of Plato and Aristotle (see pp. 45 and 60).

General Bibliographical Resources

The general guides to ancient history include Varet's *Manuel de bibliographie philosophique* (vol. 2, part 2), which is a very useful survey of the history of the philosophy of science. References to the history of ancient science are scattered throughout the bibliographies of the *Cambridge Ancient History* and are concentrated in the notes accompanying W. H. S. Jones's article, "Hellenistic Science and Mathematics," in volume 5, pp. 284–311. The serial bibliographies and bibliographically oriented periodicals in ancient history provide reasonably reliable checks on important new publications on ancient science. *L'Année philologique* and the *Bulletin signalétique* (522) have separate sections on the field, and the *Journal of Hellenic Studies* has especially excellent reviews of important new publications. The *Journal of the History of Ideas* carries occasional reviews of scholarship on ancient science and a few excellent articles in the field. The general histories of the Greek, Hellenistic, and Roman civilizations reflect the general disinterest of classicists in scientific development. An obvious exception is George Sarton, *A History of Science*. This work, including a volume on the golden age of Greek culture and one on the Hellenistic era, will be discussed below.

Nonserial Bibliographies

There are several excellent guides to the general study of the history of science, but those available for the study of ancient science are less adequate than those in modern science. General surveys of research resources in science, including the history of science, include Francis B. Jenkins, *Science Reference Sources*, and J. L. Thornton and R. I. J. Tulley, *Scientific Books, Libraries, and Collectors*. Thornton and Tulley include a history of scientific societies and scientific periodicals with biographical sketches of the leading scientists of all ages. The best recent one-volume guide to the history of science in English is K. J. Rider, *History of Science and Technology: A Selected Bibliography for Students* (see pages 1–56 for a good list of general tools in the history of science). Since the ancient period is covered in only seven pages (pp. 77–83), only the most important and obvious citations to the ancient period are included. The best of several recent works, François Russo, *Éléments d'histoire des sciences et des techniques: bibliographie,* reviews general tools (pp. 1–29), the ancient period (pp. 30–39), and classifies a treatment of the particular subdisciplines of science in Part 4. Russo's work is more useful than Rider's, but his coverage of the ancient period is not thorough. The student should turn to the excellent, albeit outdated, works of George Sarton for a detailed treatment. His *Horus: A Guide to the History of Science* is a rich source of information on writings, scientific societies, conferences, and the leading scholars in the history of science. He covers general materials (pp. 3–115) and antiquity (pp. 130–137), but his annotations are slight. There are references to each of the particular disciplines of science (pp. 149–194). Consult Sarton, *Introduction to the History of Science* (3 vols. in 4), for a detailed guide to the works and extant writings of important scientists from the beginning to the end of the medieval period. Also see the bibliographical references to ancient science in Morris Cohen and Israel Drabkin, *A Source Book in Greek Science* (pp. 559–568).

Handbooks and Encyclopedias

Two fine encyclopedias in the general history of science are being written. *The Dictionary of Scientific Biography,* edited by Charles C. Gillispie, will be invaluable as a source of biographical information and for its bibliographical aids. Eight volumes are complete and a set of 20 volumes is anticipated. The *Lexikon der Geschichte der Naturwissenschaften* has completed one volume (to "D") and will cover the chief figures and the main ideas and themes in the history of science.

The basic source for information on new literature is *Isis: An International Review Devoted to the History of Science and Civilization* (1913), with important articles, reviews, and an annual bibliography of new literature. *Isis* has been made appreciably easier to use with the appearance of *Isis: Cumulative Bibliography* (2 vols.), edited by M. Whitlow, covering from 1913–1965. *Osiris: Studies on the History of the Philosophy of Science and on the History of Learning and Culture* (1936) is a supplement to *Isis;* both were founded by George Sarton. *The History of Science: An Annual Review of Literature, Research, and Teaching* (1962), edited by Alistair C. Crombie and Michael A. Hoskin, reviews major publications and has bibliographical essays on several areas of research. Other excellent reviews in English can be found in *The British Journal for the History of Science* (1962), *Annals of Science: A Quarterly Review of the History of Science since the Renaissance* (1936), and the Anglo-American *Studies in the History and Philosophy of Science* (1970).

The *British Journal of the Philosophy of Science* (1950), *Philosophy of Science* (1934), and to a lesser but still important extent *The Monist* (1890) concentrate on the philosophy of science. These English-language journals are generally sufficient to find important new publications, and they are supplemented by two French journals, *Archives internationales d'histoire des sciences* (1919) and *Revue d'histoire des sciences et leurs applications* (1947). In addition a German source, now out of print, is recommended as a guide to literature appearing between 1902 and 1942: Karl Sudhoff, *Mitteilungen zur Geschichte der Medizin, der Naturwissenschaft und der Tecknik*. Other serial bibliographies and periodicals will be recommended under appropriate headings below.

General Surveys of the History of Science

The best known history of science is William Dampier, *A History of Science and Its Relations with Philosophy and Religion*, reprinted in 1961 with a valuable bibliographical postscript by I. Bernard Cohen. Dampier's writing is clear and enthusiastic, and he attempts to relate the development of scientific theory to the total cultural matrix. Dampier devotes little space (pp. 1–60) to ancient science, and he is much better on recent developments in the physical sciences than in biology and biochemistry. He is also criticized for too sharply dividing the history of science between clear advances and reactionary opposition, whereas recent scholarship emphasizes the continuity of scientific development and the mutual contribution of conflicting schools of thought to its advance. Dampier's work, however, remains one of the best surveys of the development of science. Charles Singer, *A Short History of Scientific Ideas to 1900*, is a balanced appreciation of the complexity of scientific progress. Singer's treatment of the ancient world (chaps. 1–4) emphasizes the physical sciences, and his treatment of the twentieth century is weak. Two other surveys of scientific thought are just as reliable and well written and improve the treatment of the modern world. Seee Stephen F. Mason, *Main Currents of Scientific Thought: A History of the Sciences,* and William P. D. Wightman, *The Growth of Scientific Ideas.* Mason's survey comments on the institutional aspects of science, e.g., modern American and Soviet institutions. His work is basically a reference source and his chapters on the ancient world (pp. 5–53) are pedestrian. Wightman's survey of chemistry, mechanics, and electricity is sound and he references ancient attitudes toward each area of science.

There are two important, but diverse, multivolume histories of science. René Taton is the general editor of a French series (now translated), *A General History of Science* (4 vols.). It is a straightforward and generally accurate summary. Volume 1 covers the ancient and medieval worlds; volume 2, 1450–1800; volume 3, the nineteenth century; and volume 4, the twentieth century. Like most collective efforts in history Taton's work is uneven in quality and lacks a general theme to make the different volumes coherent. The bibliographies are surprisingly weak for a French work, especially one of such proportions. Lynn Thorndike, *A History of Magic and Experimental Sciences* (8 vols.), has a thematic unity and a coherent development—he suggests that magic was not an obstacle to the development of science but that it actually contributed to the development of experimentation. For example, Thorndike argues that the work of alchemists was one of the foundations of empirical science. He pursues his thesis to about the year 1700 and unquestionably illuminates several cultural involvements which show that the distinction between magic and science was not as clear as many historians previously thought. Thorndike, however, tends to regard all forms of magic as being of the same intellectual quality and historical importance even though systems of magic vary markedly in both qualities. He also tends to underestimate the retarding effect of the pseudosciences, e.g., alchemy, on the development of science.

Scientists and historians of science have always been interested in the criteria to be used in judging proper scientific methods, the characteristics of scientific truths, and the validity of scientific propositions. The issue of whether scientific methods and presuppositions can be used to discover a more secure and reliable body of knowledge than other disciplines is always involved in such controversies. The dispute now centers on "verifiability" and "falsifiability," i.e., whether scientific propositions can be positively proved true or false. Does science retain an objectivity which other methods of inquiry lack?

The recent literature on the status of scientific knowledge is mountainous. The most important writings are listed and surveyed by L. Laudan, "Theories of Scientific Method from Plato to Mach: A Bibliographical Review," in *The History of Science* 7 (1968):1–64, and Jean-Dominique

Roberts, *Philosophie et science: éléments de bibliographie*. Joseph Agassi, "Towards a Historiography of Science," supplement 2 to the journal *History and Theory*, contains an interesting review of the disputes over scientific method and a criticism of science histories and philosophies. Agassi classifies most historians of science as "inductivists," those who believe there has been a clear progression in the development of science based on the accumulation of clear information and analysis by a clear method, and "conventionalists," those who see science as simply a mathematical and experimental way of looking at the world and not as a means of knowing with certainty the real character of the world. These approaches, Agassi argues, are being superseded by a relativistic and critical method which emphasizes the continuity and slow development of scientific theory and the positive value of competing schools of thought. Gerd Buchdahl, "A Revolution in the Historiography of Science?", in *The History of Science* 4 (1965):55–70, is a critical review of Agassi's work; it also reviews the important theories about the character of scientific method and discovery advanced by Thomas S. Kuhn, *The Structure of Scientific Revolutions*. Kuhn opposes the idea that scientific progress is merely an accumulation of facts, logical analysis, the purgation of errors and faulty inferences, and the construction of a universally accepted world view. Kuhn theorizes that science has progressed from one world view to another, each based on an especially dramatic example of scientific investigation and experiment. He notes that science can never fit all of the facts into any one world view but that such failures seldom amount to falsification or disproof. New approaches or world views appear which are more attractive and scientists adopt them instead of the older views. Kuhn sees progress in the known succession of dominant methods to solve puzzles and construct world views, but he rejects the notion that each new view can be neatly labelled true or false. A series of articles on the controversy appears in Imre Lakatos and A. E. Musgrave, *Criticism and the Growth of Knowledge*. The collection contains an article by Karl Popper, the proponent of the "falsifiability" theory of scientific method, "Normal Science and Its Dangers" (pp. 51–59).

There are several good surveys and anthologies on the philosophy of science, especially on the value of scientific method as opposed to other means of forming opinions about the world. The best short introduction is Stephen Toulmin, *The Philosophy of Science: An Introduction*. Morris Cohen, *Reason and Nature: An Essay on the Meaning of the Scientific Method*, is broader in its approach and defends scientific reason against the irrational philosophies of the twentieth century. The essays by the famous French mathematician Henri Poincaré in *The Foundations of Science: Science and Hypothesis: The Value of Science* are also valuable. The popular textbook on the philosophy of science by Ernest Nagel, *The Structure of Science: Problems in the Logic of Scientific Explanation*, is more complex. Nagel's discussion is largely devoted to explaining the methods and assumptions of physics and mathematics, but he includes valuable chapters on problems of method in biology and the social sciences, including history. The best anthology in the field is Sidney Morgenbesser, *Philosophy of Science Today,* and the preeminent collection of more advanced writings is Herbert Feigl and May Brodbeck, *Readings in the Philosophy of Science,* which concentrates primarily on the physical sciences. There is a well-written chapter on the "Philosophical Problems of Biology and Psychology" and an excellent bibliography (pp. 783–799).

The conflict over the proper understanding of scientific method now encompasses ancient science and even extends to the unlikely precincts of the pre-Socratics. Karl Popper, no stranger to disputes, argues in his "Back to the Presocratics" that the pre-Socratic scientists were not observationists, but rationalists. They theorized and then used observation as a check on their theories. Popper sees basic similarities in their methods with those of modern science, although he stretches the validity of their conclusions to do so. Geoffrey S. Kirk, "Popper on Science and the Presocratics," contains a detailed and effective criticism charging that Popper ignores the important preliminary role of observation in pre-Socratic speculation. These essays can be found in Furley and Allen, *Studies in Presocratic Philosophy* I:130–178. Popper replied to Kirk's criticism in *Conjectures and Refutations: The Growth of Scientific Knowledge* (pp. 153 ff.). A different approach to ancient science is taken by H. Gomperz, "Problems and Methods of Early Greek Science," in the *Journal of the History of Ideas* 4 (1943):161–176. Gomperz concentrates on the "thought patterns," analogies used by the Greeks in their first efforts to make scientific sense of the world—he found that the principal patterns were biological, political, and mechanical.

Surveys of Ancient Science

The best one-volume history of ancient science is Marshall Clagett, *Greek Science in Antiquity,* which surveys the development of scientific ideas throughout antiquity and cautiously discusses the causes of the shifting fortunes of ancient science. Clagett's discussion of the development of the sciences in late antiquity is unusually strong. A different view of ancient science is taken by Benjamin Farrington, *Greek Science: Its Meaning for Us.* Farrington gives a Marxian analysis of the origin, development, and decline of ancient science. He supposes that middle-class interests and the advance of technology inspired the development of science. Plato and Aristotle, however, reoriented science because they represented a different social order, i.e., one based on slave labor. They disdained manual labor and scorned the use of technology as a source of scientific information; hence for them science was the theoretical (rational) analysis of the world according to the standards of logical consistency. Science became a means of correctly understanding the structure and operation of the universe rather than a means of manipulating it for human advancement. Farrington develops his argument further in *Science and Politics in the Ancient World*. The reasons for the birth and decline of ancient science are also discussed by Ludwig Edelstein, "Motives and Incentives for Science in Antiquity" (pp. 15–42), in Alistair C. Crombie, *Scientific Change*. Edelstein agrees that ancient science made some contributions to a human control of nature, but he denies that it was ever primarily practical or that it was importantly fructified by technology. He argues that science was always a marginal part of ancient society. It was never sufficiently institutionalized to play a more important role in determining thought or action, that is, it did not provide careers or full-time employment for intellectuals and never had the use of a general educational system to popularize its interests. Edelstein also argues that ancient science was so dominated by philosophy that it developed no single accepted idea of scientific method—hence it was disastrously divided from within. Geoffrey E. R. Lloyd, *Early Greek Science: Thales to Aristotle*, is a sound survey of the development of the physical sciences with little coverage of the life sciences, except for chapter 5 on the Hippocratic school of medicine and its writings. There is a short bibliography (pp. 147–152). Giorgio de Santillana, *The Origins of Scientific Thought*, mostly comments on a series of long excerpts from ancient scientific writings. It is interesting and generally accurate, but there is no reason to choose it over the survey by Clagett.

The most valuable survey of ancient science is George Sarton, *A History of Science: Ancient Science through the Golden Age of Greece* and *A History of Science: Hellenistic Science and Culture in the Last Three Centuries B.C.* Sarton insisted on viewing science as a broadly cultural development. Thus his two volumes on the history of ancient science survey the entire cultural history of the Greek and Hellenistic worlds. The only weakness in his masterful survey is the rather vitriolic treatment given Plato. Plato can justly be accused of contributing to the decline of ancient science, but Sarton tends to place the major blame on Plato without recognizing that the decline of science had broad social roots. Sarton's attacks on Plato's political theories, largely taken from Fite and Popper, are superficial. On the other hand, Sarton's treatment of Aristotle is one of the best epitomes of that amazing mind ever written.

An older and still excellent French multivolume survey is A. Rey, *La Science dans l'antiquité* (4 vols.). Volume 1 is on the pre-Greek period;

volume 2 is on the youth of Greek science; volumes 3 and 4, on the maturity and spread of Greek science. The Roman period is covered in William H. Stahl, *Roman Science*.

Ludwig Edelstein, "Recent Interpretations of Ancient Science," in the *Journal of the History of Ideas* 13 (1952):573–604, is a general survey of recent scholarly trends in the study of ancient science. Edelstein essentially reviews Cohen and Drabkin, *A Source Book in Greek Science*, and in so doing denies the contention of Farrington and others that the progress of science was destroyed by a disdain for experiment, technology, and manual labor. Instead, he argues that science was retarded because researchers viewed science as a means of comprehension rather than as a means of controlling nature, and he notes that the isolation of researchers precluded the cooperative effort needed to make scientific advances. A recent collection of essays and articles by Kurt von Fritz, *Grundprobleme der Geschichte der antiken Wissenschaft*, is highly informative. His work covers the origins through Aristotle (pp. 1–327) and has superior articles on "Die Entwicklung der antiken Astronomie" (chap. 7) and "Platons Stellung zur Wissenschaft: Ideenlehre und Platonische Dialektik" (chap. 10).

The Physical Sciences: Mathematics, Physics, and Astronomy

George Sarton published an excellent guide, *The Study of the History of Mathematics*, in 1936; it is now available in a paperback edition along with *The Study of the History of Science*. The guide includes an especially valuable series of biographical sketches of important mathematicians (pp. 67–103). John E. Pemberton, *How to Find Out in Mathematics*, is also informative—chapter 8 is devoted to "Mathematical History and Biography." Consult Robert H. Whitford, *Physics Literature*, especially on the historical approach (pp. 45–60) and the biographical approach (pp. 60–73). The extensive bibliography in Morris Kline, *Mathematical Thought from Ancient to Modern Times*, is a convenient source for students.

The periodicals which specialize in the history of mathematics and physics include *Scripta Mathematica: A Quarterly Journal Devoted to the Philosophy, History, and Expository Treatment of Mathematics* (1932), *Centaurus: International Magazine for the History of Mathematics, Science, and Technology*

(1950), and *Archives for the History of the Exact Sciences* (1960). These sources must be supplemented by one of the great encyclopedias in the history of science, the *Encyclopaedie der mathematischen Wissenschaften mit Einschluss ihrer Anwendungen* (20 vols.). The articles, written by experts, have valuable bibliographical references and discuss important topics in the history of mathematics, plus many topics in the history of physics and astronomy as well. The new semiannual *Journal for the History of Astronomy* (1970), edited by Michael A. Hoskin, is devoted entirely to that field.

Mathematics

The general histories of mathematics include one which is a good introduction for nonspecialists: David E. Smith, *History of Mathematics* (2 vols.). Volume 1 surveys the development of elementary mathematics (with chronological charts and bibliographical notes); volume 2 surveys the more advanced areas of mathematics. See volume 1, chapters 1–4 (pp. 1–148), on the ancient world. Morris Kline is a contemporary writer of great skill. His best effort to popularize his subject is *Mathematics in Western Culture*, which studies the use of mathematics in western philosophy and the arts. Kline is also the author of a scholarly survey of the development of mathematics, *Mathematical Thought from Ancient to Modern Times*. Chapters 1–8 (pp. 1–183) discuss the ancient world.

Other introductions to the entire history of mathematics include Dirk J. Struik, *A Concise History of Mathematics* (see chaps. 2–5 on the ancient world); Howard Eves, *An Introduction to the History of Mathematics* (chaps. 1–6 on the ancients); and Carl B. Boyer, *A History of Mathematics* (chaps. 1–11 on the ancient world). All three include bibliographical notes at the end of each chapter. The best reference for nonmathematicians is Boyer's simply written survey, which includes illustrations and practice exercises at the end of each chapter. The multivolume histories include an interesting collection of articles on the various branches of mathematics edited by James Newman, *The World of Mathematics* (4 vols.). Some of the articles are on the history of mathematics (vol. 1, part 2); especially see the essay by H. W. Turnbull, "The Great Mathematicians" (pp. 75–168), which is a superb résumé. The more advanced standard histories include M. Cantor, *Vorlesungen über die Geschichte der Mathematik* (4 vols.)—volume 1 covers the ancient and medieval worlds to 1200—and J. E. Hofmann, *Geschichte der Mathematik* (3 vols.), which is supplemented by volume 4 by N. Stuloff, which brings the history to the present.

Two general works are indispensable for the study of mathematical thought in the ancient world: Otto Neugebauer, *The Exact Sciences in Antiquity*, and Johan L. Heiberg, *Mathematics and Physical Science in Classical*

Antiquity. These works are difficult reading for beginners because of their technical language; they are nonetheless minor classics in the study of the mathematical and physical theories of the ancients. Neugebauer's survey of the classical period is especially valuable as are his comments on the exact sciences before the rise of Greek civilization. He shows that the early Egyptians and the Babylonians in particular achieved sophisticated mathematical knowledge. See also the important essay by O. Becker, *Das Mathematische Denken der Antike,* with its examples of ancient mathematical problems.

There are also studies devoted solely to Greek mathematics. Thomas Heath, *History of Greek Mathematics* (2 vols.), has a thorough and technical discussion encompassing the whole of the Hellenistic era. Heath summarizes his two-volume work in *A Manual of Greek Mathematics.* Barthel L. van der Waerden, *Science Awakening,* is a more recent survey which relates developments through the Alexandrian period. It is easier to read than Heath's works, but it requires the reader to have a modicum of mathematical knowledge for full appreciation. "The Decay of Greek Mathematics" (chap. 8) discusses the state of mathematical skills in late antiquity. Two further works have already been cited on page 46 for their comments on Plato's mathematical philosophy. François Lasserre, *The Birth of Mathematics in the Age of Plato,* covers the development of Greek mathematics from the beginning to the late fourth century B.C. and emphasizes Eudoxus. Edward A. Maziarz and Thomas Greenwood, *Greek Mathematical Philosophy,* deals with the development of mathematics and its philosophical implications from the beginning to the "Euclidean Synthesis." Its discussions of the mathematical thought of Plato and Aristotle are especially interesting.

Physics

Stephen Toulmin and Jane Goodfield, *The Architecture of Matter: The Physics, Chemistry, and Physiology of Matter,* is a good introduction to the study of the history of physics. Chapters 1–6 (pp. 17–137) are on the ancient world. This is an excellent discussion of the conflicting ideas of the nature of living and nonliving matter from the ancient world to the modern era, but it lacks a systematic treatment of the medieval world. Toulmin and Goodfield are also the authors of *The Discovery of Time,* a valuable history of the attempt to discover the age of the earth and the universe and the impact of this attempt on science and philosophy. Ginestra Amaldi, *The Nature of Matter: Physical Theory from Thales to Fermi,* is similar in purpose and style to Toulmin and Goodfield, but only the first chapter is devoted to the ancient world. See E. J. Dijksterhuis, *The Mechanization of the World Picture,* for a still general but much more complex history of physics and astronomy together. Dijksterhuis surveys the breakdown of the Aristotelian system and its replacement in the early modern era by a mathematical idea of the universe. The best detailed history of physics is still F. Rosenberger, *Die Geschichte der Physik in Grundzugen mit synchronistischen Tabellen* (2 vols.). Rosenberger concentrates on the nineteenth century but gives some information on the ancient and medieval periods and has many valuable charts and chronological tables.

The best surveys devoted solely to the development of ancient physics are Samuel Sambursky, *The Physical World of the Greeks* and *The Physical World of Late Antiquity*. These excellent works are clearly written sources of information about ancient attitudes toward the cosmos and scientific method. The former is the most interesting because it covers the brilliant period of Greek scientific development and because it compares ancient and modern physics. "The Cosmos of Aristotle" (chap. 4) and "The World of the Continuum" (chap. 6) are noteworthy. *The Physical World of Late Antiquity* is an important contribution to the history of the mental world of late ancient philosophy and patristic theology but less valuable as a résumé of scientific information. Sambursky shows great interest in the reasons for the peculiar development and subsequent decline of ancient science as well as for its failure to achieve a method soundly based on experiment and a mathematical analysis of nature. Sambursky generally emphasizes the mental and geographical isolation of ancient scientists. On this theme see his "Conceptual Developments and Modes of Explanation in Late Greek Scientific Thought," in Alistair Crombie, *Scientific Change* (pp. 61–78). In addition consult the two basic works recommended for the study of mathematics in antiquity: Otto Neugebauer, *The Exact Sciences in Antiquity*, and Johan L. Heiberg, *Mathematics and Physical Science in Classical Antiquity*.

Astronomy

The best specialized study of astronomy for beginners is another work by Stephen Toulmin and Jane Goodfield, *The Fabric of the Heavens: The Development of Astronomy and Dynamics*. The authors explain the development of speculations on and observation of the heavens in clear and simple terms, and their explanation of why the ancient world followed a geocentric line of interpretation rather than a heliocentric theory is especially effective. Their speculations concerning the relative decline in Greek science from about 250 B.C. onward are provocative. They consider that the increasing isolation of Greek scientists made personal exchange of information and debate difficult, and they also cite the rise of antirational philosophies and religions as reasons for the decline. Part 1 (pp. 1–153) is on the ancient world and the survey then jumps abruptly to the modern age. The survey commonly considered the best in the field is A. Pannekoep, *A History of Astronomy*. Part 1 covers the ancient and early medieval periods, with a detailed, fairly technical discussion and good illustrations.

The average student will have no reason to read this work completely, but everyone should be acquainted with the magnum opus of the great French scholar Pierre Duhem, *Le Système du monde: histoire des doctrines cosmologiques de Platon à Copernic* (10 vols.). Volumes 1 and 2 deal with the ancient world, with information about astronomy and on the related areas of physics. Volume 1 covers the development of Greek astronomy through Aristotle and into the post-Aristotelian era; volume 2 (chaps. 9–13) completes Greek speculation and then summarizes the cosmology of the Christian Church Fathers (part 2, chap. 1).

The astronomical ideas of the ancient Greeks are discussed in Thomas Heath, *Greek Astronomy*, which is a collection of texts with translation and commentary, and in Heath's *Aristarchus of Samos: The Ancient Copernicus*. Part 1 briefly summarizes the development of astronomy to Aristarchus; part 2 translates and comments on Aristarchus's "On the Sizes and Distances of the Sun and the Moon." Heath is superseded by D. R. Dicks, *Early Greek Astronomy to Aristotle*, in the first of a planned two volumes. Dicks's discussion is clear and he references recent scholarship in the field. There is no bibliography, but the notes in the text are valuable references and comments on recent scholarship.

The Physical Sciences: Chemistry and Geology

Two recent surveys of the history of chemistry have extensive bibliographical notes. The easiest to use is Aaron J. Ihde, *The Development of Modern Chemistry* (pp. 759–823). It has general references and is then divided according to chapter headings. The work of James R. Partington, perhaps the most famous historian of chemistry, *A History of Chemistry* (4 vols.), is much more detailed and of greater value to the scholar. Unfortunately, volume 1 on the ancient period and the theoretical background for the early development of chemistry was incomplete when Partington died. His manuscript, however, was edited for publication and is available as a source of information and for use as a bibliographical reference.

Special serial bibliographies such as the German *Chemisches Zentral-blatt* (1830) are available. It devotes a separate section to the history of chemistry. Other periodicals publish valuable articles and sources on the history of ancient chemistry. They include *Ambix: Journal of the Society for the Study of Alchemy and Early Chemistry* (1937) and *Chymia: Annual Studies in the History of Chemistry* (1948–1967), succeeded by *Historical Studies in the Physical Sciences* (1969). There are further comments concerning the resources available for the study of chemistry in the ancient world in K. Frick, "Einführung in die alchimiegeschichtliche Literatur," in *Sudhoffs Archiv* 45 (1961):147–163, and Allen G. Debus, "The Significance of the History of Early Chemistry" (pp. 3–58), in the *Journal of World History* 9 (1965–1966). The latter extensively comments on recent literature in the field, especially on alchemy.

Chemistry

There are a number of excellent surveys of the history of chemistry, but they generally, and correctly, consider that the development of chemistry began about 1750 with the work of Lavoisier and his contemporaries. Nonetheless, these surveys are worth consulting for information about the ancient world and for an orientation in general evolution of chemistry. The progress of scientific thought in the last century can best be appreciated by comparing the recent evolution of a science such as chemistry with the intellectual efforts recorded in the previous history of humanity. A good starting place for students who lack a significant knowledge of chemistry is Isaac Asimov, *A Short History of Chemistry: An Introduction to the Ideas and Concepts of Chemistry.* Asimov is no historian, but he explains the ideas of science clearly and in simple terms. His chapter 1 on "The Ancients" and chapter 2 on "Alchemy" are especially worth reading; the remainder of the book is a summary of the later progress of chemistry. Another good introduction by highly competent historians is the already cited survey by Stephen Toulmin and Jane Goodfield: *The Architecture of Matter: The Physics, Chemistry, and Physiology of Matter.* A more detailed account can be found in Aaron J. Ihde, *The Development of Modern Chemistry,* already cited for its excellent bibliography. Chapter 1, "Prelude to Chemistry" (pp. 3–32), is a summary of the state of premodern thought in areas covered by chemistry. Two other brief surveys which attend to ancient chemical and pseudochemical ideas are Eduard Farber, *The Evolution of Chemistry: A History of Its Ideas, Methods, and Materials,* which devotes only 17 pages to the classical period, and Henry M. Leicester, *The Historical Background of Chemistry.* Robert P.

Multhauf, *The Origins of Chemistry*, has a different and interesting orientation. He first examines the relationship of chemistry to alchemy and
medicine (pp. 17–116) and concludes that the relationship to medical
theory and practice was an important influence in the development
of chemistry. Multhauf also includes an unannotated bibliography
(pp. 355–389). Volume 1 of James R. Partington, *A History of Chemistry*
(4 vols.), cited on page 97 above for its useful bibliography, is also valuable because it places the theoretical development of ancient chemistry
within the total matrix of ancient thought and relates that development
to such movements as gnosticism, magic, and astrology.

Lynn Thorndike's thesis that there was a beneficial relationship
between alchemy and experimental science may not have won general
acceptance, but it has helped focus attention on the historical importance
of alchemy. There are several excellent histories in the field. F. Sherwood
Taylor, *The Alchemists*, and John Read, *Through Alchemy to Chemistry* and
Prelude to Chemistry, are adequate surveys which outline the influence
of important personalities and ideas in the long history of this pseudoscience. Read is also the author of *The Alchemist in Life, Literature, and Art*,
a short and clear account of the principles of alchemy followed by a discussion of the alchemist's influence in literature and the arts. John M.
Stillman, *The Story of Alchemy and Early Chemistry*, is an excellent survey
of the two fields to the death of Lavoisier in 1794 and the foundations of
modern chemistry, with a bibliography of primary and secondary sources.
The best treatment of alchemy in the ancient world is found in E. J. Holm-
yard, *Alchemy*. Chapters 1–4 are an accurate and complete but unexciting
summary of the ancient world. The origins of alchemy are discussed by
Robert J. Forbes, *Studies in Ancient Technology* (vol. 1, pp. 121–143);
volumes 8 and 9 have especially relevant discussions of the history of
ancient metallurgy.

Geology

There are a few references on the history of geology in Brian Mason,
The Literature of Geology. The best source, however, is undoubtedly
G. W. White, *Annotated Bibliography for the History of Geology*. Several
histories of geology are available, but they understandably tend to concentrate on modern developments in the field. The study of geology in
the ancient world is briefly discussed in Frank D. Adams, *The Birth and
Development of the Geological Sciences* (see pp. 8–51). Robert J. Forbes
devotes volume 7 of his *Studies in Ancient Technology* to "Ancient Geology
and Mining." Chapter 1 (pp. 1–104) discusses the ancient study of geology,

and there is a chronological bibliography of ancient writings in areas relevant to geology (pp. 244–277).

Technology

The history of technological development is part of the institutional history of western civilization, but there is a great deal of recent interest in the indirect influence that technology had on the history of ideas, especially on the development of scientific theory and social attitudes which affected the development of scientific theory. This brief résumé of sources on the history of science therefore includes references to some sources of information on the history of technology. The basic bibliography is Eugene S. Ferguson, *Bibliography in the History of Technology*. Bibliographies are published annually by the Society for the History of Technology in *Technology and Science* (1959).

Thomas K. Derry and Trevor I. Williams, *A Short History of Technology from the Earliest Times to A.D. 1900*, is a survey history of technology (chaps. 1–3 on the ancient world). Another, Robert J. Forbes, *Man the Maker: A History of Technology and Engineering*, is generally inferior to Derry and Williams but is worth consulting because Forbes is an authority on the development of ancient technology and thus emphasizes that period with enthusiasm. Forbes is also the author of *Studies in Ancient Technology* (9 vols.), a series of monographs on particular areas in the field, with useful bibliographies at the end of each essay. Several surveys are devoted solely to the ancient world. See Albert Neuburger, *The Technical Arts and Sciences of the Ancients*, which covers the field in a series of topically organized discussions, and Henry W. M. Hodges, *Technology in the Ancient World*.

There are two excellent multivolume surveys of the history of technology. The best is *A History of Technology* (5 vols.; 1954–1958), under the general editorship of Charles Singer. This is a magnificent collection of articles. Volumes 1 and 2 cover the ancient and medieval worlds. Each volume is topically organized with excellent illustrations and bibliographical notes at the end of the chapters. Maurice Daumas is the general editor of a French survey now translated as *A History of Technology and Invention* (3 vols.). Volume 1, "The Origins of Technical Civilization," covers the ancient and medieval period; chapter 8, the Greeks; chapter 9, the Romans, with a bibliography (pp. 572–576). Singer's volumes are a generally more complete treatment of topics relevant to the ancient world.

Biology

Bibliographical Resources

There is no standard bibliography on the history of biology, but the beginner can refer to the notes in Marius J. Sirks and Conway Zirkle, *The Evolution of Biology* (pp. 350–365). It can be supplemented by bibliographies in other surveys of the history of biology and by citations in bibliographies recommended in the following pages for the history of medicine. See especially John B. Blake and Charles Roos, *Medical Reference Works, 1679–1966: A Selected Bibliography*, on the relation of medicine to biology, biophysics, botany, and agriculture (pp. 912–993). Consult Fielding H. Garrison and L. T. Morrison, *Medical Bibliography* (pp. 27–195), for citations of primary sources. A new journal devoted to the history of biology, *Journal of the History of Biology* (1968), has excellent articles but few reviews. *The Journal of the Society for the Bibliography of Natural History* (1936) is more bibliographically oriented, with articles and bibliographical materials on the entire range of the history of biology.

General Surveys

There is no definitive summary of ancient biology, but the standard surveys of the field provide the essential information. The best introduction to the field is Marius J. Sirks and Conway Zirkle, *The Evolution of Biology*. The history of the discipline in the ancient world is covered in chapters 1–3; chapter 3 covers the Hellenistic-Roman world. Eric Nordenskiöld, *The History of Biology: A Survey*, is a detailed, basic reference survey. Chapters 1–8 cover the ancient world; chapters 7 and 8 are a short résumé of biology in the post-Aristotelian period. There is a bibliography (pp. 617–629). The best history is by Charles Singer, *A History of Biology to about the Year 1900*. Singer is one of the great names in the history of the study of scientific development. His knowledge of science spans every period and every field, especially biology, medicine, and technology, and he has written significant histories of each. The *History of Biology* is his best book, characterized by its accuracy, writing style, and the author's enthusiasm for biology and the development of a truly scientific method in the field. Singer's enthusiasm for proper scientific method does not inhibit his true appreciation for the false byways of ancient science. Chapters 1 and 2 cover the ancient and medieval worlds and give Aristotle major attention. There is no bibliography. Singer's views on the Greeks are briefly summarized in his "Greek Biology and Its Relation to the Rise of Modern Biology," in *Studies in the History and Method of Science* 2:1–101, edited by Singer, properly emphasizing the differences between the ancient Greek idea of investigation and verification and that of modern science. This work includes an excellent sketch of the history of important manuscripts in the history of biology.

An optimistic estimate of the progress made by the Greeks toward a genuine method of scientific investigation can be found in Gustav Senn, *Die Entwicklung der biologischen Forschungsmethode in der Antike und ihre grundsatzliche Förderung durch Theophrast von Erasos.* Senn believes that ancient scientists developed a method of observation and even adopted some elements of experimentalism prior to the rise of antiscientific philosophies of metaphysics and religion. See Emanuel Radl, *The History of Biological Theories,* for further information on biological theories in antiquity. His treatment of the ancient and medieval periods is brief and accurate, but his treatment of modern theory is largely ruined because he champions the discarded vitalism of Hans Driesch.

Arthur Rook, *The Origins and Growth of Biology,* is a collection of source readings on the history of biology. Part 1, "The Beginnings of the Scientific Approach," excerpts writings from Hippocrates, Aristotle, Theophrastus, and Galen.

No general history of zoology exists in English, but there is more material on zoology than on the history of botany. This is partly because Aristotle's writings on animals survived while his research on plants was lost. The availability of information on zoology is, however, mostly the result of the important impetus given the study of anatomy and a number of other fields in the history of medicine directly related to zoology. There are, however, several good surveys of the history of botany with significant references to botany in the ancient world. Edward L. Greene, *Landmarks of Botanical History,* is not really a survey of the history of botany but rather a series of sketches of the careers and writings of some notable students of botany prior to 1562. Chapters 1–3 are on the ancient world; chapter 2 on Theophrastus is the most important. Robert J. Harvey-Gibson, *Outlines of the History of Botany,* unfortunately treats the ancient world too briefly (chap. 1). The rest of his work is well written despite the drastically out-of-date sections dealing with biochemical research. He includes a useful chart of the great names in the history of botany (pp. 268–269). H. S. Reed, *A Short History of the Plant Sciences,* is also in English but less valuable. Two additional works on the development of botany in the modern world make occasional references to the ancient world, especially to Aristotle, Theophrastus, and Pliny the Elder. They are Julius von Sachs, *History of Botany,* which includes the history from 1530–1860, and M. J. R. Green, *A History of Botany: 1860–1900,* which is a conscious continuation of Sachs's survey. A German work, Ernst

H. F. Meyer, *Geschichte der Botanik* (4 vols.), first published in 1854–1857, may also be consulted.

There is a general survey of the study of zoology by G. Petit and J. Théodoridès, *Histoire de la zoologie des origines à Linné*. Chapters 1–8 cover the ancient world. The treatment of Aristotle in chapter 4 is especially valuable. Otto Keller, *Die Antike Tierwelt* (2 vols.), is a significant collection of literary references to different animals and is of indirect value to students. Additional information can be found in slightly more specialized studies. The study of anatomy has two good surveys: Francis J. Cole, *A History of Comparative Anatomy: From Aristotle to the Eighteenth Century*, is a clear and accurate summary with valuable biographical notes; Charles Singer, *A Short History of Anatomy from the Greeks to Harvey*, has exceptionally useful illustrations. Chapters 1 and 2 cover the ancient world and are more informative than Cole's work. The classic study of the history of embryology, Joseph Needham, *A History of Embryology*, is even more valuable. Needham surveys the early scientific and philosophical conflicts concerning the genesis and development of the fetus to the eighteenth century. Chapter 1 (pp. 18–75) and parts of chapter 2 cover the ancient world. There is an excellent bibliography. Additional sources of information on generation and embryology can be found in Francis J. Cole, *Early Theories of Sexual Generation*, and volume 1 of Thomas S. Hall's excellent *Ideas of Life and Matter: Studies in the History of General Physiology* (2 vols.). The discussion of the ancient world (pp. 13–137) includes useful insights on the pre-Socratics, Aristotle, and Galen. Several important books on the modern development of embryology are reviewed by F. B. Churchill, "The History of Embryology as Intellectual History," in the *Journal of the History of Biology* 1 (1970):155–181.

Medicine

Bibliographical Resources and Periodicals

A good introduction to the literature and research resources can be found in Henry E. Sigerist, *A History of Medicine* (2 vols.). The systematic bibliographical survey in volume 1 (pp. 499–541) and the notes throughout both volumes are helpful. John B. Blake and Charles Roos, *Medical*

Reference Works, 1679–1966: A Selected Bibliography, is even more complete. This describes the general tools and surveys of the history of medicine with some brief annotations (pp. 50–92). The most complete nonserial guide is Fielding H. Garrison and L. T. Morrison, *Medical Bibliography: An Annotated Checklist of Texts Illustrating the History of Medicine*. The authors list general histories and the histories of special areas (pp. 735 ff.). The remainder of the book is largely organized organographically and is also valuable. The work includes especially important lists of primary texts relating to the development of different types of therapy. The biographies of the chief figures in the history of medicine are cited in John L. Thornton, *A Select Bibliography*, and C. H. Talbott, *A Biographical History of Medicine: Excerpts and Essays on the Men and Their Work*.

The best of several useful student guides in German is W. Artelt, *Einführung in die Medizinhistorik, ihr Wesen, ihre Arbeitsweise, und ihre Hilfsmittel*, a handbook with many bibliographical references and annotations. Artelt is one of the editors of *Index zur Geschichte der Medizin, Naturwissenschaft, und Technik* (2 vols.), with J. Strudel, which reviews the important books and articles published between 1945 and 1956.

There are several serial bibliographies which cover the history of medicine. The most valuable is the annual *The Bibliography of the History of Medicine* (1965), published by the National Library of Medicine in Bethesda, Maryland. The quarterly *Current Work in the History of Medicine: An International Bibliography* (1913), published by the Wellcome Historical Medical Library, is also an excellent source. *The Proceedings of the Royal Society of Medicine* (1913) has a historical section. These basic English-language guides can be supplemented by the multilingual *Janus: revue internationale de l'histoire des sciences, de la medicine, de la pharmacie, et de la technique* (1896–1941; new series, 1957) and the German *Sudhoffs Archiv für Geschichte der Medizin und der Naturwissenschaften der Pharmacie und der Mathematik* (1908).

The latter also publishes extremely valuable supplementary volumes on particular topics. *Janus* and *Sudhoffs* include articles, reviews, and bibliographical materials. Their reviews in the field are continuing bibliographical guides. They can be supplemented by several excellent journals in English: the *Bulletin of the History of Medicine* (1933), published by the American Association for the History of Medicine and the Johns Hopkins Institute for the History of Medicine; the *Journal of the History of Medicine and Allied Sciences* (1946), published by the Yale University Department of the History of Science and Medicine; and *Medical History: A Quarterly Journal Devoted to the History and Bibliography of Medicine and the Related Sciences* (1957), published by the Cambridge University History of Medicine Society. *Ciba Review* (1937) devotes each issue to a particular theme and includes material relevant to the history of medicine.

General Surveys

The general histories of science invariably include interesting sections on the development of ancient medicine. See especially George Sarton, *A History of Science,* volume 1, chapters 13 and 14, on the Hippocratic school, and Chapter 21, which includes information on Aristotle's medical theories. Also see volume 2, chapter 9, on "Medicine in the Third Century" and chapter 22 on medicine in the late antique period. René Taton, *A History of Science,* volume 1, part 2, chapter 5 by L. Bourgey, is on "Greek Medicine from the Beginnings to the End of the Classical Era." Chapter 5 in Book 2 by J. Beaujeu covers Alexandrian (Hellenistic) and Roman medicine. These sources provide quick and reliable surveys of the development of ancient medicine and its various therapeutic schools or doctrines. Clagett's *Greek Science in Antiquity* (chap. 4) briefly summarizes Greek biology and medicine; Santillana's *The Origins of Scientific Thought* (chap. 8) reproduces the text of "On the Sacred Disease" and discusses the conflict between science and superstition in the Hippocratic school. There is a collection of source readings in Cohen and Drabkin, *A Source Book in Greek Science* (see pp. 467–530 on medicine and pp. 530–559 on "Physiological Psychology"). Source readings are also found in Logan Clendening, *Source Book of Medical History;* see chapters 1–10 on the ancient world.

Several general histories of medicine have sections on the ancient world. The best is Charles Singer and E. Ashworth Underwood, *A Short History of Medicine.* Kenneth Walker, *The Story of Medicine* (chaps. 1–3 on the ancient world), and Ralph H. Major, *A History of Medicine* (2 vols.)— volume 1, chapters 1–3 on the ancient world—are also adequate sources of information on ancient medicine.

Several volumes are devoted solely to the history of ancient medicine. The best starting place is Benjamin L. Gordon, *Medicine throughout Antiquity.* Gordon was a practicing physician and not a trained historian, but his survey is accurate and includes summaries of the many medical schools of thought which emerged in the late ancient period. H. O. Jones, *Greek Biology and Medicine,* one of the Our Debt to Greece and Rome series, also merits attention. Jones emphasizes the interrelation between medicine and biology. W. H. S. Jones, *Philosophy and Medicine in Ancient Greece,* has a broader scope than either Gordon or Jones. E. D. Phillips, *Aspects of Greek Medicine,* is a fine detailed study of the development of Greek medicine. It competently summarizes both the theoretical and therapeutic aspects of the science.

Every student should be acquainted with the *History of Medicine* by Henry E. Sigerist, one of the great figures in the history of medicine. Sigerist originally intended his history to be a comprehensive survey of the entire development of medicine in eight volumes. Unfortunately, he died after completing volumes 1 and 2 on "Primitive and Archaic Medicine" and "Early Greek, Hindu, and Persian Medicine," respectively. These volumes include comprehensive information on the origins of medical techniques and theories. The work of Ludwig Edelstein, another master historian of ancient science in general and of medicine in particular, was also cut short by death. A collection of his opinions appears in Owsei and C. Lilian Temkin, eds., *Ancient Medicine: Selected Papers of Ludwig Edelstein.* Edelstein's thesis is that the presuppositions and techniques of ancient medicine (and ancient science in general) differed radically from modern science and that they were adversely influenced by philosophic and religious dogmas. He develops this theme in "The Relationship of Ancient Philosophy to Medicine" and "Greek Medicine and Its Relation to Religion and Magic," both included in the Temkins' collection. That collection also includes interesting articles on "The History of Anatomy in Antiquity" (pp. 247–303) and "The Dietetics of Antiquity" (pp. 303–319). Other articles on ancient medicine can be found in Ashworth E. Underwood, *Science, Medicine, and History: Essays on the Evolution of Scientific Thought and Medical Practice Written in Honor of Charles Singer* (2 vols.), especially volume 1, part 1 (pp. 3–131); and J. Longrigg, "Philosophy and Medicine: Some Early Interactions," in *Harvard Studies in Classical Philology* 67:147–177.

That portion of Roman medical practice and theory which retains historical significance was largely Greek in origin. See T. C. Allbutt, *Greek Medicine in Rome,* a chronologically organized text which relates the important areas of medical practice, and John Scarborough, *Roman Medicine,* especially the chapters on the importance of military medicine (pp. 66–76), the education and public image of doctors (pp. 94–134), and the appendix, which has excellent biographical sketches (pp. 149–161). Owsei Temkin, "Greek Medicine as Science and Craft," *Isis* 44 (1953):213–225, discusses the division in ancient medicine between physicians who were educated and used philosophical ideas and general theories in medicine and those who were uneducated. During the Greek period general ideas and theories percolated from the educated into the uneducated ranks, but in the late ancient period (from Galen on) and in the medieval period the gap between the medical scientist and craftsman was very great.

Special Studies

The more specialized studies of figures and themes in the history of ancient medicine abound. See E. J. and Ludwig Edelstein, *Asclepius: A Collection and Interpretation of the Testimonies* (2 vols.), which examines the hero and divinity of the cult of medicine. Volume 1 is a collection of translated "testimonies" (i.e., statements about cures effected through appeal to the power of Asclepius); volume 2 analyzes ancient stories about the "patron saint" of medicine and his reported cures. The evidence about Asclepius is more simply reviewed in an older essay by A. Walton, "The Cult of Asklepios," *Cornell Studies in Classical Philology* 3.

The writings of Hippocrates, traditionally and rightly considered the father of scientific medicine, appear in a collection compiled by J. Chadwick and W. N. Mann, *The Medical Works of Hippocrates*. See also Edwin B. Levine, *Hippocrates*. Levine's work is a concise résumé of evidence concerning the dating and authorship of the writings attributed to Hippocrates and the principles of his medical practice. He includes an annotated bibliography (pp. 155–168). The general histories of ancient medicine devote particular attention to Hippocrates, and at least two specialized studies should also be consulted. Max Pohlenz, *Hippocrates und die Begrundung der wissenschaftlichen Medizen*, and the best recent summary of the Hippocratic corpus, E. Joly, *Le Niveau de la science hippocratique: Contributions à la psychologie de l'histoire des sciences*, which includes a topical discussion of the elements of Hippocratic theory and therapy. The Hippocratic writings are also put into their general cultural and intellectual setting by J. Schumacher, *Antike Medizin: die naturphilosophischen Grundlagen der Medizin in der griechischen Antike*, which includes an excellent bibliography (pp. 251–298).

See George Sarton, *Galen of Pergamon*, for a short review of Galen's career and theories. More detailed studies include two works by Rudolph E. Siegel, *Galen on Sense Perception*, an analysis of Galen's extant references to the role of the senses in human life with an excellent bibliography (pp. 196–203), and *Galen's System of Physiology and Medicine*, a favorable estimate of Galen's ideas of medical treatment, also with a bibliography (pp. 383–395). See also Richard Walzer, *Galen on Medical Experience*, which translates Galen's writings (from Arabic versions) and includes comments and bibliographical notes. Charles Singer, "Galen as a Modern" (pp. 108–123), in volume 1 of *Toward Modern Science*, emphasizes that Galen judged disease from an anatomical, hence modern, point of view.

Chapter 4: *Ancient Aesthetics*

Introduction

STYLE IN THE visual and written arts in the ancient classical world had an importance which it does not have in the modern world. Classical intellectuals, especially during the period of the Roman Empire, were obsessed by a desire to express themselves properly with good style. Style and decorum were not embellishments or a form of entertainment; they were considered coeval with civilized thought and life. Obviously, this interest in style had certain adverse consequences. The adherence to a proper and highly formal mode of expression helped widen the gap between privileged and nonprivileged classes in society and reduced education in later antiquity to the exegesis and imitation of the classics. On the other hand, it created and disseminated a noble, harmonious, and concentrated conception of art which inspired western artists for the next fourteen hundred years. It also produced a common and sophisticated set of standards by which to judge art—in contrast to the multiple standards characteristic of the nineteenth and twentieth centuries.

Aesthetics is the attempt to comprehend and formulate the characteristics of beauty, art, and proper expression. It encompasses the principles and representative monuments of classical art but excludes much of the history of the development of ancient literature and the visual arts. In selecting the following references an effort has been made to reduce the number of citations to manageable proportions. Nonetheless, the general surveys and bibliographical guides cited will provide interested students a means of exploring the whole range of references to this important aspect of the history of ideas.

Bibliographical Resources and Surveys

The nonserial bibliographies in ancient history are uneven in their treatment of aesthetics, literature, and art. Neither edition of the *Guide to Historical Literature* (American Historical Association) has a section worth special consultation. Varet's *Manual de bibliographie philosophique* lacks the fine treatment given to philosophy, science, and religion. Volume 2, chapter 3 (pp. 562–608), on the "Philosophy of Art" includes several historical references organized in chronological order, with few references to the ancient period. Martin R. P. McGuire, *Introduction to Classical Scholarship*, is largely devoted to the history and the analysis of ancient literature and its treatment of ancient art is limited. McGuire includes an excellent explanation of the varying definitions and approaches to classical studies (part I) and a résumé of the "History of Classical Scholarship" (part 2, chap. 2). *Fifty Years (and Twelve) of Classical Scholarship* is an even better guide. It is a series of articles by leading British scholars on different areas of ancient literary history. The bibliographical references are current and well chosen and the explanations of recent scholarship generally avoid the supposition that the reader already knows the matter being discussed. Unfortunately, this survey is confined to literature (including philosophy) and ignores art. *The Cambridge Ancient History* has excellent chapters (each with a bibliography) covering ancient literature and art. Each chapter is written by an outstanding scholar. The following portions of *The Cambridge Ancient History* are of particular interest:

> Volume 4, chapter 14: J. B. Bury, "Greek Literature from the Eighth Century to the Persian Wars"
> Chapter 16: J. D. Beazley, "Early Greek Art"
> Volume 5, chapter 5: J. T. Sheppard, "Attic Drama in the Fifth Century"
> Chapter 15: J. D. Beazley, "Greek Art and Architecture"
> Volume 6, chapter 18: J. D. Beazley, "Greek Art and Architecture"
> Volume 7, chapter 8: E. A. Barber, "Alexandrian Literature"
> Volume 8, chapter 13: J. W. Duff, "The Beginnings of Latin Literature"
> Chapter 21: B. Ashmole, "Hellenistic Art"
> Volume 9, chapter 18: E. E. Sikes, "The Art of the Roman Republic"
> Volume 10, chapter 16: T. R. Glover, "The Literature of the Augustan Age"
> Chapter 17: E. Strong, "The Art of the Augustan Age"
> Volume 11, chapter 18: E. E. Sikes, "Latin Literature of the Silver Age"
> Chapter 20: G. Rodenwaldt, "Art from Nero to the Antonines"

Volume 12, chapter 16: G. Rodenwaldt, "The Transition to Late Classical Art"
Chapter 17: E. K. Rand, "The Latin Literature of the West from the Antonines to Constantine"
Chapter 18: J. Bidez, "Literature and Philosophy in the Eastern Half of the Empire"

Most serial bibliographies in ancient history are helpful in researching the development of aesthetics and classical literature, but they are less valuable as sources in studying the visual arts. *L'Année philologique* is notable because it devotes part 1 to serial literature on authors and texts, part 2, chapter 1, to literary history, chapter 4 to antiquities, including the history of art, and chapter 9 to the progress of classical studies.

There are several guides and surveys devoted solely to aesthetics. W. Hammond, *A Bibliography of Aesthetics and of the Philosophy of the Fine Arts for 1900–1932*, is somewhat dated and is not annotated, but it is still valuable. See chapters 1–3 which list general tools and histories useful in the study of aesthetics. Hammond can be supplemented and brought up to date by several good histories. Monroe C. Beardsley, *Aesthetics from Classical Greece to the Present*, provides bibliographies at the end of each chapter and devotes chapters 1–4 to the ancient world—mainly concentrated on Plato and Aristotle. Katherine Gilbert and Helmut Kuhn, *A History of Esthetics*, is a more detailed treatment with bibliographical notes. Greek theories are surveyed (pp. 1–87) and so are Roman theories (pp. 87–119). The recently translated W. Tatarkiewicz, *History of Aesthetics* (2 vols.), is a more detailed work valuable for its excerpted translations of passages from major sources in the history of aesthetics. Volume 1 covers *Ancient Aesthetics* and volume 2 summarizes ancient and medieval developments in the field (pp. 285–305). J. G. Warry, *Greek Aesthetical Theory*, is chiefly a study of Plato and Aristotle, with indirect references to other theories and worthwhile bibliographical notes. Warry interestingly distinguishes the beauty of art (i.e., the "callistic") from other elements in the study of art.

The best single bibliography of new serial publications in the field is published by the American Society for Aesthetics: *The Journal of Aesthetics and Art Criticism* (1941). This journal has excellent reviews and an annual bibliography. Other journals include the British Society for Aesthetics, *The British Journal of Aesthetics* (1960), the *Revue d'esthétique* (1948), and the *Bibliographische Zeitschrift für Aesthetik* (1966). Valuable articles and bibliographical surveys on aesthetics can also be found in history of philosophy journals (e.g., J. Margolis, "Recent Works in Aesthetics," in the *American Philosophical Quarterly* (1965):182–192.

Classical Literature

Literary Criticism and Scholarship

Ancient history bibliographies in general and those devoted to aesthetics in particular are rich in their coverage of literary criticism. Several surveys are devoted solely to literary criticism. William K. Wimsatt and Cleanth Brooks, *Literary Criticism: A Short History*, is a general reference work which covers the Greeks (pp. 3–77) and the Romans (pp. 77–139). Many surveys are devoted to the ancient period. The best is G. M. Grube, *The Greek and Roman Critics*, with a commentary on critical quotes from the beginning to Longinus. Chapters 4 and 5 on Plato and Aristotle are noteworthy and the bibliographical citations (pp. 358–365) recommend several periodicals not usually encountered. Other and older surveys include W. Rhys Roberts, *Greek Rhetoric and Literary Criticism*. Roberts briefly summarizes the opinions of major critics from Homer to Longinus. John W. H. Atkins, *Literary Criticism in Antiquity* (2 vols.), extends its discussion to Quintillian. Another older work, George Saintsbury, *A History of Criticism and Literary Tastes in Europe from the Earliest Times to the Present Day* (2 vols.), covers the period to the ancient world (vol. 1, books 1 and 2), but its convoluted prose makes difficult reading.

The Roman period is covered in the excellent work by John F. D'Alton, *Roman Literary Theory and Criticism*. D'Alton covers the period from the inception of Greek literary theory to the age of Horace. Several chapters discuss material omitted in other surveys; see the "Ancients vs. Moderns" (chap. 5), which cites the conflict in the Roman mind over the abilities of the older (chiefly Greek) authors versus their own abilities. Also see "Horace and the Classical Creed" (chap. 6) on Horace and his use of Greek satire and "The Supremacy of Rhetoric" (chap. 7), a superb explanation of the importance of beautiful writing and speech in the classical world.

In addition to these studies of literary criticism in antiquity, there are several valuable source collections. J. D. Denniston, *Greek Literary Criticism*, excerpts original writings and provides connecting commentary from the beginnings through Lucian. The closely related field of rhetorical principles is covered by Thomas W. Benson and Michael H. Prosser, *Readings in Classical Rhetoric*, with a topical bibliography (pp. 314–329). The collection by D. A. Russell and M. Winterbottom, *Ancient Literary Criticism: The Principal Texts in New Translations*, is even better.

Classics

The literary work of ancient Greece and Rome and the study of that work during the medieval and modern periods are identified as the "classical tradition" (i.e., the "classics"). Classical studies are also concerned with the influence of the classics on later writers; see the approach taken by Gilbert Highet, *The Classical Tradition: Greek and Roman Influences on Western Literature.* It is important to note that classical studies occupied the ancient world itself. The writing and style of ancient writers (Homer is the most obvious example) were carefully studied, preserved, and used as models for contemporary writing. This study of ancient literature was a self-conscious, complete, and sophisticated development which applied rational principles of thought and expression. An understanding of how this ancient tradition of classicism developed and was maintained is especially important to students of the history of ideas. At the same time the study of the classics encompasses an understanding of the ancient system of education—a system centered largely on rhetoric and study of the classics.

R. R. Bolgar, *The Classical Heritage and Its Beneficiaries,* is a general survey which briefly covers the ancient period. This fine work surveys the development and influence of classical scholarship from classical Greece to the end of the Renaissance. It includes an especially valuable appendix, "Translations of Greek and Roman Classics before 1600." John E. Sandys, *A History of Classical Scholarship* (3 vols.), is still invaluable. Volume 1, books 1–4, cover the ancient period with judicious and accurate summaries of the contributions of major writers and helpful chronological charts. Sandys defines classical scholarship as "the accurate study of the language, literature, and art of Greece and Rome, and of all that they can teach us as to the nature and history of man." His survey actually concerns only the literary tradition and works of highly educated ancients. R. Pfeiffer, *History of Classical Scholarship: From the Beginning to the End of the Hellenistic Age,* is a recent and excellent study.

Rhetoric (the study of persuasive and beautiful expression) was also closely related to aesthetics and literary criticism. The study of rhetoric was basic to literary criticism and it was the central theme of high Greek and Roman education. It is therefore not surprising that the same scholars who contribute to the history of education in the classical world also contribute to the history of classical rhetoric. George Kennedy, for example, surveys the development of the art in *The Art of Persuasion in Greece* and *The Art of Rhetoric in the Roman World.* Martin L. Clarke, *Rhetoric at Rome: A Historical Survey,* is also an excellent source on the ideas and influence of Cicero and Quintillian. Its interesting conclusion (chap. 15) weighs the good and bad effects of the classical emphasis on rhetoric in education.

Greek Literature

GENERAL SURVEYS

The general bibliographical resources on ancient history and the history of aesthetics devote considerable space to the development of Greek literature. However, other valuable bibliographies and surveys are available. Moses Hadas, *A History of Greek Literature*, is an accurate survey with a bibliography. The bibliographies at the end of each chapter in Albin Lesky, *History of Greek Literature*, are even better, especially in their coverage of German literature. The most important bibliographical source for scholars, however, is still the expanded version of W. von Christ, *Geschichte der griechischen Literatur* (part of the German *Handbuch der Altertumswissenschaft*). Von Christ's original contribution was published in one volume, but it has been revised and expanded by other scholars, in this case W. Schmid and O. Stahlin. Part I includes volume 1, *Griechische Literatur vor der attischen Hegemonie;* volume 2, *Griechische Literatur in der Zeit der attischen Hegemonie;* volumes 3, 4, and 5, *Griechische Literatur . . . nach dem Eingreifen der Sophistik;* and volume 6, *Die Griechische Literatur des 4. Jahrhunderts bis auf Alexander der Grosse* (in preparation). Part 2 covers the postclassical era, *Die Nachklassische Periode* (2 vols.).

These sources, combined with those recommended for the study of ancient history and aesthetics, give bibliographic coverage for the study of Greek literature. Hadas and Lesky are also valuable survey histories and both follow a general chronological organization. Lesky's work is more popular with scholars and has an especially fine treatment of the history of Greek drama. The Hadas survey, however, is more readable with chapters on "The Literature of Religion" (chap. 16) and "Lucian, the Novel" (chap. 18). Other, basically nonbibliographical surveys include Herbert J. Rose, *A Handbook of Greek Literature*. His treatment of the classical period is better than that given the Hellenistic era, and he covers every type of literary form, including historical writing. C. Maurice Bowra, *Ancient Greek Literature*, is a brief (250 pages) but more readable work with less information than either Hadas or Rose. Bowra's emphasis on the Greeks' extraordinary grasp of reality and the distinction between their artistic attitude and that of romanticism makes this a valuable introduction. Thomas B. L. Webster published a fine series of brief studies on the interrelationship of literature and the other arts: *Greek Art and Literature: 700–530 B.C., Greek Art and Literature: 530–400 B.C.,* and *Art and Literature in Fourth Century Athens.* Webster focuses on literature, but his attention to philosophy and art is also valuable. He makes excellent use of the artistic character of Greek vases of the archaic era. Webster has also done a study of the Hellenistic era, *Hellenistic Poetry and Art,* which improves the older reference style work by Frederick A. Wright, *A History of Later Greek Literature from the Death of Alexander to the Death of Justinian*. The famous French work by Alfred and Maurice Croiset, *Histoire de la littérature grecque* (5 vols.), has been translated in a condensed version, *An Abridged History of Greek Literature*.

References to Homer, Hesiod, and the archaic age prior to the fifth century B.C. are generally omitted here to allow greater attention to the dramatists and literary theory. A few basic references, however, are necessary. See Moses I. Finley, *The World of Odysseus*, on the general social and cultural background and two works by Andrew R. Burn, *The World of Hesiod* and *The Lyric Age of Greece*. The epic form of poetry found in Homer and Hesiod is covered by Gilbert Murray, *The Rise of the Greek Epic*. John A. Symond's admiring *Studies of the Greek Poets* (2 vols.) is a broader study of poetic forms, with a survey to Theocritus. C. Maurice Bowra's *Greek Lyric Poetry from Alcman to Simonides* and *Early Greek Elegists* concentrate on the period prior to the fifth century. Hermann Fränkel, *Dichtung und Philosophie des fruhen Griechentums: eine Geschichte der griechischen Epik, Lyrik, und Prosa bis zur Mitte des funften Jahrhunderts*, is a vital survey from Homer to Pindar with excellent treatment of Homer, Hesiod, and the older lyric poets (chap. 4).

GREEK TRAGIC DRAMA

The Athenians of the late sixth and fifth centuries B.C. invented drama. Exactly how they created this art form is one of the intriguing and ultimately insoluble problems of the history of ancient literature. The problem is not integral to the history of ideas as defined in the introduction, but a review of the question is in order to illustrate the scholarly energy and skill devoted to the subject. This review will focus on the careers and significance of the three great dramatists of Athens: Aeschylus, Sophocles, and Euripides.

The problems associated with Greek drama and recent literature in the field are briefly outlined by Thomas B. L. Webster, "Greek Tragedy," in *Fifty Years (and Twelve) of Classical Scholarship* (pp. 88–122). See the bibliographical notes in Schmid-Stahlin, *Geschichte der griechischen Literatur* (vols. 1–3), and Albin Lesky, *History of Greek Literature and Greek Tragedy*. The latter has a bibliography (pp. 213–224) revised to include more English titles. Also see Lesky, *Die Tragische Dichtung der Hellenen*, which contains a superb summary of the problem of the origins of the drama (pp. 11–39). There is also a bibliography and discussion of the development of tragedy in Margarete Bieber's well-illustrated *The History of the Greek and Roman Theatre*. The continuous reviews of literature on Greek tragedy in *Classical World, Lustrum, Anzeiger für Altertumswissenschaft*, and the annual *L'Année philologique* (the last named lists works separately under the names of the three great tragedians) are also vitally important references.

The handbooks and encyclopedias on the general ancient period and classical literature in general are supplemented by handbooks devoted solely to Greek drama. Two of them deserve special mention. Philip W. Harsh, *A Handbook of Classical Drama*, has an introductory chapter on the origins and general setting of Greek drama and an author-by-author, play-by-play résumé of Greek drama. The bibliographical notes in this older work are by no means completely outdated and Harsh's references to accepted facts and opposing theories are clear and stimulating. John Ferguson, the author of studies of ancient morality and religion, contributes *A Companion to Greek Tragedy*, which has a short, not altogether satisfactory chapter on the background and excellent résumés of the individual works of Aeschylus, Sophocles, and Euripides. He includes a bibliography of periodical and book literature (pp. 573–604).

The general histories of Greek literature invariably contain substantial comments on the development of Attic drama. In addition, there are several excellent surveys devoted to drama alone. The student will find Margarete Bieber, *The History of the Greek and Roman Theatre*, to be an excellent, carefully written, and lavishly illustrated survey and introduction. Bieber's range precludes detailed discussion, but she includes bibliographical notes which direct readers to other sources. Donald W. Lucas, *The Greek Tragic Poets: Their Contribution to Western Life and Thought*, is another, somewhat more detailed introduction. Chapter 1 is devoted to the background and development of drama; chapter 2 describes the general character of the drama; and most of the remainder of the work surveys the work of Aeschylus, Sophocles, and Euripides.

There are other excellent, and more detailed guides including Albin Lesky, *Greek Tragedy*, and H. D. F. Kitto, *Greek Tragedy: A Literary Study*. Lesky is the most authoritative German scholar on the history of Greek literature. His survey deals fully with the periods preceding and following the classical stage of the fifth century B.C. and it is filled with original insights and suggestions. Kitto's survey, however, is more balanced in judgment and concentrates on the three great dramatists—indeed, his book is a complete survey of the extant plays. Kitto's general argument concerning the development of the history of tragedy is that the dramatists exhibited a progressive emancipation of the individual from control by the gods and the impersonal government of justice (*dike*). Kitto's treatment of "The Philosophy of Sophocles" (chap. 6) and "The Euripidean Tragedy" (chap. 8) are especially important.

Before starting a detailed study of the dramatists students are advised to read two short works by R. Lattimore, one of the most successful translators of classical literature. *Story Patterns in Greek Tragedy* is a criticism of critics' description of the elements that supposedly give tragedy its distinctive character. Lattimore shows that these elements (e.g., the fatal flaw in heroic characters) are rarely present. Instead, he argues that Greek drama followed an intrinsic logic which required certain dramatic situations to be resolved and pursued in certain ways. Lattimore's

The Poetry of Greek Drama is less important, but his explanation of how the discipline of strict poetic forms helped develop the Greek dramatic genius and provided a flexible and severe vehicle for writing tragedy is worth reading.

Jacqueline de Romilly, *Time in Greek Tragedy*, can hardly be called a general survey of Greek drama, but it is an acute study of a theme which persists in the extant plays and therefore places the dramatists in the context of general Greek philosophical development. This work reviews the use of the word and the idea of time in the works of Aeschylus, Sophocles, and Euripides (see chaps. 3, 4, and 5). Aeschylus, she argues, considered the inevitable justice of the gods over the course of time to be a teacher of humanity—thus others who desired to learn from the fates of the wicked and the unfortunate were given prudent examples. Time in the work of Sophocles was not so much a source of divine justice as a bringer of the tragic instabilities of life against which the heroic must struggle and as the revealer of a person's true character and circumstances. Romilly considers that time was a psychological category in the work of Euripides. The characters' appreciation of time and their references to it are used to bring out their emotional characters. Time is a source of instability in life, but it is also a healer which brings forgetfulness. Romilly's distinction between the attitudes of the three great dramatists may be too sharply drawn, but it is a superb example of how intellectual history can be developed by closely explicating literary texts. Max Pohlenz,, *Die Griechische Tragödie* (2 vols.), has not appeared in English, but it emphasizes the political and historical background of the development of the plays. Volume 2 includes informative notes on special subjects.

Particular theories about the origins of Attic drama abound. The older theories tend to explain those origins in terms of seasonal and vegetative cycles and the Greek reverence for traditional heroes. Several scholars (e.g., Lewis Farnell, Gilbert Murray, Francis M. Cornford) believe that the protodrama represented a conflict between summer, represented by Dionysus who was thought to be associated with fecundity, and winter. Pantomimes of this sort appear in some modern Balkan societies. This interpretation has the advantage of connecting the drama with natural habits in primitive societies and with Dionysus, at whose festival Athenian drama began. Other scholars (e.g., W. Ridgeway) argue that drama originated in the liturgies and protoplays of the earlier Greeks presented at the tombs of heroes to commemorate heroic deeds. This theory explains the central role of important heroic figures in drama, but it does not explain the role of Dionysus or the exact origin of the chorus so important in the developed Attic form. Lesky plausibly suggests that a likely explanation can be found in a combination of the two themes. Attic drama, he argues, was first sponsored by tyrants (Peisistratus, for instance) who encouraged the festival of Dionysus and the combination of representations of heroic deeds with the chorus. These broad theories do not exhaust speculation about the origins of drama. Some recent speculation is inclined to emphasize drama's immediate political importance. George Thomson, *Aeschylus and Athens,* presents a Marxian argument that drama evolved from tribal initiation ceremonies and that the transformation of this ubiquitous institution was in accord with Greek urban society. Recently Gerald F. Else, *The Origin and Early Form of Greek Tragedy,* traced the drama to recitation from the Homeric epics. These recitations, according to Else, were transformed into drama by Thespis and Aeschylus. Thespis added a chorus and a spokesman who discussed the tragic turning point in the hero's career. Aeschylus, who was inspired by the Persian Wars and hoped to inspire a broader heroic spirit, expanded the role of actors to exploit the Athenians' confidence and interest in the heroic.

Most of the theories concerning the origin of Attic drama are brilliantly criticized by Arthur W. Pickard-Cambridge in *Dithyramb, Tragedy, and Comedy.* Thomas B. L. Webster revised the second edition.

Aeschylus

The reader interested in Aeschylus can turn to a number of fine works in addition to the appropriate sections of general works. J. T. Sheppard, *Aeschylus and Sophocles: Their Work and Influence,* is a sound starting place. See "The Work of Aeschylus" (chap. 1, pp. 3–40) and "The Work of Sophocles" (chap. 2, pp. 40–82). The rest of the volume is devoted to the influence of the two poets on later ancient and modern writers. Gilbert Murray, *Aeschylus: The Creator of Tragedy,* is another informative and well-written survey. Murray was one of the authors of the theory that Greek tragedy evolved as a poetic and dramatic representation of the primitive conflict between winter and summer, the growth and death of vegetation. His devotion to that theory, however, does not spoil his summary of the genius of Aeschylus. Herbert W. Smyth, *Aeschylean Tragedy,* is an introductory survey which rejects the use of anthropological canons.

Additional information on Aeschylus can be garnered from commentaries on his extant plays. Simple and effective commentaries are found in the Prentice-Hall Greek Drama series, especially those by Hugh Lloyd-Jones on the *Agamemnon, The Eumenides,* and *The Libation Bearers.* Herbert J. Rose, *A Commentary on the Surviving Plays of Aeschylus* (2 vols.), is generally excellent, especially on religion. Another and even more valuable commentary is that of the German scholar Eduard Fraenkel on the *Agamemnon* (2 vols.). Fraenkel includes a detailed phrase-by-phrase commentary on the play and the environment in which it was produced.

Fraenkel's comments on religion are also perceptive. Finally, essays from the writings cited in this section can be read in a collection by M. H. McCall, *Aeschylus: A Collection of Critical Essays.*

During this century there has been interest concerning the influence of Greek politics and thought on the master tragedians. This line of inquiry has chiefly busied itself with Aeschylus's possible interest in the Athenian political scene and in traditional religion. George Thomson, *Aeschylus and Athens* (cited above on p. 117), argues that Aeschylean drama urbanized the social ceremonies of the tribal order. Gerald Else, *The Origin and Early Form of Greek Tragedy* (also cited on p. 117), interprets Aeschylean drama as a form of political education partly inspired by Greek victories in the Persian Wars. Anthony J. Podlecki, *The Political Background of Aeschylean Tragedy,* identifies Aeschylus as a political ally of Themistocles, whom *The Persians* was meant to help, and as an opponent of tyranny, which *Prometheus Bound* was designed to attack. These studies suggest but do not establish a possible interest on the part of Aeschylus in the political life of Athens. The passages which might be interpreted as references to politics are too scattered, too indefinite, and too easily given other meanings to prove such arguments. Eric A. Havelock always makes interesting and provocative contributions to any area of Greek thought to which he turns his attention. His *The Crucifixion of Intellectual Man* is a translation of the *Prometheus Bound.* Havelock argues that the play is a paradigm of the conflict between the power drive and reason in history. Havelock's book is chiefly valuable as a basis for discussion of the play and for an appendix on the lost plays of this trilogy which gives much information on the religious themes used by Aeschylus.

There are many more specifically religious than political elements in the plays of Aeschylus, but scholars also dispute his religious attitudes. The important theories range from claims that he held a primitive and crude religious position to the idea that his theology evolved from a primitive to a relatively advanced form and finally to the position that his plays present a sophisticated idea of divinity. Among the scholars who insist that Aeschylus's idea of Zeus was primitive in character is Hugh Lloyd-Jones in his "Zeus in Aeschylus" in the *Journal of Hellenic Studies* 76 (1956):55–67 and his "The Guilt of Agamemnon," *Classical Quarterly* 12 (1962):187–199. Lloyd-Jones's argument is also briefly outlined in the introduction to his translation and commentary, *"Agamemnon" by Aeschylus,* one of the Prentice-Hall Greek Drama Series. The idea of a primitive Zeus in Aeschylus is also supported by D. Page and J. D. Denniston in their comments in *Aeschylus's "Agamemnon"* and by Friedrich Solmsen. In his "Strata of Greek Religion in Aeschylus" (pp. 121–136) in volume 1 of *Kleine Schriften,* Solmsen identifies the two strata of Aeschylus's gods of the family and gods of the city and the central role of *dike* (justice) as the expression of Zeus's will. In his "The Erinys in Aischylos' Septem" in *Transactions of the American Philological Association*

58 (1937):197–211, Solmsen argues that the *erinyes* or demons are the leitmotif of the play and shows that Aeschylus took this primitive element in Greek religious tradition seriously. See also Solmsen's *Hesiod and Aeschylus,* in which Solmsen finds Aeschylus an heir to themes apparent in Hesiod and Solon. Solmsen also believes, however, that Aeschylus had the character of Zeus evolve and improve from its tyrannical form in the *Prometheus Bound* to a more humane outlook in the rest of the trilogy and as in the *Agamemnon.* Aeschylus meant that Zeus actually improved in the course of time. Other scholars (e.g., D. W. Lucas) also argue that Aeschylus's Zeus was meant to evolve from a primitive and tyrannical character into a just and benign deity.

Karl Reinhardt, *Aischylos als Regisseur und Theologe,* argues that Zeus in the plays of Aeschylus is both tyrannical and cruel as well as just and benign. This contradictory representation of Zeus simply reflects the divided aspect of the universe and shows that Aeschylus believed that the character of divinity transcends human comprehension. Eduard Fraenkel, *Agamemnon* (3 vols.), argues that Aeschylus reinterpreted the traditional stories about Zeus and the other gods in order to improve those stories, making them theologically acceptable to fifth-century Athens and generally freeing them of primitive and superstitious meanings. Leon Golden, *In Praise of Prometheus: Humanism and Rationalism in Aeschylean Thought,* makes Aeschylus an enlightened believer in humanism and human progress. Golden argues that Aeschylus's Zeus represents both the ordered rules of human society and the raw, ungoverned elements of harsh nature. Zeus stands, therefore, for the hidden forces which cause everything which happens in the universe. Eric R. Dodds, "The *Prometheus Vinctus* and the Progress of Scholarship," in *The Ancient Concept of Progress* (pp. 26–44), convincingly argues that Aeschylus meant the tyrant Zeus of *Prometheus Bound* to progress morally and be reconciled with Prometheus in the remaining two plays of the trilogy. Scholars have normally missed this point because they have wrongly taken Plato and Aristotle's idea of the unchanging character of divinity as typical of Greek religious thought. Dodds comments extensively on various scholarly interpretations of the *Prometheus Bound.*

Sophocles

The bibliographies to be found in the general studies of Greek literature and Greek drama are useful sources on Sophocles. Also see H. F. Johansen's review of writings on Sophocles from 1939–1959 in *Lustrum* 7 (1962). There are a number of interesting collections of scholarly articles on Sophocles: Albert Cook, *"Oedipus Rex" and the Critics;* T. Woodward, *Sophocles: A Collection of Critical Essays;* Michael J. O'Brien, *Twentieth Century Interpretations of "Oedipus Rex": A Collection of Critical Essays;* and H. Diller, *Sophokles.*

The best introductory surveys are J. T. Sheppard, *Aeschylus and Sophocles*, and Sinclair M. Adams, *Sophocles the Playwright*. George H. Gellie, *Sophocles: A Reading*, is a more detailed and exceptionally well-written work. Each of the plays is analyzed, and there is a chapter on "The Gods" which effectively argues that for Sophocles the gods sanctioned the normal and the customary balances of life and punished anyone who upset those balances regardless of their motives. Thus he gives a salutary warning that the Greek idea of divinity was quite different from the modern one. See also Thomas B. L. Webster, *An Introduction to Sophocles*, a clearly written topical survey. Chapter 2 is devoted to "Sophocles' Thought." Webster argues that Sophocles was basically optimistic and that he purified traditional religion while defending it against skeptical attacks. He further argues that Sophocles generally promoted aristocratic ideals inherited from his predecessors Aeschylus and Pindar. Sophocles took the idea that *hubris*, or excessive pride, leads to calamity from Aeschylus and the ideals of personality and *sophrosyne* (i.e., the safe-mindedness which avoids upsetting excess) from Pindar.

Much of the literature on Sophocles, both general and specialized, deals with his attitude toward the gods. C. Maurice Bowra, *Sophoclean Tragedy*, analyzes each of the extant plays and argues that Sophocles believed the gods imposed suffering on apparently innocent people, such as Oedipus. Their actions appear unjust to human beings because human beings are ignorant of the full purpose and context of the gods' actions. Sophocles' plays teach caution and moderation in prosperity, for even unintentional acts can destroy anyone. H. D. F. Kitto, *Sophocles: Dramatist and Philosopher*, surveys the interaction of human and divine will in the plays. The gods represent the overpowering elements in human life; justice is the force which acts throughout the universe to prevent encroachment by one element in the sphere of another. Thus life is governed by reason (i.e., *logos*), although its government is often hidden from human understanding. Cedric H. Whitman, *Sophocles: A Study of Heroic Humanism*, argues that Sophocles was a humanist who concentrated on the heroism of human beings in the face of adversity. It was not the gods who imposed suffering on a hero, but the hero's own *arete*, or special excellence, which leads to excess and to destruction. B. M. Knox, *The Heroic Temper: Studies in Sophoclean Tragedy*, is a series of lectures also focused on the heroes in Sophocles. These figures are distinguished by their refusal to yield to fate or to accept the limitations of human nature. Arthur J. A. Waldock, *Sophocles, the Dramatist*, is chiefly valuable for its critical remarks on other interpretations of Sophocles. Waldock denies that Sophocles exhibited any strong religious ideas in his plays. Such a work as *Oedipus Rex* is best regarded as an artistic representation of the power of accident and of human power to bear the misfortune of life. Eric R. Dodds, "On Misunderstanding the *Oedipus Rex*," in *The*

Ancient Concept of Progress and Other Essays on Greek Literature and Belief (pp. 64–78), gives an interesting review of interpretations of the play and concludes that Sophocles meant Oedipus to be morally innocent. The play represents him as freely choosing the acts which lead to his downfall, while at the same time fate has predetermined his fall. The important didactic function of the play is to reinforce reverence for oracles against skepticism.

M. B. O'Connor, *Religion in the Plays of Sophocles*, systematically reviews the religious references in the extant plays, and Karl Reinhardt, *Sophokles*, also focuses on the idea of piety and the relations of human beings to gods. Reinhardt also comments on each of the plays. The general question of Sophoclean pessimism is well introduced by J. C. Opstelten, *Sophocles and Greek Pessimism*. Opstelten believes that Sophocles was a "pessimist in his thought or rational insight, but an optimist by temperament" (pp. 227–228). Thus Sophocles followed a normal Greek attitude in believing that human wishes are ultimately vain and are defeated by fate and that this pessimism was not a sign of passivity; rather it encouraged a heroic effort. Opstelten thus considers that the plays recognize human limits and simultaneously portray heroic human endurance—they are a victory over pessimism. Victor Ehrenberg, *Sophocles and Pericles*, is a study of the personal connections between these two men and their representation of fifth-century Athenian society. Ehrenberg considers them both good representatives of the society and he argues that they shared a belief in the perfectability of human nature but they also conflicted sharply because Sophocles was conservative and religiously inclined while Pericles was a rationalist. These general discussions are supplemented with interesting comments on the role of rulers in Sophocles' plays (especially Creon and Oedipus) and with a valuable introduction on "Tragedy and History."

Euripides

Frank L. Lucas, *Euripides and His Influence*, one of the Our Debt to Greece and Rome series with a brief but interesting sketch of the influence of Euripides on later literature (p. 39 ff.), and D. J. Conacher, *Euripidean Drama: Myth, Theme, and Structure*, are both useful introductions to Euripides and his works. Thomas B. L. Webster, *The Tragedies of Euripides*, comments on the plays. Webster is mainly devoted to the chronological reconstruction of the composition of all the plays, extant and lost. Gilbert Murray, *Euripides and His Age*, has now been generally supplanted. Murray clearly discusses the plays in chronological order and includes an interesting discussion of Euripides' artistic techniques (chaps. 8 and 9). The student should also read Gilbert Norwood, *Essays on Euripidean Drama*, especially the essay on "Towards Understanding Euripides."

General studies of Euripides tend to pay almost disproportionate attention to his attitude toward religion, specifically on the question of whether he was a rational skeptic or a basically conservative thinker. The most common interpretations are well summarized and criticized by L. H. Greenwood in *Aspects of Euripidean Tragedy*. The argument that Euripides was a rationalist skeptical of religion is the obvious subject of Arthur W. Verrall, *Euripides the Rationalist: A Study in the History of Art and Religion*. Verrall argues that Euripides wrote superficially conventional plays which contained elaborate indirect and ironical attacks on religion. Verrall's arguments are ingenious, but they depend on his supposition that the audiences which heard the plays were incredibly astute in their interpretations. Paul Decharme, *Euripides and the Spirit of His Dramas*, is a better balanced and more persuasive attempt to represent Euripides as a rationalist. Decharme devotes part 1 to a study of "The Critical Spirit in Euripides" and part 2 to "Dramatic Art in Euripides." Decharme believes that Euripides was a rationalist in the sense that he was personally critical of the traditional social and religious institutions of Athenian society. He does not, however, claim that Euripides constructed an elaborate system of double meanings and twin plots to express his rationalism. G. M. A. Grube, *The Drama of Euripides*, is a well-balanced and informative survey which takes particular exception to Verrall. Most of his book is a consideration of the Euripidean writings and the introductory essays are excellent. The chapter on "The Gods" (pp. 41–63) shows that the Greeks did not think gods were necessarily good or evil, but they were nonetheless immortal. Thus many of the Euripidean representations of misbehavior on the part of the gods were not as contrary to the idea of divinity as modern readers suppose. Consequently, Euripides did not necessarily employ a rationalist critique or irony. The most brilliant commentary on an individual play is Eric R. Dodds, *Bacchae*, which is a detailed commentary on the text of the play and its background. Geoffrey S. Kirk, *The "Bacchae" by Euripides*, one of the Prentice-Hall Greek Drama Series, is a simpler commentary well suited for the reader without a knowledge of Greek. Eric Dodds's "Euripides the Irrationalist" in *The Ancient Concept of Progress and Other Essays on Greek Literature and Belief* (pp. 78–92) argues that Euripides was a skeptical pessimist convinced that emotions rule human life. Thus Euripides opposed the rationalism of Socrates, which supposed the rule of reason over the passions and the rational structure of the universe.

The scholarly anthologies on Euripides are of uneven quality. The best is in German, E.-R. Schwinge, *Euripides*, one of the Wege der Forschung series. The articles by eminent students of the field are all worthwhile: e.g., Albin Lesky, "Psychologie bei Euripides" (pp. 79–101). The Twentieth Century Interpretations collection on *Euripides's "Alcestis"* is edited by John R. Wilson. *Euripides: A Collection of Critical Essays*, edited by Eric Segal, includes G. M. A. Grube's excellent "Euripides and the

Gods" from his *The Drama of Euripides*. Several of the articles are either too narrow in scope for the student or too clever in the manner of literary criticism.

Roman Literature

BIBLIOGRAPHICAL RESOURCES AND GENERAL SURVEYS

Herbert J. Rose and Moses Hadas have both published surveys of Roman literature which are the equal of their surveys of Greek literature. Herbert J. Rose, *A Handbook of Latin Literature*, is a reference guide with a bibliography (pp. 534–561) brought up to date by E. Courtney. It covers the period from the beginnings of Roman literature to the death of Trajan (i.e., the close of the Silver Age), although chapters 14 and 15 provide some information on later literature. Moses Hadas's survey, *A History of Latin Literature*, has a short bibliography and is an accurate, well-written history. The most complete bibliographical references are to be found in the *Handbuch der Altertumswissenschaft*. M. Schanz began *Geschichte der römischen Literatur* in four volumes, but it has since been revised and brought up to date. Volumes 1 and 2 are by C. Hosius; volumes 3 and 4, part 2, by C. Hosius and G. Kruger. Volume 4, part 1, is Schanz's original work. The entire work is a magnificent reference and bibliographical source.

The most delightful introduction to Roman literature for the beginner, aside from those recommended as bibliographical sources, is Gilbert Highet, *Poets in a Landscape*. Highet sketches his travels through Italy and describes the lives and writings of Catullus, Vergil, Propertius, Horace, Tibullus, Ovid, and Juvenal. The book is immensely entertaining and also illuminates the general cultural environment of literature in the early Roman Empire. The best conventional introduction is Michael Grant, *Roman Literature*. This effective survey is especially valuable for its explanation of the metrical system of poetry in Latin. Tenny Frank, *Life and Literature in the Roman Republic*, is a more restricted survey (up to Lucretius and Cicero). Every student should be acquainted with John W. Duff's two-volume general survey: *A Literary History of Rome from the Origins to the Close of the Golden Age* and *A Literary History of Rome in the Silver Age: From Tiberius to Hadrian*. Duff discusses every important aspect of Roman literary history and includes a happy distribution of comments on the lives, style, and cultural environments of Roman authors. Frank O. Copley, *Latin Literature from the Beginnings to the Close of the Second Century A.D.*, covers the same general ground as Duff.

Gordon Williams, *The Nature of Roman Poetry*, is restricted to a survey of poetry from the beginning to the death of Horace in 8 B.C. His *Tradition and Originality in Roman Poetry* covering the same time span, is a fuller survey in 810 pages with detailed comments on lengthy excerpts and translations. Clarence W. Mendell, *Latin Poetry*, is a three-volume work which covers the period from the first century B.C. to the second century A.D. The author analyzes numerous excerpts from Roman poetry and drama.

VIRGIL (VERGIL)

There is a succinct review of Virgil by T. E. Wright in *Fifty Years (and Twelve) of Classical Studies* (chap. 11, pp. 387–395) and in a short pamphlet by Gordon Williams, *Virgil* (1967), one of the New Survey of the Classics series published by the Classical Association. The *Classical World* publishes periodic résumés of new literature. The most recent is G. E. Duckworth, "Recent Works on Vergil: 1940–1956," in volume 51:89 ff. See volume 57 (1964):193 ff. for a list of work published during 1957–1963; also see *Vergilius*, the journal of the Vergilian Society of America. There is a recent survey by A. G. McKay, "Vergilian Bibliography: 1968–1969," in volume 1 (1969):42–52. *L'Année philologique* publishes a separate and indispensable section on Virgil.

The general histories of Latin literature include a good treatment of Virgil in Herbert A. Rose, *A Handbook of Latin Literature* (see chap. 9, "Vergil and Augustan Poetry"), Moses Hadas, *A History of Latin Literature* (chap. 8), and John Duff, *A Literary History of Rome* (vol. 1, part 3, chap. 1). The older but still useful surveys include John W. Mackail, *Virgil and His Meaning to the World of Today*, Tenny Frank, *Vergil: A Biography*, Terrat R. Glover, *Virgil*, and William Y. Sellar, *The Roman Poets of the Augustan Age*.

The student interested in uncovering the literary devices used by Virgil in the construction of his poetry (especially in the *Aeneid*) will find Henry W. Prescott, *The Development of Virgil's Art*, to be a good starting point. Prescott shows how Virgil used and modified traditional Greek forms. The bulk of Prescott's interpretation (as he points out to the reader in his preface) is based on R. Heinze, *Virgil's epische Technik*, which is a classic detailed study of the chief themes in the *Aeneid* and of Virgil's artistic principles. Edward K. Rand, *The Magical Art of Virgil*, is a broad analysis which attempts to replicate the approach taken by John Livingston Lowes in *The Road to Xanadu*, his study of Coleridge. Rand attempts to uncover the sources of Virgil's themes and ideas and the literary genres used by the author. Lowes had materials from Coleridge to facilitate his research and since Rand had no comparable references, his task was more difficult. Rand, however, has contributed a creditable survey of the sources available to Virgil. Rand's approach is broader than Prescott's because he is interested in all of the themes and ideas Virgil used in composing his poems. Rand's work is a sound argument for Virgil's basic originality. Another excellent study of Virgil is by the eminent scholar, W. F. Jackson Knight; his *Roman Virgil* combines interesting comments on the general cultural, political, and literary environment of the poet.

Knight, however, has been justly accused of a tendency to judge the psychological qualities which he alleges influenced Virgil's poetry. The final chapter on "Vergil and After" is a résumé of Virgil's reputation and his literary influence immediately after his death and in the subsequent history of western literature. On Virgil's religion see Cyril Bailey, *Religion in Virgil*, which surveys the magic, animism, anthropomorphism, and philosophy contributing to Virgil's religion. W. Wade Fowler, *Religious Experience of the Roman People* (chap. 18), is another excellent summary.

There are a large number of studies focused on the *Aeneid*. Brooks Otis, *Virgil: A Study in Civilized Poetry*, is a complex work concentrating on the *Aeneid* as the best of Virgil's works. Otis carefully reviews the sources of Virgil's forms and ideas and gives special attention to his use of symbols. W. A. Camp, *An Introduction to Virgil's "Aeneid,"* explains the epic's social and literary background and its chief themes and events. Kenneth Quinn, *Virgil's "Aeneid": A Critical Description*, is a detailed examination chiefly of the literary quality of the epic. Two important works are critical of the theory, especially advanced by Heinze, that Aeneas was meant to be a Stoic hero. C. Maurice Bowra disagrees with this theory in his *From Virgil to Milton*. Bowra shows that Aeneas was "essentially a creature of his emotions" and lacked the heroic self-control important to the Stoic ideal. Viktor Pöschl, *The Art of Vergil: Image and Symbol in the "Aeneid,"* also argues that Aeneas was not a Stoic hero. Instead he combined *magnitudo animi*, or "greatness of soul," with *humanitas*, or love for humanity. The most important treatment of a single book in the *Aeneid* is E. Norden, *Aeneis: Buch VI*, giving the text and a translation plus a wealth of material on the eschatological ideas available to Virgil.

On the *Eclogues* see Herbert J. Rose, *The "Eclogues" of Vergil*, which is an interesting general summary, and *Vergil's Messianic "Eclogue": Its Meaning, Occasion, and Sources*, which translates the fourth *Eclogue* and includes articles by J. B. Major, W. Wade Fowler, and R. S. Conway. They note that this poem foresaw the birth of a savior of humanity (the Christians interpreted it to be a pagan presage of the birth of Jesus, but it was a reference to Augustus or a member of his family).

There are interesting and contrasting estimates of Virgil's literary value to be found in two articles. Victor Pöschl, "The Poetic Achievement of Virgil," in *Classical Journal* 56 (1960–1961):290–299, considers Virgil and his *Aeneid* to be the sum of ancient civilization, especially of ancient moral values. Robert Graves, "The Virgil Cult," in *The Virginia Quarterly Review* (1962):13–35, argues that Virgil is overrated as a poet and a human being. Other articles can be found in Stielo Commager, *Virgil: A Collection of Critical Essays*. This is a collection of scholarly articles of uneven value to students. Also see D. R. Dudley, *Virgil*, a collection of contributions by eminent scholars. The most interesting article is R. D. William, "Changing Attitudes to Virgil" (pp. 119–138).

HORACE

Bibliographical references to Horace can also be found in T. E. Wright, "The Augustan Poets," (pp. 399–405), in *Fifty Years (and Twelve) of Classical Scholarship*, and in part 1 of *L'Année philologique*. Also see Kenneth Reckford, *Horace* (pp. 164–167), one of the Twayne World Author series.

The surveys of Latin literature invariably emphasize the work of Horace. See Herbert Rose's *Handbook of Latin Literature*, "Vergil and the Augustan Poets" (chap. 9); Moses Hadas's *A History of Latin Literature* (chap. 9); John Duff's *A Literary History of Rome* (vol. 1, part 3, chap. 3); and John D'Alton's *Roman Literary Theory and Criticism*, which includes an especially brilliant study of "Horace and the Classical Creed" (chap. 6).

An older short study of the life and writings of Horace by G. Showerman, *Horace and His Influence*, one of the Our Debt to Greece and Rome books, is worth reading for its survey of "Horace through the Ages" (pp. 69–127). Alfred Noyes contributed a highly readable biography, *Horace: A Portrait*, which has been criticized for being unreliable in its details. Noyes wrote as a lover of poetry rather than as a scholar, and that approach evokes the beginner's interest. The reader is advised to read Noyes and then refer to one of the more scholarly surveys: either the competent scholarly survey by the American Henry D. Sedgwick, *Horace: A Biography*, or that of the French Jacques Perret, *Horace*. The beginner is reminded that Gilbert Highet, *Poets in a Landscape*, includes a chapter on Horace.

There are several detailed and scholarly studies of Horace. The following are recommended: William D. Sellar, *The Roman Poets of the Augustan Age: Horace and the Elegiac Poets*. Pages 1–201 are devoted to Horace. John F. D'Alton, *Horace and His Age: A Study in Historical Background*, is still one of the best books available on Horace. D'Alton pays less attention to Horace's use of the literary genres of his age than Sellar, but he surveys those ideas in every area of thought which may have influenced Horace. D'Alton avoids the common tendency to make Horace appear more philosophical and intellectual than he was, but his work lacks a clear focus— and the reader may be overwhelmed by its detail. Several surveys concentrate on explanations of the metres and literary forms used by Horace. See L. P. Wilkinson, *Horace and His Lyric Poetry*, and Charles O. Brink, *Horace on Poetry: Prolegomena to the Literary Epistles*, which has a bibliography (pp. 273–286) and a fine introduction to Horace's poetic theories and techniques. Brink's *Horace on Poetry: The "Ars Poetica"* (2 vols.) gives a detailed introduction and commentary on Horace's discussion of the standards of literary excellence. Brink should be supplemented by A. Y. Campbell, *Horace: A New Interpretation*, which treats Horace as a moral teacher of society and suggests that ancient literary theory assumed that poetry had to be understood in those terms. See especially "The Function of Poetry in the Ancient World" (chap. 2). The best detailed study is Eduard Fraenkel, *Horace*, a brilliant résumé of every aspect of

Horace's life, career, sources, ideas, and modes of expression. C. D. N. Costa, *Horace,* is a collection of useful articles on Horace's art.

The Visual Arts

Bibliographical Resources

M. W. Chamberlin, *Guide to Art Reference Books,* and E. L. Lucas, *Art Books: A Basic Bibliography,* reference the basic sources and several serial bibliographies also reference literature in the visual arts. The Wilson Company publishes the *Art Index: A Cumulative Author and Subject Index to Fine Arts Periodicals* (1929), which can be supplemented by the *Architectural Index* (1950). The *Art Index* adequately covers archaeology and art history, but it lacks annotations and its references to foreign journals are limited. American Bibliographical Center-Clio, Inc. publishes *Artbibliographies: Current Titles* (1972). *Artbibliographies: Current Titles* reproduces the table of contents pages of nearly 250 journals in the history of art and design—including the most important foreign-language publications.

There are several invaluable foreign-language guides. The *Répertoire d'art et d'archéologie,* published by the Comité internationale d'histoire de l'art (1910), lists books and articles according to country of publication and chronology and provides occasional short annotations. The *Répertoire* includes a section on the general history of art and architecture. The *Zeitschrift für Kunstgeschichte* (1932) provides an annual bibliography of books and articles, unannotated. Also see the *Kunstgeschichtliche Anzeiger,* published semiannually (1904–1913; 1955). The Italian *Annuario bibliografico di storia dell'arte* (1952) reviews books and periodicals. It is organized according to country of publication and by artist, with short summaries.

The important journals include book reviews and bibliographical essays. The most important American journals are the *Art Bulletin* (1913) and the *Art Quarterly* (1938). The most important British journal is *The Journal of the Warburg and the Courtauld Institutes* (1937), which specializes in the study of iconographical materials. The *Journal of the Society of Architectural Historians* (1941) is devoted entirely to that field. The *Papers of the American Association of Architectural Bibliographers* (1965) is published annually and discusses a variety of topics.

HANDBOOKS AND ENCYCLOPEDIAS

By far the best one-volume guide is the *Oxford Companion to Art,* edited by Harold Osbourne. It has succinct and accurate articles and a fine bibliography (pp. 1231–1277). The recently translated *Larousse's Encyclopedia of Art* is one of the best multivolume guides. Volume 1 covers "Prehistoric and Ancient Art" and includes fine illustrations and articles written by experts. Its historical organization is particularly advantageous. A recently translated Italian encyclopedia is not as conveniently organized, but it includes some excellent articles on the history of art: *The Encyclopedia of World Art* (15 vols.). The Germans (during the prewar era) have produced the most erudite encyclopedia in the field, the *Allgemeines Lexikon der bildenden Kunstler* (37 vols.). The Italian *Enciclopedia dell'arte antica: classica e orientale* (6 vols. and 1 supplementary vol.) is also valuable and concentrates on the field of ancient art.

Art history and art criticism are well covered in *Art and Archeology*, one of the Humanistic Scholarship in America series edited by James S. Ackerman and Rhys Carpenter. Part 2 is by Ackerman on "Western Art History." U. Kultermann, *Geschichte der Kunstgeschichte: der Weg einer Wissenschaft*, is a more detailed and systematic study of the development of art criticism.

General Surveys

There are several competent surveys of the history of art, and the following accurate and clearly written works are recommended. Sheldon Cheney, *A New World History of Art*, includes useful bibliographical notes. Chapters 1–10 (pp. 1–225) cover the ancient period—including Asia. Helen Gardner, *Art through the Ages*, is an older and deservedly popular survey which has been revised by the Yale Department of the History of Art. Chapters 5–7 (pp. 114–280) cover the classical world, with good bibliographies for each chapter. Horst W. Janson, *History of Art*, is more difficult to use but more informative than either Cheney or Gardner. Part 1 (pp. 18–185) is entirely devoted to the ancient Near East, Greece, and Rome, with a competent introduction to the major styles and monuments of art. The bibliographies are useful but unannotated.

The following works deal with particular themes in western art from the Greeks to the contemporary era. They are worth consulting as general histories of art and for their useful treatment of the classical era. Benjamin Rowland is the author of *The Classical Tradition in Western Art*. His work traces the influence of artistic standards and techniques established during the Greek and Hellenistic eras. The ancient period is dealt with directly (pp. 1–96) and the author provides a simple definition of classicism. Kenneth Clark, *The Nude: A Study in Ideal Form*, is difficult to read, but it is worth the added effort. Clark includes a series of chapters on Apollo, Venus, Energy, Pathos, and Ecstasy and explains the role of the nude in western art and how it differs from a simply naked body. He considers that the nude was always an ideal motif which transcended the mundane reality of the human body. Arnold Hauser, *The Social History of Art* (2 vols.), is a different type of general topical study from Rowland and Clark. Hauser ruthlessly applies Marxian analysis to the history of art and is determined to show that art reflects the evolution of social and economic forces. He discusses all of the fine arts with emphasis on the visual arts. Volume 1, part 2 (pp. 71–131), covers the art of Greece and Rome. The excellent survey by Giovanni Becatti, *The Art of Ancient Greece and Rome: From the Rise of Greece to the Fall of Rome,* covers the ancient classical period. It is beautifully illustrated, with several comments on the artistic theories of the ancient world. See especially "The Severe Style and Its Artistic Concept" (chap. 5), "The Classical Style and the Achievement of an Ideal Organic Naturalism" (chap. 6), and "The Art of the Fourth Century and the Humanization of the Classical Idea" (chap. 7).

Most source collections in art tend to ignore the ancient period, but two important exceptions must be mentioned. The *Sources and Documents in the History of Art* includes two excellent anthologies of sources from the classical world by J. J. Pollitt with extensive comments. See *The Art of Greece: 1400–31 B.C.* and *The Art of Rome: 753 B.C.–337 A.D.* Harold Spencer, *Readings in Art History* (2 vols.), is a collection of scholarly articles on the development of art. Volume 1 (entries 1–10) deals with the history of ancient art.

Since 1945 several important multivolume series on the history of art and architecture have been published. They expand the resources available to the student and the scholar enormously. Their analyses and magnificent plates make them especially valuable. See the Pelican History of Art series under the general editorship of Nicholas Pevsner, which is scheduled to be completed in about 50 volumes. This series includes detailed texts and excellent bibliographies and is more suited for scholarly reference than for casual reading. The French series now being translated as The Arts of Mankind is oriented toward the discussion of plates. This series, under the general editorship of André Malraux, is scheduled for completion in about 40 volumes. The Art of the World series also discusses beautiful plates, and it includes geographically and historically organized volumes. It normally includes historical charts and bibliographical notes. A somewhat narrower series with less material on the ancient world is the Great Centuries of Painting. Several volumes from these series and others will be cited below.

Greek Art

The preeminent handbook survey of Greek art is Gisela Richter, *A Handbook of Greek Art.* It is a topically organized guide to all aspects of the visual arts with acute comments accompanying fine illustrations. John D. Beazley and Bernard Ashmole, *Greek Sculpture and Painting to the End of the Hellenistic Period,* is despite the title essentially a survey of the classical period which includes a systematic chronology of the period (pp. 35–50). A more recent survey, Raymond V. Schoder, *Masterpieces of Greek Art,* is essentially a series of plates with short and judicious comments. John Boardman, *Greek Art,* is less detailed. Boardman also contributed to a collective one-volume survey, *Greek Art and Architecture,* which is a topical discussion of the different types of art. Boardman's survey of the development of architecture (pp. 7–116) is especially well done, and the book is distinguished by the plates arranged by Max Hirmer.

The multivolume series invariably include important studies of Greek art. The Arts of Mankind series has three superb volumes produced jointly by J. Charbonneaux, R. Martin, and F. Villard, *Archaic Greek Art: 620–480, Classical Greek Art: 480–330,* with a bibliography (pp. 367–376), and *Hellenistic Art: 330–50 B.C.* Part 4 of the latter is an invaluable collection of charts and bibliographies. The Art of the World series includes Frederick Matz, *The Art of Crete and Early Greece,* and most importantly Karl Schefold, *The Art of Classical Greece.* Schefold's survey is useful because it covers the most important period in the development of Greek art and because it includes notes, charts, and maps, plus an introduction entitled "Prerequisites of Classical Art." Thomas B. L. Webster, *Hellenistic Art,* is a sympathetic exposition of what used to be considered the decadent stage of Greek art. C. Mitchell Havelock, *Hellenistic Art: The Art of the Classical World from the Death of Alexander the Great to the Battle of Actium,* is a topical survey of all art forms with comments concerning the plates.

The history of sculpture is well covered in the detailed study by Reinhard Lullies and Max Hirmer, *Greek Sculpture.* Also see the older studies including Arnold Lawrence, *Classical Sculpture,* which is most useful as a reference work; Gisela Richter, *The Sculpture and Sculptors of the Greeks;* Margarete Bieber, *The Sculpture of the Hellenistic Age;* Arnold Lawrence, *Later Greek Sculpture and Its Influence on East and West,* which is a short work with commentary accompanying the plates and a sketch of the later Greek artistic principles; and a short lecture by Bernard Ashmole on *The Classical Ideal in Greek Sculpture.*

Several works concentrate on the theoretical principles involved in the visual arts. Percy Gardner, *The Principles of Greek Art,* has an excellent introduction plus chapters on "The Grammar of Greek Art" (chap. 1) and "Naturalism and Idealism in Greek Art" (chap. 21); he succinctly summarizes the theoretical bases of Greek art and its distinctive elements compared to earlier forms and modern attitudes toward representation. Robert M. Cook comments extensively on the theory of Greek art throughout his recently published *Greek Art: Its Development, Character, and Influence* and he includes an annotated bibliography. Robert L. Scranton discusses the principles of art in the ancient world in his *Aesthetic Aspects of Ancient Art*. Scranton surveys the art of Egypt, "Hither Asia," the Early Aegean period, the classical art of Greece and Rome, and early Christian art. He comments on the basic elements of artistic presentation (e.g., "signification," the use of literal or symbolic communication, configuration, dynamics, system, focus, and cohesion). His work would be improved if he had more clearly related those general principles to the illustrative plates. The works of Rhys Carpenter, *The Esthetic Basis of Greek Art of the Fifth and the Fourth Centuries B.C.* and *Greek Art: A Study of the Formal Evolution of Style*, are even more interesting. Carpenter considers that the Greeks were a visually oriented people in art and other fields of thought and that this orientation is the key to understanding their art. Their visual orientation, he believes, was the basis of art forms which reflected a fidelity to actual appearance. Carpenter further argues that the Greeks perceived the essential structure and formal elements of the things represented in their art and concentrated on those basics rather than on details. He considers that it was the function of Greek artists to fathom the basic structural configurations of objects, to synthesize them, and through composition impose these formal elements on their art forms. Thus Greek art was a kind of *"mimesis* metamorphosed by formalization."* Carpenter considers that the more photographic forms which appeared after the classical period represented a degeneration of Greek art. His volumes have excellent chapters on the evolution of Greek architecture. J. J. Pollitt, *Art and Experience in Classical Greece*, is a most interesting examination of the characteristics of high classical art in the period 480–320 B.C. Pollitt finds classical art to have taken a variety of forms but always to have given a balanced representation of the generic and the specific in life. Hellenistic art in contrast focused on the concrete specifics of experience. Pollitt seeks to correlate this evolution of art with other areas of Greek cultural development. R. Ross Holloway, *A View of Greek Art*, also relates the development of art and other areas of thought. He surveys from the archaic period to the Hellenistic period and argues that only in the later era did the artist gain a genuine independence from convention and use art for the purpose of expressing strong emotional interests.

Two references to Greek architecture are also informative regarding Greek art theory. R. D. Martienssen, *The Idea of Space in Greek Architecture: With Special Reference to the Doric Temple and Its Setting*, is an interesting albeit controversial argument that the Greeks developed a sense of spatial relations basic to the systematically integrated (or organic) harmony characteristic of their architecture. Vincent Scully, *The Earth, the Temple, and the Gods: Greek Sacred Architecture*, is a study of Greek temples and their integral relationships with their settings. Scully departs from widely held opinion to argue that landscapes were vitally important to the Greeks, who considered them to be the embodiment of divine forces. Landscapes were essential to the temple's function as a sacred building and the two combined to create the desired symbolic and spiritual environment. For this reason, he argues, Greek temples did not create an important "interior space"; rather they occupied an "exterior space," including landscapes.

Roman Art

Eugenie Strong, *Art in Ancient Rome* (2 vols.), is an older handbook on Roman art and antiquities. George M. A. Hanfmann, *Roman Art: A Modern Survey of the Art of Imperial Rome,* parallels Schoder's survey of Greek art with a series of comments on brilliant plates. The Arts of Mankind series includes two works on the Roman period by Ranuccio B. Bandinelli, *Rome: The Center of Power* and *Rome: The Late Empire.* The Art of the World contribution by Heinz Kahler, *The Art of Rome and Her Empire,* has an especially interesting essay, "The Fundamental Characteristics of Roman Art" (chap. 1), and valuable bibliographical notes and charts (p. 216 ff.). The Skira series includes an essay by Amedeo Maiuri entitled *Roman Painting.*

The development of early Christian art (as part of Roman art) has always received special attention. That field is obviously important to the study of the development of medieval art, and an analysis of Christian iconography provides valuable insights into the thought of the ancient Christians themselves. See F. van der Meer, *Early Christian Art,* which is a sound introduction, and Walter Lowrie, *Art in the Early Church.* Lowrie's work is contentious and unsystematic but informative. It is organized topically and comments on the chief monuments of Christian art and architecture and includes a bibliography (pp. 233–243). The Arts of Mankind series includes an essay by André Grabar, *Early Christian Art: From the Rise of Christianity to the Death of Theodosius,* with an introductory chapter on the general characteristics of Christian art. The Pelican History of Art includes J. Bechwith, *Early Christian and Byzantine Art,* who writes on the ancient church (chaps. 1–4) and includes excellent bibliographical notes. Also see W. Fritz Volbach, *Early Christian Art,* which is a good review of the development of art forms to the seventh century. Pierre Du Bourguel, *Early Christian Art,* is the best complex survey. G. Schiller, *Iconography of Christian Art* (2 vols.), is a historical analysis devoted to symbols of the life of Jesus (vol. 1) and the symbols of the crucifixion (vol. 2).

Several generally controversial studies of the place of Roman art (including architecture) in its cultural setting are worth consulting. The most interesting studies are by Hans P. L'Orange, including *Art Forms and Civic Life in the Late Roman Empire,* in which L'Orange correlates the development of political and artistic forms. He does not claim that changes in the social and political environment caused the late ancient changes in artistic style, but he argues that those evolutions were similar because they were caused by fundamental changes in thinking. The older classical ideal of the harmonious whole and carefully articulated details was replaced by simplified, massive forms with stereotyped details transformed into symbols. Late ancient artists sought "a static world of types and eternal orders" and thus prepared the way for the transcendent art of the medieval period. Similar studies of the relationship between social and artistic motifs can be found in L'Orange, *Studies on the Iconography of Cosmic Kingship in the Ancient World,* and in a collection of his writings, *Likeness and Icon: Selected Studies in Classical and Early Medieval Art.* See the especially interesting articles, "The Antique Origin of Medieval Portraiture" (pp. 91–103) and "Apotheosis" (part 3). A different analysis of late ancient changes in style can be found in Wladimiro Dorigo, *Late Roman Painting: A Study of Pictoral Records, 30 B.C. to A.D. 500.* Dorigo agrees there was a change in style during the late ancient period but attributes it chiefly to the emancipation of the native Roman art form from Hellenic domination and to "expressionism," which ended the a priori order of the classical period. These reorientations more accurately represented the social and political environment of the western Empire and art thus eventually assumed forms appropriate to the medieval world. Dorigo comments on the influence of Plotinus and Augustine, whose ideas reflected this new orientation. R. Brilliant, *Gesture and Rank in Roman Art: The Use of Gesture to Denote Status in Roman Sculpture and Coinage,* studies the imperial use of art as propaganda and the use of gestures to dramatize human figures and to signify status.

Architecture

General Surveys

In addition to the coverage given the development of architecture in general surveys of art history, there are several histories devoted entirely to architecture. Nicholas Pevsner, *An Outline of European Architecture,* is detailed and accurate, but it mostly analyzes particular buildings and does not treat the development of broad architectural styles. British architecture receives exaggerated attention and, most importantly, virtually nothing is included on ancient architecture. Other one-volume surveys include readable accounts of architecture in the classical period and the chief styles. Talbot Hamlin, *Architecture through the Ages*, covers the ancient world in books 1–3 (pp. 3–213). Hamlin includes excellent illustrations. Joseph Watterson, *Architecture: A Short History*, has a useful treatment of ancient architecture (chaps. 1–4, pp. 3–64). Every student should also be acquainted with Bannister Fletcher, *A History of Architecture on the Comparative Method*, an elaborately illustrated reference work. Part 1 (pp. 5–271) discusses ancient architecture. Another older classic must be mentioned: Frederich M. Simpson, *A History of Architectural Development* (3 vols.). Simpson's style is clear and less detailed than Fletcher's. Volume 1, revised by H. Plommer, covers ancient architecture.

Surveys of Ancient and Greek Architecture

The indispensable work in this field is Donald S. Robertson, *A Handbook of Greek and Roman Architecture*, which includes valuable appendices containing chronological charts and bibliographies.

Volume 1 of Simpson's *History of Architectural Development*, revised by H. Plommer, and Bruce Allsopp, *A History of Classical Architecture: From Its Origins to the Emergence of Hellenesque and Romanesque Architecture*, are excellent treatments of architecture during the ancient period. Allsopp covers important developments in a loosely chronological order. The history of Greek architecture includes the following indispensable works. W. B. Dinsmoor, *Architecture of Ancient Greece*, is an accurate and clear account of the development of Greek architecture and it has valuable bibliographical notes. Arnold L. Lawrence, *Greek Architecture*, is detailed and accurate with an extensive bibliography; however, the treatment of the early stages of Greek architectural development is markedly superior to that given to later periods. Lawrence is too advanced for most students and nonspecialists except as a reference. See Robert L. Scranton, *Greek Architecture* (one of the Great Ages of World Architecture series), which is less advanced. John Boardman et al., *Greek Art and Architecture*, is also suitable for the beginner.

Roman Architecture

Frank E. Brown, *Roman Architecture*, in the Great Ages of World Architecture series, is a good introduction to the field, and so are G. T. Rivoira, *Roman Architecture and Its Principles of Construction under the Empire*, and Mortimer Wheeler, *Roman Art and Architecture*. Despite the title, Wheeler treats architecture as the basic Roman artistic form—he believes Roman art was chiefly intended to decorate architecture. William L. MacDonald, *The Architecture of the Roman Empire,* is a detailed study of the change from the "sculptured linear" to the "canopied volume" style which occurred between 50–150 A.D. He introduces evidence adduced from a detailed examination of Nero's palaces, Domitian's palace, Trajan's market, and the Pantheon. The Pelican history by Axel Boethius and J. B. Ward-Perkins, *Etruscan and Roman Architecture,* surveys Etruscan art (chaps. 3 and 4). Part 3 describes the chief monuments and remains in the provinces. There is also a bibliography (pp. 587–605).

General histories of ancient and Roman art are informative on the development of Christian architecture, but several specialized surveys are worth consulting. The Great Ages of World Architecture series includes William L. MacDonald, *Early Christian and Byzantine Architecture.* This work concentrates on the Byzantine period, but it includes comments on ancient Christian developments. Another of the Pelican series by Richard Krautheimer, *Early Christian and Byzantine Architecture,* also concentrates on the Byzantine era, but it also has information on the late antique period. Krautheimer's work is detailed, accurate, and includes a bibliography. John G. Davies, an expert on the general development of the ancient church, concentrates on the cultural and liturgical environment in *The Origins and Development of Early Christian Architecture.* J. Strzygowski, *Origins of Christian Architecture,* has an outdated but still interesting argument on Christian architecture. Strzygowski propounds the theory that the distinctive features of Christian architecture came from the East, especially from Iran, and that Christian art was a new development and not a fulfillment of Roman art.

Classical Music

Bibliographical Resources

The general bibliographical guides to ancient history and ancient aesthetics are singularly weak in their coverage of publications on ancient music. There are, however, several serial and nonserial guides specializing in music and its history. An overview of the available resources is found in Vincent Duckles, "Music Literature, Music, and Sound Recordings," in *Library Trends* 15 (1967):494–521. Duckles also wrote the excellent

Music Reference and Research Materials: An Annotated Bibliography, which includes general resources (pages 1–73), histories and chronologies (pp. 73–92), and bibliographies of music literature (pp. 99–142). L. B. Spiess, *Historical Musicology: A Reference Manual for Research in Music*, is also a sound reference, but the best one-volume nonserial guide is J. H. Davies, *Musicalia: Sources of Information in Music*.

Several valuable serial bibliographies supplement the nonserial guides. *The Music Index* is a basic American source which covers periodical literature (including book reviews) and includes a separate section devoted to the history of music. The *Répertoire internationale de littérature musicale* (1967), a quarterly by the International Musical Society and the International Association of Music Libraries, is an excellent source. Despite the title, *RILM* is in English and it abstracts new publications in all areas of the study of music, including history. The American Bibliographical Service, *Quarterly Check-List of Musicology*, is less valuable than either of these two sources.

Several English-language journals are rich in bibliographical coverage and critical reviews. One of the best is *Notes: The Quarterly Journal of the Music Library Association* (1943). It is mostly devoted to book lists, reviews, and comments on new recordings or printings of musical scores. The Yale School of Music's *The Journal of Musical Theory* has bibliographies of new publications in every issue. *Current Musicology* (1959), by the Columbia University Department of Music, carries many reviews of scholarship on various areas in the history of music. Finally, each issue of the *Music Quarterly* (1915) carries a list of new publications in all languages on the history and current status of music.

The English-language sources can be supplemented by the German *Bibliographie des Musikschriftums* (1936–1940; 1949), which includes coverage of the history of music (part C) and unannotated lists of books and articles. Also see the *Archiv für Musikwissenschaft* (1918) and the French *Revue de musicologie* (1927).

HANDBOOKS AND ENCYCLOPEDIAS

There are many good guides to music, but the two best and most readily available are *The Oxford Companion to Music*, edited by Percy A. Scholes, and the *Harvard Dictionary of Music*, edited by Willi Apel. Both accurately and clearly cover the important aspects of the history of music. Scholes's "Reader's Synopsis of the Contents" is a useful summary, and "The History of Music" (section 13) lists all of the articles that should be consulted to comprehend the volume's contributions on that subject. The bibliographical references are scant in comparison to Apel. His articles end with judiciously chosen references for further reading. *The International Cyclopedia of Music and Musicians*, first edited by Oscar Thompson, merits attention. It includes chapters by experts on all the major composers and especially valuable and clear lists of the works of the composers.

Two multivolume encyclopedias of music must be continually used by students of the history of music. In English, see *Grove's Dictionary of Music and Musicians* (10 vols.), edited by Eric Blom. *Grove's* is informative about all aspects of music, past and present, and the fifth edition concludes each article with a bibliography. The masterful German *Die Musik in Geschichte und Gegenwart: allgemeine Enzyklopädie der Musik* (14 vols.) is a worthy supplement to *Grove's*.

General Surveys

One of the best introductions to the history of music is the joint work of Horst W. Janson and Joseph Kerman, *A History of Art and Music*. The entire work is written simply and clearly. Kerman, professor of the history of music at the University of California, Berkeley, covers the history of music (book 2, pp. 211–293). Unfortunately, the ancient development of music is treated too briefly (pp. 211–220), but the book is easy to read and its parallel development of art and music history makes it a fine starting place for students. Another brief survey of the history of music is by Alfred Einstein, *A Short History of Music*. Einstein devotes even less space to ancient music than Kerman (pp. 6–14), but his appendix includes 39 examples of musical scores which exhibit the points made in the main text. Students with more advanced knowledge of music will find the following textbook surveys useful: Donald J. Grout, *A History of Western Music*, and Jack A. Westrup, *An Introduction to Music History*. Grout assumes that his readers have some prior knowledge of music and he proceeds to emphasize the importance of different musical styles. He includes chronological charts and an annotated bibliography. Donald H. van Ess, *The Heritage of Musical Style*, discusses the development of musical theory and techniques; see "The Greco-Roman Era" (chap. 2). His writing style is clear and he includes excellent illustrations and charts. Paul H. Lang, *Music in Western Civilization*, is another standard American survey. Lang makes an effort to place the development of music in the context of western social and cultural development. He includes a good booklist bibliography (pp. 1045–1067). Lang is a better reference work than survey. The ancient period is discussed in chapters 1–4 (pp. 1–62). Oliver Strunk, *Source Readings in Music History: From Classical Antiquity through the Romantic Era*, is a good collection of source materials on the history of music. "The Greek View of Music" (chap. 1) and "The Early Christian View of Music" (chap. 2) are especially interesting.

Every student should be acquainted with the multivolume *The Oxford History of Music* (7 vols.). Four volumes of a revised edition are complete. The full revised set will be in 11 volumes. The revised edition's first volume includes a chapter by I. Henderson on "Ancient Greek

Music" (chap. 9, pp. 336–404), another by J. E. Scott on "Roman Music" (chap. 10, pp. 404–421), and a fair chapter-by-chapter bibliography (pp. 479–504). *The Oxford History of Music* is advantageously supplemented by a series of records produced by RCA Victor as examples of the music discussed in the history: *History of Music in Sound* (10 vols.). The first volume, edited by E. Wellesz, covers the ancient period.

Greek and Roman Music

Several studies focus solely on the development of music in the ancient world, or more precisely, on the development and elaboration of Greek music in ancient times. Some of the most important recent publications are reviewed by R. P. Winnington-Ingram, "Ancient Greek Music: 1932–1957," in *Lustrum* 3 (1958):5–58. Winnington-Ingram is the author of a study of the technical structure of Greek music, *Mode in Ancient Greek Music.*

See Ingemar Düring, "Greek Music: Its Fundamental Features and Its Significance," in *The Journal of World History* 3:1 (1956):302–330, for a quick overview of Greek music within its cultural context, and the broader study by Curt Sachs, *The Rise of Music in the Ancient World: East and West.* Sachs reviews the development of Greek music in the Roman era and in the classical and Hellenistic eras and compares it to the development of oriental music. E. A. Lippman, *Musical Thought in Ancient Greece,* surveys the role of music in Greek philosophical development through the Hellenistic era. Lippman includes interesting essays on "Theories of Musical Ethics" (chap. 2) and "The Philosophy and Aesthetics of Music" (chap. 3), plus a bibliography (pp. 177–201). Also see Warren D. Anderson, *Ethos and Education in Greek Music: The Evidence of Poetry and Philosophy.* Anderson surveys the Hellenic (classical) period and concludes there was no general theory concerning the characteristics ("ethos") of good music or its ethical and educational effects at that time. He suggests that at most there was agreement that music might either help or corrupt a developing mind. He includes excellent bibliographical notes (pp.197–285). H. Kohler, *Musik und Dichtung im alten Griechenland,* also places Greek music into a cultural context. He compares and explains the distinctive qualities of Greek and Near Eastern music. M. Wegner, *Das Musikleben der Griechen,* is a cautious and judicious account of Greek music based on original sources rather than on later commentaries; it is therefore especially interesting to scholars. Wegner discusses literary and other forms of archaeological evidence. The student will find some value in an older work, A. Gavaert, *Histoire et théorie de la musique de l'antiquité* (2 vols.).

Chapter 5:   *Ancient Religion*

Introduction

RELIGION EXERCISED AN authority in the ancient classical period unimaginable to most educated people in the twentieth century. Educated people in this century may consider religion to be an important facet of their lives, but it rarely shapes their world view. The modern view of the universe is determined largely through the methods of science, and technology and medicine are dominant factors in most modern social relationships. Religion is usually an uncomfortable guest in the house of science. Modern theology tends to adjust itself to the demands of science and theologians rarely expect to influence the scientist and his methods. During the ancient period, especially during late antiquity, these roles were generally reversed. Philosophy competed with theology effectively during the classical period, but religion overcame that influence and came to dominate the thinking of educated people toward the end of the ancient period.

The spiritually charged atmosphere characteristic of ancient history tends to inhibit understanding of the history of ideas in antiquity. This problem is exacerbated because the study of pagan religion and the study of Judaeo-Christian history have been traditionally divided in scholarly curricula. Since Judaeo-Christian history was once assumed to be sacred, it was exempted from the normal standards of historical analysis. Few modern scholars make that distinction, so historical methods are increasingly applied to the study of the two fields—yet, Judaeo-Christian studies are still influenced by scholars who do not always apply objectively historical canons of evidence and judgment.

General Bibliographical Resources

The traditional division of classical history into two broad areas—the institutions and culture of Greece and Rome and the development of Christian religion—is reflected in the bibliographical resources available for the study of ancient religion. The general bibliographical guides to ancient history listed in the introduction are of little use to the student of Christian history, but they are invaluable in the study of the non-Christian religions of the classical world. A remarkable series of bibliographies, handbooks, encyclopedias, and periodicals cited below (p. 160 ff.) specialize in the history of Christianity and they are reliable guides to new literature. The user should, however, remain aware of the religious bias which influences many writers (and reviewers) on Christian history.

The 1931 edition of the *Guide to Historical Literature* has many citations relevant to the history of ancient religious thought, including a section on the history of Christianity (pp. 233–276) by W. H. Allison. Varet's *Manuel de bibliographie philosophique* devotes volume 1, part 2, to Christian philosophy and volume 2, chapter 2, to the philosophy of religion. Both contain important references to the ancient world. The *Cambridge Ancient History* devotes several chapters (vols. 3–12) to ancient religion and each has an excellent bibliography. The most complete serial bibliography of works on the history of pagan religions and Christianity is the *Revue d'histoire ecclésiastique,* but *L'Année philologique* (part 2) contains a section on the history of religion with citations of writings on both pagan and Christian development. The indispensable *Journal of Hellenic Studies* and the *Journal of Roman Studies* both have fine critical reviews of important works in the history of Greek and Roman religious development. The *Journal of Roman Studies* reviews some works relevant to Christian history, but it is a more useful contribution to non-Christian developments. The German and French-language journals which have valuable bibliographical coverage cite and review some works in ancient Christian history but chiefly concentrate on pagan history—see the *Anzeiger für Altertumswissenschaft, Gnomon,* the *Revue des études anciennes,* the *Revue des études grecques,* and the *Revue des études latines.*

The bibliographical guides to ancient history and the handbooks and encyclopedias for the entire field comment on the development of pagan religion and largely ignore Judaic and Christian history. The *Oxford Classical Dictionary* is a fine guide to pagan religious institutions and their development, and both Whibley's and Sandys's *Companion* guides contain useful information. In Whibley see "Mythology and Religion" (chap. 5); in Sandys's see "Religion and Mythology" (chap. 4) by the eminent historian of religion, W. Wade Fowler. The *Real-Encyclopädie* covers major figures in the history of ancient Christianity, but its general orientation is pagan culture and religion.

The relevant general bibliographies, periodicals, and reference works in ancient history can be supplemented by guides which specialize in religious history. There is no entirely satisfactory nonserial bibliography on ancient religious history, but several guides are worth consulting. The bibliography in Kenneth Latourette, *A History of the Expansion of Christianity: The First Five Centuries* (vol. 1, pp. 370–402), and the notes at the end of each volume of the *Histoire générale des religions* (4 vols.) are helpful sources. The *Histoire* covers Greece and Rome (vol. 2) and Judaism and Christianity (vol. 3). The references to paganism and Judaeo-Christian development in Shirley Jackson Case, *A Bibliographical Guide to the History of Christianity*, are useful. R. P. Morris, *A Theological Book List*, is weak on the ancient period but more up to date than Latourette or Case. There are more useful serial bibliographies than there are nonserial guides, largely because periodicals devoted to early Christian history also review literature on pagan religious development. The most general sources include *The International Bibliography of the History of Religion* (1954). See "The Religions of Antiquity" (chap. 3) and the chapters on Judaism (chap. 4) and Christianity (chap. 5). Also consult the reviews and bibliographical essays in *Numen: International Review for the History of Religions* (1954). The *Harvard Theological Review* (1908) is an indispensable English-language periodical with scholarly articles on the entire range of religious history; it is less valuable as a bibliographical source. Better review coverage can be found in two British journals, the *Journal of Theological Studies* (1899) and the *Journal of Ecclesiastical History* (1950). The American *Church History* (1932) is also valuable, and *Vigiliae Christianae* (1947) provides articles and reviews chiefly (but not entirely) in English.

The most valuable bibliographical reports are carried in foreign-language (or multilingual) journals. The important French-language sources are the *Revue de l'histoire des religions* (1908), *Revue d'histoire et de philosophie religieuse* (1921), *Revue des sciences philosophiques et théologiques* (1907), *Recherches de science religieuse* (1910), and the *Revue philosophique de Louvain* (1894). The multilingual *Recherches de théologie ancienne et médiévale* (1929) is narrower in scope but exceptionally useful. The valuable German-language journals include *Theologische Rundschau* (1928), *Theologische Literaturzeitung* (1876), *Theologische Revue* (1902), *Theologische Zeitschrift* (1945), the *Zeitschrift für Theologie und Kirche* (1891), *Zeitschrift für Kirchengeschichte* (1889), and the *Zeitschrift für katholische Theologie* (1877). The *Zeitschrift für Religions und Geistesgeschichte* (1948) is a less useful bibliographical source with excellent articles on the development of western religious thought. It is a successor to the famous *Archiv für Religionswissenschaft* (1898–1936), now available in a Kraus reprint.

Handbooks and Encyclopedias

The encyclopedias of ancient history include some relevant material on religion, and other reference works devoted solely to the history of religion are also good sources for students and scholars. Several of the latter show a marked bias in judgment, but when used with prudence they are valuable sources of information.

Samuel G. F. Brandon, *Dictionary of Comparative Religion,* is an excellent introduction with judicious articles by eminent authorities which conclude with bibliographical notes. The resources available for the study of comparative religion cannot be fully reviewed here, but a few citations may be helpful to indicate the results attained in the field and the methods commonly applied to the study of the ancient religions. Charles J. Adams, *A Reader's Guide to the Great Religions,* does not directly cover the "dead" religions of Greece and Rome, but it clarifies the general religious environment of the ancient period and the development of comparative religion as a field of inquiry. The development of the discipline is also found in the work of a French master H. Pinard de la Boullaye, *L'Étude comparée des religions;* volume 1 is *Son histoire dans le monde occidental.* One of the most famous works in the study of the evolution of religion, W. Schmidt, *Der Ursprung der Gottesidee,* is also informative. It was first completed in 12 volumes and is available in a one-volume translation, *The Origin and Growth of Religion.* Schmidt, a Catholic scholar, argued that religion began with a primitive monotheism later corrupted by agricultural interests into polytheism. Schmidt's thesis is not generally accepted today, but his discussions of alternative theories of religious development are worth reading. Raffaele Pettazzoni, *The All-Knowing God,* is a scholarly critique of the Schmidt thesis.

The most valuable multivolume encyclopedia is Samuel M. Jackson's revision of a famous German work, *The New Schaff-Herzog Encyclopedia of Religious Knowledge,* first done in 12 volumes in 1908–1914 and brought up to date by the two-volume *Twentieth Century Encyclopedia of Religious Knowledge.* James Hastings, *Encyclopedia of Religion and Ethics,* 13 volumes first completed in 1908–1927, is an even better Protestant but historically oriented work. The English-language *Oxford Dictionary of the Christian Church,* edited by Frank L. Cross, is an indispensable guide to the history of the ancient Christian church, and so is *The New Catholic Encyclopedia* (15 vols.). The latter's Catholic orientation is evident in such articles as those on Mary and the papacy, but it is well written, informative, and the articles generally include bibliographical suggestions. It can be supplemented by the *Sacramentum Mundi: An Encyclopedia of Theology* (4 vols.), edited by Karl Rahner and translated from the German, and the still incomplete *A Catholic Dictionary of Theology.* These encyclopedias should be compared to a new Jewish encyclopedia, *Encyclopaedia Judaica* (16 vols.), edited by Cecil Roth.

Advanced work in the field requires the use of French and German reference guides. The most important French work is the *Dictionnaire de théologie catholique* (15 vols. with 3 supplementary vols.). The *Dictionnaire* is consciously committed to a defense of Catholic theology, but it is too valuable to be ignored. Two German sources, one Protestant and one Catholic, are invaluable guides for the scholar: *Die Religion in Geschichte und Gegenwart* (7 vols.), and *Lexikon für Theologie und Kirche* (11 vols. plus 3 supplementary vols.). An even more valuable tool for the study of religion in the ancient period is the *Reallexikon für Antike und Christentum*, which includes the first eight volumes under the editorship of T. Klauser. The companion publication to the *Reallexikon*, the *Jahrbuch für Antike und Christentum* (published annually), includes articles and book notices on ancient religion and advance copies of articles to appear in forthcoming volumes of the *Reallexikon*. The important Italian work, the *Enciclopedia delle religione* (5 vols.), has exceptional bibliographical notes.

Greek Religion

General Surveys

Herbert J. Rose, *Ancient Greek Religion*, is a good starting place and general handbook for the study of ancient Greek religion. It is available in paperback with Rose's *Ancient Roman Religion* under the title *Religion in Greece and Rome*. Rose is workmanlike, and he attempts to be accurate and thorough rather than entertaining in his treatment of Greek religious development. He cautiously deals with theories about archaic Greek religion that have poured from the presses in this century—but he fails to explain his reason for caution in accepting those theories. His history of Greek religion includes the beginning of the Christian era, but his history of the archaic and classical periods (generally 800 B.C. to 300 B.C.) is best. Gilbert Murray's *Five Stages of Greek Religion* is broader in scope and more evocative in style. Murray was a British scholar of the early twentieth century interested in applying anthropological theory to an analysis of Greek religion. He also used that approach to analyze the origins of Greek drama. The first chapter ("Saturnia Regna") illustrates his method. He properly emphasizes the importance of vegetative fertility to Greeks and other ancient peoples, but generally speaking this section of the work is oversimplified because Murray's knowledge of anthropology was not sufficient to do full justice to the complexities of primitive traits. The later chapters on the history of classical Greek religion and its evolution to the end of the ancient period are superior. "The Failure of Nerve" (chap. 4) describes the loss of confidence in human effort and the growth of anxiety inclining the ancients to choose emotional and magically oriented religions. William K. C. Guthrie, *The Greeks and Their Gods,* differs from Rose and Murray. Guthrie limits his history to the period ending with Plato and Aristotle and describes the religious attitudes of educated rather than ordinary Greeks—though chapter 10 is on the "Hopes and Fears of the Ordinary Man." Guthrie notes that the Greeks believed that man and the gods were inseparably different (humans therefore should never attempt to compete with the gods), and yet many of their institutions assumed a physical and spiritual contact between them—human beings could even be deified. Guthrie traces the former attitude to the Olympian religion the Greeks brought with them when they entered Greece, and he credits the second attitude to the chthonic (i.e., fertility) religions active before they arrived. He concludes that classical Greek religion merged these basically different attitudes. Guthrie is a recognized expert on the Orphic religion, so it is not surprising that the "Orphics" (chap. 11) is excellent.

The recommended general histories of Greek religion necessarily include an old standard by the masterful British scholar, Lewis R. Farnell, *The Higher Aspects of Greek Religion.* Farnell's work is especially interesting because he disagreed with Jane Harrison, Francis Cornford, and other scholars who tended to believe that the Olympian stage of Greek religion was basically an unemotional degeneration of the earlier, chthonic stage. Farnell emphasizes the anthropomorphic grandeur of the Olympic religion and its potential for inspiring moral improvement. Farnell is also author of the five-volume survey, *Cults of the Greek States,* still valuable despite its age. His treatment of the development of the Dionysus cult (vol. 5) is exceptionally well done.

The preeminent treatment of the development of Greek religion is Martin P. Nilsson, *Geschichte der griechischen Religion* (2 vols.). This masterful survey includes all of the important literary and archaeological evidence from the beginning to the age of Alexander the Great (vol. 1) and from Alexander to the end of the ancient period (vol. 2). It is difficult to single out particular parts of this work for special attention because Nilsson exhibits uniformly exemplary scholarship throughout. This work is untranslated, but Nilsson's *History of Greek Religion* gives the essential elements of volume 1 and his *Greek Piety* covers the same ground as volume 2. Two other general histories of Greek religion, also in German, are useful sources. Ulrich von Wilamowitz-Moellendorff capped his career in the field of Greek history with his *Der Glaube der Hellenen* (2 vols.). Wilamowitz employed relatively old-fashioned methods. He was aware of anthropological theories and techniques as they applied to his study, but he consciously rejected their use on the grounds that he did not know

people other than the Greeks well enough to benefit from the comparative method. Hence his methodology retained the philological tradition
of the nineteenth century. The chief defect of his work is not related to his
failure to use specific anthropological theories. It is the result of archaeological evidence subsequently accumulated on the Minoan-Mycenaean
period of Greek religious history. This weakness was partially corrected
by his student Otto Kern in *Die Religion der Griechen* (3 vols.), which covers the entire period from the archaic age to the end of the Roman Empire.
Kern is more sympathetic, though still cautious, in his use of new anthropological methods. Kern's work rests almost entirely on German scholarship for secondary support and thus it ignores important French and
English sources. His nationalistic orientation is evident in his addenda,
"Von Aristoteles zu Wilamowitz" (vol. 3), which sketches German contributions to the field completely and largely ignores the contributions
of scholars from other countries. Arthur B. Cook, *Zeus: A Study in Ancient
Religion* (3 vols. in 5), is the most comparable work in English. Cook
surveys every important aspect of classical Greek religion (the title
is misleading). His study is divided into two parts: an examination of
Zeus as the bright sky and an examination of Zeus as the dark, threaten-
ing, and fertilizing sky. This classic provokes discussion in every area of
Greek history. The "Entretiens I" of the Foundation Hardt series, *La
Nature du divin depuis Homère jusqu'à Platon*, comments extensively on the
history of Greek religion. The introduction by Herbert J. Rose is followed
by the remarks of some leading scholars in the field.

Olympian and Chthonic Gods

Scholars devote considerable attention to the great division between
Greek gods. Some are called chthonic (from the Greek for "earth") and
are related to fertility and to the dead buried within the earth. The chthonic
gods are usually associated with the pre-Greek Minoan and Mycenaean
civilizations. The Olympian gods (e.g., Zeus, etc.) supposedly entered
Greece with invading tribes and had little or nothing to do with the earth's
fertility and less to do with the dead. Classical Greek religion was allegedly a fusion of these two groups.

At the start of the twentieth century several scholars, chiefly British,
became interested in applying anthropological theory to the study of
the Greeks. Jane Harrison, Francis Cornford, and Gilbert Murray were
the leaders of that movement. Harrison and Cornford were especially
interested in the theories of the French anthropologist Emile Durkheim.
Harrison interpreted archaic Greek religion to be a symbolic representation of the collective consciousness of society. She considered the
chthonic rituals to be the religious equivalents of the rites of passage

common to all primitive societies; other religious ideas she thought represented vegetative cycles. The tendency to disdain the later Olympian stage of Greek religion as an abstract and cold degeneration of the emotional vitality of the chthonic stage was a corollary of this British movement. Jane Harrison expounded her ideas moderately in *Prolegomena to the Study of Greek Religion* and more pointedly in *Themis: A Study of the Social Origins of Greek Religion*. Lewis Farnell wrote an informative critical review of Harrison's thesis in the *Year's Work in Classical Studies* (1912):59–63. Gilbert Murray used a similar approach in his *Five Stages of Greek Religion* (chap. 1). The use of archaeological and anthropological evidence to reconstruct archaic Greek religion is more recently indicated in Martin P. Nilsson, *Minoan-Mycenaean Religion and Its Survival in Greek Religion*, and in the studies listed by C. Picard in his *Les Religions préhelleniques (Crete et Mycènes)*, one of the French Mana series.

Dionysus and Orpheus

General references to these closely related figures in the development of Greek religion can be found in William K. C. Guthrie, *The Greeks and Their Gods* (chaps. 6 and 11); in Lewis R. Farnell, *Cults of the Greek States* (vol. 5); and (rather uncritically) in Jane Harrison, *Prolegomena to the Study of Greek Religion* (chaps. 8–12). There are also special studies on Dionysus; see H. Jeanmaire, *Dionysus: histoire du culte de Bacchus*, and Martin P. Nilsson, *Dionysiac Mysteries of the Hellenistic and Roman Age*. Nilsson demonstrates that the cult was not absorbed by the Orphic movement but continued a lengthy and separate existence in Greece and Italy where its sanction of sensual pleasure appealed to the upper classes of later antiquity. There is a good critical review of the historical evidence on Orpheus and Orphism in L. Moulinier, *Orphée et l'orphisme à l'époque classique*. Two works take contradictory positions on the existence of a distinct Orphic religion: William K. C. Guthrie, *Orpheus and Greek Religion*, and I. M. Linforth, *The Arts of Orpheus*. Guthrie is agnostic concerning the existence of Orpheus, but he argues that a community of Orphic reformers existed as early as the sixth century B.C. and imposed its doctrines on individuals and other cults. Linforth denies the existence of a self-conscious Orphic religion and argues that it is unlikely that such a separate movement ever existed. He suggests that the name of Orpheus was used by various cults to add to their spiritual pedigree. Guthrie and especially Linforth provide excellent reviews of historical records.

The worship of Dionysus and the Orphic reform have posed other questions about the character and evolution of Greek religion. Erwin Rohde raised some of them in 1893 in one of the monumental works in the history of Greek religious thought: *Psyche: The Cult of Souls and Belief in Immortality among the Greeks.* Rohde argued that Homer represented an atypical Greek religious attitude because he virtually ignored the chthonic cults native to Greece. Homer, therefore, gives the impression that the Greeks believed the gap between humanity and divinity was unbridgeable and that the idea of an afterlife was only vaguely present. Rohde believed that the Greek idea of personal immortality and their notion of the imperishability and spirituality of the soul developed through the worship of chthonic gods such as Dionysus. The Dionysians and the Orphics, he also notes, did not believe there was an immovable gap between humanity and the gods. On the contrary, their ritual ecstasies made it possible for them to break free of the limitations of human flesh and be elevated to a higher level. Rohde argues that the development of asceticism and cult loyalty was the next evolution in the search for a way for humanity to break free of this world altogether and to live imperishably in another.

The older Olympian religion and popular Greek attitudes provided another institution intended to close the gap between the human and the divine: the cult which venerated and worshipped heroic figures at their graves. This mode of veneration tended to weaken the distinction between the human and the divine, and in time the Greeks believed that some important heroes became gods, that is, death was for them a kind of apotheosis. The best work on Greek heroes is still Lewis R. Farnell, *Greek Hero Cults and Ideas of Immortality.* Farnell did not believe the hero cults originated the idea of human immortality but that they strengthened the idea and prepared the way for the later apotheosis of Hellenistic rulers.

Roman Religion

Herbert J. Rose wrote an excellent brief account of the development of Roman religion, *Ancient Roman Religion,* which is available in a paperback edition under the title *Religion in Greece and Rome.* (His *Ancient Greek Religion* appears in the same edition.) It covers the period from the beginnings to the age of Augustus but includes some comments on the later period. Rose's work is well written and factually accurate; however, it must be used with caution because his theory concerning the origins of Roman religious thought is not generally accepted. He theorizes that early Roman religion was predeistic, i.e., there were no personal gods or myths about gods. Instead, early Roman religion was a means of recognizing and exploiting the spiritual power in nature (called "mana" by anthropologists). Rose identified "mana" with the Latin *numen*. Rose argues that the later importation of Greek ideas influenced the Roman development of a pantheon of personal gods to characterize their Augustan cults. The argument has been widely discussed by twentieth-century historians and the discussion is surveyed in A. K. Michels, "Early Roman Religion, 1945–1952," in the *Harvard Theological Review* 48 (1954–1955): 25 ff. Rose is credited with the development of the predeistic theory and the role of *numen*, but a survey by W. Wade Fowler, *The Religious Experience of the Roman People*, predates Rose's book. Fowler also theorized that early Roman religion experienced a predeistic stage and that magic played a dominant role in that period. Fowler believed that the development of a genuinely theistic type of Roman religion involved the evolution of a formalized theology and an elaborate, mechanical, and magical cultic system. He suggests there was a period of spiritual and intellectual reaction against this older system beginning in the late Republic. Fowler's treatment of the religious ideas of Virgil (chap. 18) is brilliant. The role of *numen* in early Roman religion, and a specific development of the Rose theory, appears in H. Wagenvoort, *Roman Dynamism: Studies in Ancient Roman Thought, Language, and Custom*, translated from the Dutch by Rose himself. Wagenvoort carefully examines the philological meaning of *numen*, but most scholars are still not convinced that it occupied the central role he and Rose assigned to it.

Several general histories of Roman religion differ with Rose and are available in English. F. Altheim, *A History of Roman Religion*, is a survey ending with the age of Augustus, with a final chapter on the late imperial period. Altheim believes the early Romans had highly developed gods and myths which were not simply representations of natural forces but symbolic projections of human experience. Rose's comments on Altheim are in a review published in the *Harvard Theological Review* 27 (1934):33–51. Georges Dumézil, *Archaic Roman Religion* (2 vols.), has a better criticism of the predeistic theory and is translated from the French. Dumézil argues that the philological and archaeological evidence shows that the Romans always had myths and gods and that *numen* was an important part of Roman thought since it was always *numen dei*, the power of a particular god, rather than an independent or superior force (see "Numen or Deus," vol. 1, chap. 3). Additional comments on the *numen* theory can be found in S. Weinstock's remarks in the *Journal of Roman Studies* 39 (1949):166–167.

Two of the most important scholarly surveys of the history of Roman religion are as yet untranslated from the German. Both are parts of the *Handbuch der Altertumswissenschaft*. G. Wissowa, *Religion und Kultus der Römer*, has an authoritative description of the cult in Roman history (including worship and sacrifice ceremonies), but it relies on literary rather than archaeological evidence and exaggerates the crass, mechanical character of the Roman use of sacrifices. The *Handbuch* editors called on Kurt Latte to supplement and update but not to replace Wissowa. Latte's *Römische Religionsgeschichte* follows a generally chronological order and clearly covers the essential aspects of Roman religious development. Latte includes a history of research into the history of Roman religion (chap. 2, p. 9–18).

A few other works valuable to the undergraduate student merit mention. Robert M. Ogilvie, *The Romans and Their Gods,* is a fine summary of the essentials of Roman religion. Ogilvie explains the major elements of Roman religion in the time of Augustus, and the result is an excellent introduction to the entire middle and later periods of Roman religious history. Frederick C. Grant, *Roman Hellenism and the New Testament,* is a survey neither systematic nor clear in presentation. The author is argumentative and fails to explain the issues to his readers. Yet the work includes many fascinating comments on the religious attitudes of the early Empire, which are mostly ignored in other works. For example, Grant emphasizes the importance of sin as a kind of pollution or semi-material disease in the ancient period. Grant edited two collections of source materials for Roman religious development with his typically interesting comments and bibliographical suggestions: *Hellenistic Religions: The Age of Syncretism* and *Ancient Roman Religion*. Michael Grant has recently published two books on myths. *Myths of the Greeks and Romans* summarizes the influence of classical myths on later literature. His *Roman Myths* is even better suited to student reference. He suggests that myths were "imposed from above" by the ruling classes and did not originate at the popular level—myths were therefore meant to sanction political and moral traditions. The novel by Walter Pater, *Marius the Epicurean,* evokes the religious atmosphere of the supposedly dead civic religions of the early Empire.

Religion in the Roman Empire

The general histories of Roman religion just listed tend to treat the period from the beginning to about the time of Augustus and pay little attention to the imperial period. This approach is logical because the distinctively Roman period of religious development largely ended with Augustus. After Augustus, religion in Italy was dominated by Greek and oriental beliefs—the latter entered the Roman world directly from the East or they were mediated by a prior synthesis with Greek ideas. As a result many of the best books on the development of religion in the Empire have little or nothing to do with the history of distinctively Roman themes. They are histories of Greek religious development or histories of Christianity and other oriental religions. Thus Nilsson's

Geschichte der griechischen Religion (vol. 2) is far more valuable to the student of the imperial period than either Wissowa or Latte. Gilbert Murray, *Five Stages of Greek Religion*, also has valuable comments on the imperial period, and so does another general work, Samuel Angus, *The Spiritual Quests of the Graeco-Roman World*. The Angus survey relies too heavily on literary evidence and secondary works, but it has interesting things to say about every aspect of later Roman religion. Its discussion of sacramental institutions and therapeutic magic are especially good (see pages 127–254 and 414–438). André-Jean Festugière, *Personal Religion among the Greeks*, is a less systematic but equally valuable work. Festugière argues that there was a common idea of personal relations with deities from the earliest periods. He believes, however, that religion flourished best in the Roman Empire and among the upper classes. His treatment of Lucius and Isis (chap. 5) and Aelius, Aristides, and Asclepius (chap. 6) is outstanding.

John Ferguson, *Religions in the Roman Empire*, is the best starting place for a study of religion in the Roman Empire. Ferguson covers the period from Augustus to about the end of the second century. His style of writing is not especially lucid and his use of archaeological evidence makes his work difficult to read. Nonetheless, he surveys all the important recent evidence on early imperial religion aside from Christianity and Judaism. Terrot R. Glover, *The Conflict of Religions in the Early Roman Empire*, is a different approach to the same subject which Ferguson says inspired his survey. Glover's evidence is taken almost entirely from literary sources and he has a strong bias in favor of Christianity in contrast to Ferguson's consideration of all types of evidence and balanced treatment. The new collection by Z. Stewart of the best writings of Arthur D. Nock, *Essays on Religion in the Ancient World* (2 vols.), is important. The essays cover all ancient religions, but most deal with the religious developments of the Roman Empire. They are invaluable as sources of information and as an exacting investigation of ancient history.

THE MYSTERY CULTS

The history of mystery cults during the ancient period is important as part of the history of Roman religion and because of their possible influence on early Christianity. Brief reviews of relevant scholarship can be found in J. R. Hinnells, "Christianity and the Mystery Cults," in *Theology* 571 (1968) 20–26; in Bruce Metzger, "Methodology in the Study of the Mystery Religions and Early Christianity," in his *Historical and Literary Studies: Pagan, Jewish, and Christian* (pp. 1–25); and in Hugo Rahner, *Greek Myths and Christian Mystery* (pp. 3–45).

John Ferguson, *Religions in the Roman Empire* (chap. 7), and Karl Prumm, *Religionsgeschichtliches Handbuch* (chap. 3, pp. 213–357), summarize the chief features of the cults in the Roman Empire. The older works by Samuel Angus, *The Spiritual Quests of the Graeco-Roman World* and *The Mystery Religions and Christianity: A Study in the Religious Background of Early Christianity,* provide further discussions of the general principles and development of the mysteries. Angus relies heavily on literary evidence, but the concurrent use of more recent studies (e.g., Ferguson's *Religions in the Roman Empire)* provides adequate compensation for that defect. Angus is therefore an excellent summary of the cults, their principles, and their appeal. The masterpiece by Franz Cumont, *Oriental Religions in Roman Paganism,* is another indispensable supplement to Angus. Cumont organizes discussion geographically and includes an excellent discussion of the means used by the cults to spread their gospels (chap. 2). The reasons for the successful spread of the cults is discussed by Arthur D. Nock in his general *Conversion: The Old and the New in Religion from Alexander the Great to Augustine of Hippo* and in a disjointed but more specific way in his *Early Gentile Christianity and Its Hellenistic Background.* Nock does not deny that the cults influenced Christianity but emphasizes the lack of evidence to validate it. Harold Willoughby, *A Study of Mystery Initiations in the Graeco-Roman World,* deals with the theologies of the cults, which theme is so basic that the reader becomes well acquainted with the general principles and tone of the mysteries. Willoughby weakens his analysis by depending solely on literary sources. The best systematic studies of the mystery cults are in German. Martin P. Nilsson, *Geschichte der griechischen Religion,* is a masterful survey of existing evidence relating to all areas of classical religion, including the cults. Nilsson also provides valuable bibliographical notes on research resources in volume 1 (pp. 440 ff. and 619 ff.). Richard Reitzenstein, *Die Hellenistischen Mysterienreligionen nach ihren Grundgedanken und Wirkungen,* and Wilhelm Bousset, *Kyrios Christos: Geschichte des Christusglaubens von den Anfangen des Christentums bis Irenaeus,* are nearly as valuable and more controversial because they both assume that the mysteries influenced Christianity. Both Reitzenstein and Bousset argue that the pagan world exerted a broad influence on nascent Christianity, generally making Christianity part of the syncretistic movements of the period. Reitzenstein emphasizes the possible Iranian influence on Christianity, but that view has been difficult to sustain and it dates his work in comparison to Bousset. The best study of the broad and varied influences of pagan thought on the early development of Christianity is Carl Schneider, *Geistesgeschichte des antiken Christentums* (2 vols.). Schneider's work has been criticized in some quarters because of his unwarranted speculation concerning possible pagan influences on Christianity. It is nonetheless a brilliant analysis of the interaction of thought and emotion in the Christian and the pagan worlds. Some scholars (Reitzenstein, Bousset, and Schneider, for instance) have dealt with the important influence of the cults on Christianity, but a new, shorter survey of the problem in English is needed for students. Since no such survey is available the student is forced to use out-of-date sources. The arguments that the cults strongly influenced Christianity appear in J. Glasse, *The Mysteries and Christianity*, and Shirley Jackson Case, *The Evolution of Christianity: A Genetic Study of First Century Christianity in Relation to Its Religious Environment*. The argument against that influence appears in C. Clemen, *Primitive Christianity and Its Non-Jewish Sources*.

GNOSTICISM

Two German scholars, Rudolph Bultmann and Richard Reitzenstein, led the inquiry concerning the role of gnosticism in the ancient period, especially the possibility that gnosticism directly influenced first-century Christianity. Bultmann advanced his belief that a coherent gnostic theology predated Christianity and had an important influence on the later development of Christianity. See his *Primitive Christianity in Its Contemporary Setting* (pp. 162–175) for a summary. His *Theology of the New Testament* (2 vols.), provides more complete explanations and detailed argument. His *The Gospel of John: A Commentary*, suggests that the fourth gospel, *John*, was influenced by gnostic sentiments. Bultmann believes that the author of *John* was influenced by Mandaean gnosticism and that he actively tried to counter the development of a full, heretical Christian gnosticism. Reitzenstein considered that gnosticism was pre-Christian in origin, the product of a synthesis of Iranian and other eastern ideas. His view is developed in his writings, for example, in *Die Hellenistischen Mysterienreligionen*. Reitzenstein's basic research in support of that view included studies of the Mandaean sect of the Near East and the esoteric Hermetic literature of the ancient Christian era. The question of the origins and character of ancient gnosticism is one of the most hotly debated issues in New Testament scholarship. The key issues concern whether gnosticism was a pre-Christian phenomenon or a Christian heresy and whether it originated in pagan redeemer myths or in Judaic eschatological speculation. The lines of recent discussion are outlined in James P. Hyatt, ed., *The Bible in Modern Scholarship* (pp. 252–294), with articles by three of the outstanding experts in the field, G. Quispel, R. M. Wilson, and Hans Jonas. There is also an excellent summary of the current state of scholarly discussion in G. van Groningen, *First Century Gnosticism: Its Origins and Motifs* (chap. 1). The rest of the book is less useful except that it suggests there was a link between gnosticism and "scientism" (i.e., a desire to control and use supernatural power on earth). Van Groningen fails to emphasize that "scientism" was identified with all late ancient religions, including Christianity.

Several books provide broad interpretations of the gnostic movement. G. Quispel, *Gnosis als Weltreligion*, is a short and convincing analysis which differentiates between gnosticism and Christianity and other forms of late ancient philosophy and theosophy. The American Robert M. Grant has edited a collection of gnostic writings, *Gnosticism: A Sourcebook of Heretical Writings from the Early Christian Period*, and he is the author of *Gnosticism and Early Christianity*. Grant believes that gnosticism resulted from the failure of Judaism to realize hopes of freedom in this world. Those disappointed adherents thus turned to eschatological and gnostic dreams. His study surveys Judaic literature for evidence of developing gnosticism. The relationship between gnosticism and Judaism is also explored by a British scholar, Robert M. Wilson, *Gnosticism and the New Testament*. Wilson surveys the evidence for a gnostic theme which may have influenced the writers of the New Testament, especially Paul and "John." In *The Gnostic Problem: A Study of the Relations between Hellenistic Judaism and the Gnostic Heresy*, Wilson surveys Diaspora (or Dispersion) Judaism for evidence of the existence of gnosticism in that religious world. He concludes that a fully integrated and self-conscious gnosticism only developed in the Christian era but that the elements of gnosticism, a "proto-gnosticism," were being drawn together by the syncretistic tendencies of the first century. Gnosticism was an "atmosphere," or tendency, to assimilate elements from pagan, Judaic, and Christian thought without restraint. Judaism and Christianity were restrained in sharing this syncretistic tendency, though a Jew like Philo and a Christian like Paul can be considered gnostics in a broad sense. Gershon G. Scholem, *Jewish Gnosticism: Merkabah Mysticism and the Talmudic Tradition*, takes a different approach. Scholem finds that the esoteric speculations and exegesis of the Pharisees and late ancient rabbis were one source of gnosticism.

In addition to Grant's *Gnosticism: A Sourcebook of Heretical Writings from the Early Christian Period* just cited, there are other collections of gnostic writings. Werner Foerster, *Gnosis: A Selection of Gnostic Texts*, includes gnostic texts and references from the patristic period (vol. 1). Volume 2 will include selections from the Nag Hammadi library. Also see Robert Haardt, *Gnosis—Character and Testimony: An Anthology of Hellenistic Gnosticism*.

The study of late antique gnosticism centers on the Hermetic literature, which was probably completed by the third century A.D. The scholarly critical edition of these writings is Arthur D. Nock and André-Jean Festugière, *Corpus Hermeticum* (4 vols.), which includes the Greek text and a French translation on facing pages. The standard English translation is Walter Scott, *Hermetica: The Ancient Greek and Latin Writings Which Contain Religious or Philosophical Teachings Ascribed to Hermes Tresmegistus* (4 vols.). A. S. Ferguson collaborated on volume 4. André-Jean Festugière, *Hermetisme et mystique païenne*, is a general study citing the importance of Hermeticism to the development of Christian and higher pagan thought as well as in alchemy and astrology. Festugière's *La Révélation d'Hermes Trismégiste* (4 vols.) has a detailed examination of the writings and system. Volume 4 treats "the unknown God" and knowledge directly concerned with gnosticism. Volumes 1 to 3 cover astrology and the occult science, the "cosmic god," and the ancient doctrine of the soul.

For a résumé of recent work on the full range of gnosticism, see K. Rudolph, "Gnosis and Gnosticism," in *Theologische Rundschau* 34 (1969): 121 ff. and 36 (1971):1 ff.

JUDAISM

Two branches of Judaism influenced first-century Christianity. The traditional Palestinian Judaism produced Jesus and the development of a Judaeo-Christian wing of the church headed by James, the brother of Jesus. Diaspora Judaism, the Judaism of the Jews dispersed outside of Palestine, was a collection of religious attitudes influenced by the religious environment of the surrounding pagan world. The readings suggested for Judaism will be divided to reflect these broad historical groupings.

The Old Testament was basic to all Jewish religious thinking. It is impossible to include a lengthy review of scholarship on the Old Testament here, but a few suggestions may be helpful in understanding Judaism in the Roman era. The current status of Old Testament scholarship is briefly reviewed in two paperback publications: *Biblical Criticism* by Robert Davidson and Alfred R. C. Leaney (pp. 25–169), and George E. Wright and Reginald Fuller, *The Book of the Acts of God: Contemporary Scholarship Interprets the Bible* (pp. 13–228). These are competently written references which miss nothing of importance in the field. Harold H. Rowley, *The Old Testament and Modern Scholarship,* and Herbert F. Hahn, *The Old Testament in Modern Research,* are more advanced. Hahn's work is organized anthropologically and religio-historically to facilitate scholarly Old Testament study. Nonserial and serial bibliographies relevant to the Old Testament are recommended on pages 160–161 below. They are also useful references to early Christian and New Testament history.

There are several good surveys of the writings and ideas of the Old Testament. See Bernard Anderson, *Understanding the Old Testament,* and Norman Snaith, *The Distinctive Ideas of the Old Testament.* Anderson generally follows a historical sequence, with summaries of the various writings of the Old Testament and the type of literature it includes. He treats the gradual evolution of Judaic religion as it was influenced by the restless history of the Jews. Snaith's approach is more topical. He reviews the chief ideas of the Old Testament and their historical development with less detail than Anderson. As a result his impression of Old Testament unity and coherence is exaggerated. A similar topical approach emphasizes the historical evolution of Judaic ideas, H. Emerson Fosdick, *A Guide to Understanding the Bible.* Fosdick follows the key ideas, such as the idea of life after death, from their Old Testament beginnings to their New Testament "fulfillment." Robert Pfeiffer, *Introduction to the Old Testament,* is an advanced and difficult work cited on page 160 for its bibliography. Pfeiffer's careful and detailed review of the literature of the Old Testament explains the differences between the various genre of writings which make up that composite work. Two prestigious German studies of Old Testament theology have recently been translated into English: Walther Eichrodt, *Theology of the Old Testament* (2 vols.), and Gerhard von Rad, *Old Testament Theology* (2 vols.) Eichrodt has been strongly and justifiably criticized for interpreting the Old Testament with a decidedly Christian bias. He sees a basic unity in Old Testament theology which he explicates in terms of the covenant between God and Israel. He argues that the New Testament was a logical fulfillment of the Old Testament. Von Rad is historically better since he does not claim there was a logical unity to Old Testament theology. Instead, he sees the Old Testament as a record of various Judaic creeds concerning the historical intervention of God for the salvation (and punishment) of his people. Thus von Rad sees the history of salvation (*Heilsgeschichte*) as the unifying theme of the Old Testament. That idea admits there was a genuine historical development and von Rad insists that the creed of Israel about God developed under varied historical circumstances and included diverse forms. Von Rad argues that the prophetic movement found existing statements about God unsatisfactory and so recast it to meet its particular needs. This, von Rad argues, was the crucial factor in improving Judaic thought. The New Testament represents the last and in a sense culminating state of prophetic criticism and updating.

Palestinian Judaism evolved into the forms which constituted the religious environment of Jesus during the last two centuries B.C. The overlapping institutions of that period included those of the Pharisaic-Rabbinic tradition, the apocalyptic movement, and the closely related Zealot movement. It is not possible to provide a detailed review of the extensive literature available on each of these areas, but some general works are sufficient to acquaint readers with the basic ideas. Palestinian Judaism in the time of Jesus is reviewed in two French works, J. Bonsirven, *Palestinian Judaism in the Time of Jesus Christ,* and Marcel Simon, *Jewish Sects in the Time of Jesus.* Bonsirven's work (the English translation of the abridged original French version) summarizes the elements of dogmatic and moral theology. Simon's work reviews various schools of Judaism in the first century B.C. and has an especially good treatment of Alexandrian Judaism (chap. 5).

See the short pamphlet by W. D. Davies, *Introduction to Pharisaism,* on Pharisaism and the rabbinic tradition that grew out of it. Davies had promoted considerable interest in the Pharisees, especially in his *Paul and Rabbinic Judaism: Some Rabbinic Elements in Pauline Theology.* Davies and many other scholars lately tend to underestimate the influence of pagan ideas on figures like Paul. Two older introductions, Solomon Schechter, *Some Aspects of Rabbinic Theology,* and Robert T. Herford, *The Pharisees,* are adequate introductions. Schechter, a British Jew of phenomenal erudition, surveys the key ideas found in the *Mishnah* and *Talmud* and reconstructs the basic theology of the Pharisees. Herford's study is a basic and sympathetic survey of the Pharisees. The best recent survey, Jacob Neusner, *From Politics to Piety: The Emergence of Pharisaic Judaism*, is a simple summary of Neusner's monumental *The Rabbinic Traditions about the Pharisees before 70* (3 vols.). He examines and evaluates all of the evidence on the Pharisees. The development of Judaism after 70 A.D. is covered in George Foote Moore, *Judaism in the First Centuries of the Christian Era* (3 vols.). Moore attempts to define rabbinic Judaism as the normative form of that faith. Another informative source, the anthology edited by Claude G. Montefiore and H. Loewe, *A Rabbinic Anthology*, has excellent excerpts. The authors, however, fail to warn the reader that the essays represent a wide variety of interpretations and extensive evolution in Judaic thought. Jacob Neusner has made several important contributions to late ancient Judaic history; the short edition of *Formation of the Babylonian Talmud: Studies in the Achievement of Late Nineteenth and Twentieth Century Historical and Literary-Critical Research* is an excellent sample of his work.

The basic and fascinating question of the degree and kind of Judaic influence exercised on the New Testament is considered in the works on the New Testament recommended below. One basic source, equally essential to the study of Judaism, must be mentioned: H. L. Strack and P. Billerbeck, *Kommentar zum Neuem Testament aus Talmud und Midrash* (6 vols.). This indispensable tool lists the relevant Judaic sources or parallels for every line of the New Testament but unfortunately does not refer to the Dead Sea Scrolls.

The Judaic apocalyptic movement, the expectation of an imminent end to the world, developed beginning in the second century B.C. It strongly influenced Jesus and the early Christians—they probably expected the end to come soon. Several relevant studies will be discussed later as part of the treatment of Jesus and the New Testament. A few general titles are cited here. David S. Russell, *The Method and Message of Jewish Apocalyptic*, is a thorough survey of the development and basic principles of Jewish apocalyptic thinking. Other works concerning the Essene sect responsible for the Dead Sea Scrolls are also insightful regarding apocalyptic thought. The Essenes apparently believed that their age was the last, but it is less clear that they believed the end was imminent. The literature concerning the scrolls is extensive and includes several readily understandable and competent introductions. The best, Helmer Ringgren, *The Faith of Qumran: Theology of the Dead Sea Scrolls*, deals topically and prudently with the writings and archaeological remains of the Qumran sect. Lucitta Mowry, *The Dead Sea Scrolls and the Early Church*, devotes attention to the possible influence of Qumran on early Christianity. William S. La Sor, *The Dead Sea Scrolls and the New Testament*, competently reviews the evidence and concludes that the Essenes and the Christians were disparate Jewish sects that had no direct influence on each other. La Sor comments on the work of other scholars in the field and includes an annotated bibliography (pp. 265–269). The student can best understand the sect by referring directly to its writings. See the collection of Geza Vermes, *The Dead Sea Scrolls in English,* which has excellent notes and introductions.

The Zealot movement, which probably dated from the second century B.C., believed that Jews should use force to gain their independence from any pagan power. The movement is an important facet of ancient religion because of its role in the development of Judaism and because some scholars believe that Jesus himself may have been sympathetic to that cause. The standard survey of the history of the Zealot movement at the start of the Christian era is M. Hengel, *Die Zeloten: Untersuchungen zur judischen Freiheitsbewegung in der Zeit von Herodes I bis 70 n.Chr.* Hengel's opinions are summarized in English in his Facet pamphlet, *Was Jesus a Revolutionist?* Hengel's answer is a rather more emphatic "no" than his evidence would seem to call for. The opposite conclusion that Jesus was either part of the Zealot movement or sympathetic to it is supported by R. Eisler and his student Samuel G. F. Brandon. Eisler's *The Messiah Jesus and John the Baptist* develops the argument that Jesus expected the end of the world and believed that he should lead the Jews into the desert as they had done in Exodus. Since such an exodus could only be made against the will of the Romans, the use of force would have been inevitable. Brandon's *Jesus and the Zealots* does not specifically claim that Jesus was a Zealot; it does argue that he was aware of the Zealot movement, was sympathetic to it, and that active Zealots were among his disciples. According to Brandon, these sympathies were expunged in Christian records to allay Roman suspicions. The pros and cons of the argument are well presented by Oscar Cullmann, *The State in the New Testament.* "Jesus and the Resistance Movement of the Zealots" (chap. 1) and "Jesus' Condemnation of the Roman State" (chap. 2) develop Cullmann's argument that Jesus was not a Zealot, but they concede that he may have had a number of Zealot disciples.

There has been a great deal of interest in this century in the "Diaspora," the dispersion of Jews living outside of Palestine. The important issue is whether this Judaism differed from the Judaism of Palestine, in particular whether it blended with pagan thought in any important way. Answers have varied. It has been claimed that there was no substantial difference between these areas of Judaism, either because Diaspora Jews remained basically conservative or because Palestinian Jews were strongly influenced by pagan ideas. It is also claimed that there were basic differences. The scholars who argue the latter usually conclude that Diaspora Judaism became a major force, acting especially through Paul to change Jesus' purely Jewish message into one compatible with pagan thought.

Victor A. Tcherikover, *Hellenistic Civilization and the Jews,* provides the most general background information on the Diaspora. See the progress of hellenization in Palestine (part 1) and its progress in the Diaspora (part 2). "The Cultural Climate" (pp. 344–381) is an excellent résumé. There is an excellent review of the distinctive character of Diaspora Judaism in Hans J. Schoeps, *Paul: The Theology of the Apostle in the Light of Jewish Religious History* (pp. 24–37). Schoeps consistently refers to the relative importance of Jewish and pagan ideas on Paul. He concludes that Diaspora Judaism was basically different from Palestinian Judaism and influenced Paul toward the construction of a theology with non-Jewish elements. In elevating Jesus to divinity Schoeps believes that Paul departed from every species of Judaism. Many excellent comments on Diaspora Judaism appear in a work by Robert M. Wilson (already cited on page 153), *The Gnostic Problem: A Study of the Relations between Hellenistic Judaism and the Gnostic Heresy.* Erwin R. Goodenough was an American scholar greatly influenced by the question of the blending of pagan and Jewish ideas and the effect of the resulting attitude on nascent Christianity. Goodenough believed that Jewish civilization in general was influenced by pagan thought and that this influence was evidenced by the symbols current in the Roman world occupied by Jews. Goodenough collected and explained these symbols in *Jewish Symbols in the Graeco-Roman Period* (13 vols.). He argues that these symbols constituted a kind of ancient lingua franca which allowed the Jews to represent their religious institutions as basically similar to those of the pagans. Volume 12 summarizes Goodenough's position.

One of the best Jewish thinkers obviously influenced by pagan thought was Philo of Alexandria (d. 50 A.D.). See Wilson's *The Gnostic Problem*, which contains excellent material on Philo. Erwin R. Goodenough made a major contribution on this subject in *An Introduction to Philo Judaeus* and *By Light, Light: The Mystic Gospel of Hellenized Judaism.* Goodenough's *Introduction* is a short and highly readable account of the general religious and social environment of Philo's thinking, accompanied by a good bibliography. *By Light, Light* argues that Philo was strongly influenced by Hellenistic pagan thought. Harry A. Wolfson, *Philo: Foundations of Religious Philosophy in Judaism, Christianity, and Islam* (2 vols.), is a different approach which suggests that Philo constructed his theology essentially out of Jewish elements in the rabbinic tradition. As such Philo was the first thinker to consider carefully the question of a relationship between reason and faith as revealed in the scriptures. Thus Wolfson argues that Philo founded a tradition by combining two types of truth which dominated Jewish, Christian, and Islamic thought from then until the early modern period.

THE WORLD OF MAGIC AND ASTROLOGY

During the late ancient period (ca. 200–500 A.D.) a prominent feature of religious thought was interest in the magical exploitation of supernatural power as a guarantee of good fortune or as an aid in securing salvation. Religious and nonreligious thought was increasingly dominated by magic and by closely allied forms of pseudoscience, e.g., astrology.

Lynn Thorndike, *A History of Magic and Experimental Science* (vol. 1), is a general study which puts magic in its full cultural perspective. Introductions to the theme include Shirley Jackson Case, *The Origins of Christian Supernaturalism,* and Nilsson, *Greek Piety* (especially see pp. 92–186). More detailed histories include Nilsson's *Geschichte der griechischen Religion* (vol. 2) and André-Jean Festugière's *La Révélation d'Hermes Trismégiste* (4 vols.).

The general studies cited above include references to astrology. In addition, see the recent summary in D. Pingree's article in the *Dictionary of the History of Ideas* 1:118–126. The relevant literature and evidence on the study of astrology in the ancient period can be found by consulting W. and H. G. Gunkel, *Astrologumena: die astrologische Literatur in der Antike und ihre Geschichte,* supplement 6 to *Sudhoffs Archiv für Geschichte der Medizin und der Naturwissenschaften der Pharmazie und der Mathematik* (1966). Ancient astrology is surveyed in two older works: Franz Cumont, *Astrology and Religion among the Greeks and the Romans,* and F. Boll and C. Bezold, *Sternglaube und Sterndeutung: die Geschichte und das Wesen der Astrologie.* Cumont's study is a general survey which argues that the Olympic (the most anthropomorphic) stage of Greek religion effectively limited the influx of Near Eastern astrological ideas. Following the demise of this stage of Greek religion and its replacement by more abstract religious themes, Chaldean astrology expanded rapidly in the West. Boll and Bezold survey the entire history of astrology (see chaps. 1, 2, and 3 on the ancient period) and summarize its major elements as a pseudoscience. There are, however, many valuable references to ancient astrology throughout the supplementary comments in the fourth edition by W. Gundel. Jack Lindsay, *Origins of Astrology,* surveys the period from the beginnings of recorded history to the end of the ancient period. He emphasizes the Babylonian stage and its fusion with Greek mathematics. His work is extremely detailed; it cites all of the relevant literature and is excellently illustrated. It fails, however, to carefully explain the basic principles of astrology and its cultural setting. The conclusion includes a specious attack on post-Galilean science. The astrology of the Greek (mathematicized) period is covered in A. Bouché-Leclercq, *L'Astrologie grecque.* The attitudes skeptical about astrology are well covered in D. Amand, *Fatalisme et liberté dans l'antiquité grecque.* Amand summarizes the influence of the antifatalistic arguments of Carneades (d. ca. 128 B.C.) on later philosophers and the Christian church.

The ancient period lacked public hygiene and medical technology, so the people of that era were obsessed by disease and its cure. Many of the works recommended in chapter 3 (ancient medicine) reference the ancient interest in the use of magic and other such means to gain good health. A few additional citations may be helpful. See Samuel Angus, *The Spiritual Quests of the Graeco-Roman World* (pp. 414–438) for a discussion of ancient cures. Angus was cited on page 151 above in reference to the general study of ancient religion. Also see Eric R. Dodds, *Pagan and Christian in an Age of Anxiety*. Dodds includes an especially interesting discussion of the mental conditions which led to the late ancient interest in spiritual power as well as a discussion of Aristides and his attempts to effect cures through religious and magical means (chap. 2). André-Jean Festugière, *Personal Religion among the Greeks*, cited on page 151, discusses Aristides and the cult of Asclepius (pp. 85–105).

During the ancient period people sought supernatural power to achieve good health but also to ensure moral purity and salvation. Gerhard Ladner, *The Idea of Reform: Its Impact on Christian Thought and Action in the Age of the Fathers*, includes several references to the latter idea. Festugière's *La Révélation d'Hermes Trismégiste* references the ideas of personal renewal and salvation throughout his multivolumed work; especially see volumes 3 and 4. J. Gross discusses the subject and includes bibliographical notes (pp. lx–xviii) in his study of deification as the key to salvation, *La Divinisation du Chrétien d'après les pères grecs*, as does M. Lot Borodine, *La Déification de l'homme selon la doctrine des pères grecs*. Borodine discusses the special eastern and Byzantine view of Jesus as a deified man-god as opposed to the crucified Jesus emphasized in the West. See the interesting foreword by Jean Danielou.

The Origin and Development of Ancient Christianity

General Bibliographical Resources

A brief bibliography on the Old and the New Testaments is included in the *Revue d'histoire et de philosophie religieuse* 51 (1971):265–360. The Old Testament is covered bibliographically in Robert Pfeiffer's excellent *Introduction to the Old Testament* (pp. 849–876) and in two collections based on the book lists of the Society for Old Testament Study: Harold H. Rowley, *Eleven Years of Bible Bibliography 1946–1956*, and E. W. Anderson, *A Decade of Bible Bibliography: 1957–1966*. The best New Testament starting place is John C. Hurd, *A Bibliography of New Testament Bibliographies,* which includes a collection of biographical sketches and references on leading New Testament scholars. J. L. Schreiber, *Primitive Christian Traditions . . . A Selective Bibliography,* concentrates on the complex structure of the first church. The annotations on the disputes between Paul and the Judaic church in Jerusalem are especially useful. See the important series New Testament Tools and Studies, especially the following: Bruce Metzger's *Index to Periodical Literature on Christ and the Gospels* and *Index to Periodical Literature on the Apostle Paul* and A. J. and M. B. Mattill's *A Classified Bibliography of Literature on the Acts of the Apostles.* All are excellent guides to periodical literature on the New Testament.

On the history of the ancient church after the New Testament era see Owen Chadwick, *The History of the Church: A Select Bibliography.* Chadwick lists the essential citations and includes brief annotations. Shirley Jackson Case, *A Bibliographical Guide to the History of Christianity,* also provides excellent lists. Patristics, the study of writers in the ancient church, is the subject of J. L. Stewardson, *A Bibliography of Bibliographies in Patristics.* J. Quasten, *Patrology* (3 vols; to be completed in 4), is a most important guide to the literature of Christian antiquity with copious bibliographical notes. It is available in most libraries.

Readers interested in church history should read P. Meinhold, *Geschichte der kirchlichen Historiographie,* which includes excellent biographies of the most important Christian historians. There is also a bibliography (pp. 600–616).

Several serial bibliographies specialize in the history of Judaism and Christianity. One of the most important, the *Elenchus Bibliographicus Biblicus* (1919), covers books and articles without annotations. The German *Evangelische Theologie* issues a series of supplementary volumes over a two-year cycle which review scholarship in various areas. Those relevant to the history of ideas include the Old Testament, the New Testament, and church history. *New Testament Abstracts* (1956) is in English and generally available in American libraries. It has excellent résumés of articles in the field. Its coverage of new books and book reviews is also competent. The period of the ancient church is covered in the unannotated *Bibliographia Patristica: internationale patristische Bibliographie* (1956). See also the *Bulletin Signalétique* (section 527), the *Index to Religious Periodical Literature* (1953), and the well-annotated *Internationale Zeitschriftenschau für Bibelwissenschaft und Grenzgebiete* (1952) for additional coverage of periodical literature.

HANDBOOKS AND ENCYCLOPEDIAS

The intense interest of Christians in the history of their religion has produced excellent guides and encyclopedias to the study of the Bible —literally too many to mention. A few of the best scholarly efforts must be discussed. One of the many one-volume guides, Alan Richardson,

A Theological Word Book of the Bible, has accurate and judicious reviews of the chief terms and ideas of the Old and New Testaments. Two classics are still valuable. James Hasting's *Dictionary of the Bible* has been revised and reedited by Frederick C. Grant and Harold H. Rowley. *Peake's Commentary on the Bible* has also been revised by Harold H. Rowley and Matthew Black. Peake's commentary includes a verse-by-verse commentary and succinct background articles.

There are two outstanding multivolume dictionaries of the Bible. *The Interpreter's Dictionary of the Bible* (4 vols.) has articles on the important ideas and institutions of the Bible and the ancient religious environment. It is one of the best examples of American Biblical scholarship. The German work being translated and edited by Gerhard Kittel and G. Friedrich, *Theological Dictionary of the New Testament* (now 7 vols.), includes scholarly examinations of the use of key words in pagan literature, the Old Testament, and the New Testament. Hence it is a dictionary of key ideas. No important investigation of New Testament ideas can avoid using this masterful source.

There is a wide range of quality and historical value among multivolume verse-by-verse commentaries. *The Interpreter's Bible* (12 vols.), readily available in American libraries, is an excellent reference to biblical scholarship for the lay person. The Old Testament is covered in volumes 1–6 and the New Testament in volumes 7–12. The background articles are mostly well written and the text includes a scholarly analysis of the historical meaning of the text with a parallel devotional and exhortatory commentary. The *Moffatt New Testament Commentary* (18 vols.) is an older British publication. The Moffatt commentary is out of date, but it includes the works of some of the great biblical scholars of the century, e.g., Charles H. Dodd, Thomas W. Manson, and F. J. Foakes-Jackson. The best recent commentary is *Harper's New Testament Commentaries* (13 vols.).

One foreign-language commentary and encyclopedia with valuable supplementary volumes (its original volumes are out of date) needs to be cited: *Dictionnaire de la Bible.* The original work was completed in five volumes, and seven supplementary volumes have been completed; all are of high scholarly quality with bibliographical notes.

The New Testament

Two surveys listed as guides to scholarship on the Old Testament have valuable sections on the New Testament. In *Biblical Criticism,* the section by Leaney (pp. 169–341) covers the New Testament. Also see Reginald Fuller's treatment of the New Testament in *The Book of the Acts of God* (pp. 229–361). In addition Stephen Neill, *The Interpretation of the New Testament: 1861–1961,* is a provocative description of New Testament scholarship spiced with personal anecdotes which uniquely capture the excitement of British scholarship. The work, however, must be used with caution since Neill largely ignores the central role of German New Testament scholarship and unduly elevates British scholars. Neill pictures many of the latter as veritable heroes battling the forces of skepticism and he distorts the work of scholars whose theories he considers mischievous. For example, the German Rudolph Bultmann is widely accepted as the leading New Testament scholar. Yet Neill minimizes Bultmann's ideas and advises his reader that Bultmann's expert knowledge of classical literature and philosophy makes him worth reading.

The excellent history of New Testament scholarship by Werner G. Kummel, *The New Testament: The History of the Investigation of Its Problems*, is based on an analysis of lengthy quotes of scholars. Kummel's work is a general survey which includes a "History of Religions School of New Testament Interpretation" (part 5) and biographies of the chief scholars in the field (pp. 466-499).

Most general surveys of the New Testament are hindrances to students interested in an objective, historical treatment of that body of writings. The following references, however, are generally objective and informative.

Reginald Fuller, *A Critical Introduction to the New Testament*, is a brief and accurate review of the textual history and problems of the New Testament corpus. See Howard C. Kee, Franklin W. Young, and K. Froehlich, *Understanding the New Testament*, for an introduction to the contents of the writings, the historical background, and the theology of the New Testament. The second edition should be used since the first edition's treatment of Jesus is superficial. Two standard references are more advanced but still readable accounts of the New Testament which concentrate on its theological development. See Frederick C. Grant, *An Introduction to New Testament Thought*, which clearly describes the ideas contributing to the multifaceted New Testament theology. Grant's analysis of the social and economic roots of Jesus' beliefs is interesting but unacceptable. He believed that Jesus represented the opinion (common to the rural poor of any age) that the poor of the countryside are more pious than the people of the city and that God intervenes to protect his faithful poor. Johannes Weiss, *Earliest Christianity: A History of the Period A.D. 30-150* (2 vols.), was first published in 1914. Weiss was a pioneer in modern New Testament study. He, more than Albert Schweitzer, established the theory that the career of Jesus was dominated by a belief that the world was about to end through the intervention of God. *Earliest Christianity* deals with the development of Christian literature, the geographic spread of Christianity, and the development of the first Christian theologies.

A review of more recent works of special value necessarily includes Rudolph Bultmann. Bultmann is the leading New Testament scholar. He was one of the founders of "form criticism" or "form history," the study of the structure of the New Testament which attempts to establish

the elements of oral tradition out of which the gospels were woven. Bultmann's contributions to the study of gnosticism and the mystery cults
in the development of Christian thought are also important. Bultmann
estimates that pagan ideas exerted considerable influence on Paul. His
Primitive Christianity in Its Contemporary Setting is an excellent short
introduction to his thought. See *Theology of the New Testament* (2 vols.)
for a more detailed summary of Bultmann's argument. This standard
work has an especially complete treatment of Paul's theology and the
influence of gnostic themes and mystery cults on him. Two other works
focus on Christology (the theory concerning the place of Jesus in God's
plans) but also cover all important issues of New Testament theology.
Oscar Cullmann, *The Christology of the New Testament*, carefully considers
what is known about Jesus' attitude toward his traditional roles. Cullmann's conclusions are controversial, but his review of the evidence is
excellent. Reginald Fuller, *The Foundations of New Testament Christology*,
accords greater weight to the changing perceptions of Christians regarding Jesus' ideas about himself. It is the best work of its kind available.

Jesus

There are even more books about Jesus than there are general surveys of the New Testament. Most of them are positively misleading.
Those listed here are worth reading by anyone interested in the career
of Jesus. See Hugh Anderson, *Jesus and Christian Origins*, for a review
of scholarly work on Jesus. Anderson includes most important references
up to 1964 and is most interested in the scholarly search for the historical
Jesus, i.e., how reliable is the reconstruction of the life and career of Jesus
considering the limited evidence available. His résumé of recent interpretations of the resurrection story (chap. 5) is excellent. Albert Schweitzer, *The Quest of the Historical Jesus*, is a seminal study of the ideas of Jesus
which also includes much information on the interpretation of Jesus.
The best collection of essays concerning the "new quest" for the historical
Jesus, the effort to reach satisfactory conclusions about him, is by Carl
E. Braaten and Roy Harrisville, eds., *The Historical Jesus and the Kerygmatic Christ: Essays on the New Quest of the Historical Jesus*.

STUDIES OF JESUS

Joseph Klausner, *Jesus of Nazareth: His Life, Times and Teachings*, is a
good starting point. Klausner (a Zionist) suggests that Jesus remained
generally within the orbit of Judaism yet exaggerated certain of its pre-
cepts—he notes especially that Jesus claimed to be the messiah. Klausner's work is ambivalent; he claims that the ethical teaching of Jesus was
one of the best products of Judaism, yet he condemns his overall career.
The book is written by an eminent scholar from an openly Jewish point of

view and it has an excellent review of the relevant Jewish literature about Jesus. Two valuable French studies judiciously survey the available evidence and reach cautious conclusions about the life and teachings of Jesus. See Charles Guignebert, *Jesus,* and Maurice Goguel, *Jesus and the Origins of Christianity.* For an example of a "liberal" history of Jesus which discards the supernatural to find valuable bits of information in the modest residue, see Morton Enslin, *The Prophet from Nazareth.* Enslin carefully and sensibly judges the evidence and convincingly concludes that Jesus did not claim to be the messiah, only a prophet of the final days of the world.

During the three decades prior to 1960 the "form criticism" school (especially Rudolph Bultmann) dominated thinking about the gospels, and the possibility of writing a useful biographical study of Jesus was viewed with skepticism. Surprisingly, one of Bultmann's students, Gunther Bornkamm, published a brief sketch of the mature Jesus: *Jesus of Nazareth.* Bornkamm is more cautious than his predecessors, but even his conclusions are not all validated by the evidence.

An extensive listing of books on the teachings of Jesus is impossible in this brief bibliography, but good résumés of his ideas can be found in the surveys listed above, especially in Grant's *An Introduction to New Testament Thought,* Weiss's *Earliest Christianity* (vol. 1), Bultmann's *Theology of the New Testament* (vol. 1), and Oscar Cullmann's *Christology of the New Testament.* Also see the standard survey, Thomas W. Manson, *The Teachings of Jesus.* Manson's well-written survey covers the major elements in the reconstructed theology of Jesus; however, his theory concerning Jesus' understanding of the role of the Son of Man is questionable. Manson argues that Jesus understood the Son of Man to be a collective symbol for those faithful to God and that the faithful were led by Jesus and his disciples. This theory is ingeniously based on Old Testament precedents, but it lacks New Testament evidence.

Several specialized works deal with the eschatological expectation of Jesus, i.e., his expectation that the world was about to end. Norman Perrin, *The Kingdom of God in the Teachings of Jesus,* reviews the many theories on this issue and includes an annotated bibliography. The classic argument that the expectation of an imminent end to the world strongly influenced Jesus can be found in Albert Schweitzer, *The Quest of the Historical Jesus.* Schweitzer's detailed analysis of the expected end is strongly disputed, but his assumption that it was vitally important to the theology of Jesus is generally accepted. Charles H. Dodd, *The Parables of the Kingdom,* analyzes the parables dealing with the Kingdom of God and argues for the theory of "realized eschatology": that Jesus believed that the Kingdom of God had come in his career rather than that it was imminently due in the future. Recently efforts have been made to reconcile the majority opinion of scholars who believe that Jesus expected the end of the world in the imminent future and those who believe that the coming of the Kingdom of God meant no future *eschaton* to Jesus but rather a Kingdom present in his own life. A German scholar, Walther G. Kummel, suggests in his *Promise and Fulfillment: The Eschatological Message of Jesus,* that Jesus held both positions. Kummel argues that most gospel passages suggest that Jesus believed that the Kingdom of God was about to be fully realized in the imminent future and that it was present in his career and thus part of human history.

There are more books on the ethical teachings of Jesus than on his eschatological teachings. Laurence H. Marshall, *The Challenge of New Testament Ethics,* is an interesting commentary which recognizes important differences between Jesus and Paul—a factor diminished by other scholars. Marshall, however, follows the unfair technique used by many of his Christian colleagues: he tends to compare the worst elements of pagan moral behavior to the ideals of Christianity. The ethics of Jesus, the Pharisees, and the rabbis are compared in the appropriate sections of Claude Montefiore, *The Synoptic Gospels* (2 vols.). Montefiore comments verse by verse on the first three gospels and notes the parallel between Judaism and New Testament ideas. The most important major work on the ethics of Jesus in W. D. Davies, *The Setting of the Sermon on the Mount.* Davies exhaustively examines Jesus and non-Jewish sources of the ideas and the composition of the Sermon on the Mount. His work is therefore a study of thinking in the first church and the ethical beliefs of Jesus. The work is available in a paperback edition, *The Sermon on the Mount.*

Paul and the First Church

Most of the reliable information about the theology of the first Christians concerns Paul of Tarsus. Information concerning the first Christian church in Jerusalem is meager; the book of *Acts* is a later and deliberately irenic account of that community. Some reasonably reliable information about Jerusalem can be inferred from references in the letters of Paul and other fragments in the New Testament. *The Beginnings of Christianity* (5 vols.), edited by F. J. Foakes-Jackson and Kirsopp Lake, is a dated but still excellent source of information. It is a classic collection of major contributions to the study of the first church organized as commentaries and exegeses of *Acts.* Volume 1 surveys the religious environment of the first church, and volume 5 contains feature articles on crucial problems in its history. Maurice Goguel, *The Birth of Christianity,* is a balanced one-volume synopsis.

Samuel G. F. Brandon, *The Fall of Jerusalem and the Christian Church,* is an earlier expression of the theory Brandon propounded in *Jesus and the Zealots.* Brandon argues that the Christians were as patriotic as their Jewish compatriots until the fall of Jerusalem to the Romans in 70 A.D., but when they abandoned the city prior to its fall they earned the hatred of other Jews. In turn the Christians renounced loyalty to Judaism and tried to convince the Romans that they were not seditious. Brandon's argument is interesting and plausible though not conclusive. His work, however, includes material on the relationship between the Jerusalem church and Paul. Brandon convincingly argues that there was a basic conflict between Paul and the Jerusalem church headed by James, the brother of Jesus, and that the fall of Jerusalem in 70 A.D. destroyed the power of its church and gave the upper hand to the followers of Paul. The general character of the church in Jerusalem is also examined in two works by Wilfred L. Knox, *St. Paul and the Church of Jerusalem* and *St. Paul and the Church of the Gentiles*. The first work examines the conflict between Paul and the "Hebrew-Christians," who required fulfillment of the Jewish law by all Christians. Knox, however, underestimates the support which James gave to the Judaizing position. *St. Paul and the Church of the Gentiles* is a far more valuable contribution to the history of ideas. According to Knox, Paul began preaching to the gentiles apocalyptic ideas common to Jesus and the Jerusalem church. He demonstrates that those ideas were once common throughout the Mediterranean world (chap. 1). By the time of Paul's preaching, however, the apocalyptic interests of the gentiles had faded and Paul's original message was unsuccessful in converting the Athenians. Paul then recast his message in nonapocalyptic, gentile terms by emphasizing the role of Jesus as a heavenly lord and giver of divine power and revelation. Paul did not entirely give up the distinctively Judaic elements of his original message. The process of accommodating gentile ideas was, however, important later in converting Christianity into a gentile cult. The British scholar Charles H. Dodd examines the relationship of biblical Christianity to gentile thought in his monumental *The Interpretation of the Fourth Gospel*. Dodd believes the fourth gospel contained important Judaic and earlier Christian themes and that it was also partly inspired by "higher paganism" (later and independently expressed in Hermetic literature) (see p. 153 above). The theme of higher paganism was enlightenment and occult knowledge as a means of achieving salvation (gnosis).

Paul and the First Church

The literature on Paul is nearly as extensive as that on Jesus. The New Testament bibliographies listed on p. 160 ff. are suitable guides to the material and so is the survey by E. Best, "Recent Pauline Studies," in *Expository Times* 80 (1960):164–167. The important recent literature and the problems involved in interpreting Paul are reviewed by E. Earle Ellis, *Paul and His Recent Interpreters*. Albert Schweitzer reviews previous interpretations in *Paul and His Interpreters: A Critical History*. The scholarly dispute concerning Paul's relation to Jesus is reviewed by V. P. Furnish, "The Jesus-Paul Debate: From Bauer to Bultmann," in *The Bulletin of the John Rylands Library* 47 (1965):342–381.

The general surveys of New Testament thought contain substantial comments on Paul and his theology. Weiss's *Earliest Christianity*, Bultmann's *Theology of the New Testament*, and Fuller's *Foundations of New Testament Christology* deserve special reference. Mention has already been made of Knox's excellent *St. Paul and the Church of the Gentiles* and Brandon's *The Fall of Jerusalem and the Christian Church*, which emphasizes the basic differences between Paul's theology and the Judaizers in Jerusalem. The general studies of Paul's theology include the convenient summary by D. E. H. Whiteley, *The Theology of Paul*. Whiteley reaches some dubious conclusions, for example, that Paul did not believe in predestination or in the vicarious propitiation of an angry God the Father. Hans J. Schoeps, *Paul: The Theology of the Apostle in the Light of Jewish Religious History*, is less systematic but otherwise better than Whiteley. Schoeps examines Paul's theological principles in terms of the Diaspora and the Pharisaic-rabbinic tradition and identifies those which indicate his break with Judaism—for instance, the elevation of Jesus to divinity. W. D. Davies, *Paul and Rabbinic Judaism: Some Rabbinic Elements in Pauline Theology*, is narrower in subject, but it covers all of Paul's theology. Davies attempts to show that Paul was influenced by Greek thought but attributes his basic ideas to Judaism. According to Davies the apocalyptic and the Pharisaic-rabbinic traditions influenced the construction of Paul's theology. Schoeps thus denies that Paul found a basis for the divinity of Jesus in Judaism, while Davies argues that Paul simply reapplied to Jesus the terms Judaism applied to the *Torah* and *Wisdom*. Davies's argument fails, but his exposition of rabbinic ideas and his survey of the relationship of Paul to pagan and Judaic thought are immensely informative.

Albert Schweitzer's interest in Paul has already been cited. Schweitzer, like Davies, believed that the roots of Paul's theology were Judaic rather than pagan, but he believes Paul's eschatology bound him to Jesus and the church in Jerusalem. Schweitzer believes that Paul awaited an imminent end to the world (a Jewish idea) and that his theology follows from that expectation. Thus, others interpreted Paul's mysticism as the use of a pagan idea, but Schweitzer believes the eschatological spirit bound his believers together. The argument is more fully developed in *The Mysticism of Paul the Apostle*. Against the arguments of Davies and Schweitzer that Paul was primarily Judaic in his theology, see Bultmann, *Theology of the New Testament*, Reitzenstein, *Die Hellenistischen Mysterienreligionen*, Hans Lietzmann, *An Die Korinter*, and Kirsopp Lake, *The Earlier Epistles of St. Paul*. See Erwin R. Goodenough, "Paul and the Hellenization of Christianity" (pp. 23–71), in *Religions in Antiquity: Essays in Memory of Erwin Ramsdell Goodenough*, for an analysis of the book of *Romans*.

General Histories of Ancient Christianity

The best general history of the institutional and theological development of ancient Christianity is Henry Chadwick, *The Early Church*. Chadwick covers the development of the church from the end of the New Testament period to about 500 A.D. and summarizes the important institutional developments. His treatment of theological developments is less useful but still worth reading. His style is concise, urbane, and often witty. John G. Davies, *The Early Christian Church*, is useful but badly organized. Davies divides the history of the church periodically and surveys each branch of Christian thought according to period. The result gives a disjointed impression. Christian architecture and art, however, receive unusual treatment. Robert M. Grant, *Augustus to Constantine: The Thrust of the Christian Movement into the Roman Empire*, is less detailed, but it will hold the lay reader's interest. Leonard E. Elliott-Binns, *The Beginning of Western Christendom*, is more complex in style. The best multivolume survey of the ancient church is Hans Lietzmann, *A History of the Early Church* (4 vols.). Lietzmann's view of Christianity is learned and rational. His expert analyses of the institutional development of the church cover areas commonly overlooked in other general histories—e.g., see "Popular Christianity in the Fourth Century" (vol. 4, chap. 5). Augustin Fliche and V. Martin, *Histoire de l'église*, openly favors a Catholic point of view but is still valuable for its basic information. Volumes 1–6 are now translated as *The History of the Primitive Church* (vols. 1–4) and *The Church in the Christian Roman Empire* (vols. 5–6). Volumes 1–4 are by Jules Lebreton and Jacques Zeiller; volumes 5 and 6 by Pierre C. de Labriolle, Gustave Bardy, L. Brehier, and R. Plinval. Two studies of the life and thought of Augustine of Hippo, F. van der Meer, *Augustine the Bishop: Church and Society at the Dawn of the Middle Ages*, and Peter Brown, *Augustine of Hippo: A Biography*, contain a wealth of information on the late ancient church.

The Ancient Church: Christian Thought

The researcher will find little interesting information on the development of Christian thought in general histories. Fliche and Martin, *Histoire de l'église*, includes several volumes with comments on ancient doctrine, but their Catholic bias contorts the history of that field. Several histories of Christian thought, however, deal with the ancient church from various points of view. The patristic period (i.e., the age of the Church Fathers) and its theological development was distinguished by an emphasis on the scriptures. The resulting discourses on theology and exegesis do not mean that the leaders of the ancient church were fundamentalists committed to the literal infallibility of Scripture. On the contrary, they developed the techniques of allegorical interpretation used in pagan and Judaic circles for the use of Christians. Origen (d. 254 A.D.) was the outstanding exponent of the allegorical method. Two studies of allegory emphasize the influence of Origen and summarize the allegorical method used during the pagan, Judaic, and Christian periods: Robert M. Grant, *The Letter and the Spirit*, and Richard P. C. Hanson, *Allegory and Event: A Study of the Sources and Significance of Origen's Interpretation of Scripture*. Once acquainted with patristic exegesis students can turn to the development of patristic thought. The best starting place is the work of Maurice Wiles, *The Making of Christian Doctrine* and *The Christian Fathers*. In the first work Wiles considers the forces and interests that caused the changes in belief necessary to the evolution of Christian doctrine in the ancient church. He recognizes the influence of social forces and emphasizes the effects of tradition, habits of worship, and doctrinal "feedback." The second work topically surveys the opinions of the Fathers on theology. He necessarily simplifies Christian theology and theological disputes, but his work is an accurate and valuable introduction. After reading Wiles, one can profitably turn to Martin Werner, *The Formation of Christian Dogma*. Werner emphasizes the importance of the fading eschatological expectation of the early ancient church to the development of Christian thought. He also clearly analyzes the conflicting ideas of Paul and the church in Jerusalem. John N. D. Kelly, *Early Christian Doctrine*, is an excellent survey of the major doctrines from the period of the New Testament to the Council of Chalcedon (451). Kelly chronologically divides the patristic period and deals with each major doctrinal development in turn. The result accurately emphasizes the variety as well as the conflict of different patristic ideas. Sidney H. Mellone, *Leaders of Early Christian Thought*, is a topically organized survey which attempts (sometimes unconvincingly) to rationalize the theological principles discussed. Jaroslav Pelikan, *The Emergence of Catholic Tradition: 100–600*, is a useful reference to the development of ancient theology. Pelikan's comments are supplemented by marginalia and bibliographical references, but his explanations are too complex for the average student. Harry A. Wolfson, *The Philosophy of the Church Fathers*, was meant to be the first volume of a complete survey of the development of major Christian doctrines. It does not attempt to review the history of all doctrines in detail but is limited to a treatment of the doctrines of the trinity and the incarnation. It is, however, a useful and clear analysis of those basic ideas. Wolfson is an expert on the history of ancient philosophy and Jewish thought, and he explains the use of philosophy by Christian theologians to explicate doctrines and defend them against their pagan opponents. Adolph Harnack was one of the great German scholars in the tradition of nineteenth-century liberalism. His *History of Dogma* (7 vols.) is still useful. Harnack's disdain for later eastern Christianity and for Roman Catholicism is evident throughout this masterful survey and so is his admiration for Martin Luther. Nonetheless, his erudition repays repeated reading. He vigorously analyzes all of the important writings and ideas, yet his work is deliberately focused on the history of dogma (i.e., those doctrines declared official by church leaders). He thus fails to accord the "losing" doctrines in the history of the church a detailed and sympathetic treatment. Harnack's short survey of the ancient church, *The Mission and Expansion of Christianity in the First Three Centuries*, is one of the best available. In this work he explains the syncretism of Christianity and its growing interest in superstition during the late ancient period. An excellent older Catholic work is available in translation and should be consulted: Joseph Tixeront, *History of Dogmas* (3 vols.), which surveys the key doctrines to the medieval period but lacks Harnack's detailed analysis.

Christianity and Classical Culture

Several sections in this chapter dealt directly with the relationship between Christianity and classical culture, especially the degree of influence exerted on Christianity by pagan thought. The literature on that topic was recently reviewed by Rudolph Bultmann in *Theologische Rundschau* 33 (1968):1–18 and in the bibliographical notes in Jean Danielou, *Gospel Message and Hellenistic Culture*. The *Reallexikon für Antike und Christentum* is an indispensable source for scholars in the field.

Introductions to the topic include Henry Chadwick, *Early Christian Thought and the Classical Tradition*, a study of the classical themes used by Justin Martyr, Clement, and Origen; and Arthur H. Armstrong and Ralph A. Marcus, *Christian Faith and Greek Philosophy*, a topical review of classical and Christian thinking in key areas, e.g., "God and the World," "The Material Universe," and "Knowing and Understanding." It clearly presents the issues and its graceful style makes it the best starting place for students. Edwin Hatch, *The Influence of Greek Ideas and Usages upon the Christian Church*, is a still valuable survey. Hatch includes especially good treatment of "Christianity and Greek Philosophy" (chap. 5) and "Greek and Christian Ethics" (chap. 6). Jean Danielou, *Gospel Message and Hellenistic Culture*, describes the Christian missionary appeal to the Hellenistic mind and the Christian use of Homer, Plato, and Aristotle. James Shiel published an anthology of materials on *Greek Thought and the Rise of Christianity*, one of the Problems and Perspectives in History series. Shiel selects ancient writings and interlaces them with informative notes, but his selection of modern authors is quite disappointing. He prefers to discuss the opinions of Nietzsche, Jung, and Toynbee instead of writings by authorities in the field.

Carl Schneider, *Geistesgeschichte des antiken Christentums* (2 vols.), is systematic, encyclopedic, and in some ways the most interesting of the studies of the relationship of Christianity and paganism. Schneider views the history of ancient Christianity as the progressive Hellenization of the original message of Jesus, the adoption of specific Greek ideas, and the Christian appeal to the emotions of the Hellenistic world. His argument has been vigorously attacked since he sometimes speculates about the evidence, but it is generally convincing. His work was reviewed by H. Karpp in *Theologische Rundschau* (1967):89–99. Cochrane's *Christianity and Classical Culture* is also informative (see p. 19 above). Cochrane's image of classical thought is distorted and his flattering impression of late ancient Christian thought ignores the alliance of Christian theology with the superstition and irrationalism of that age.

Several studies of the interaction of Christian and classical thought in other areas are available. The following are a sample. D. S. Wallace-Hadrill, *The Greek Patristic View of Nature*, is an interesting study of the patristic attitude toward the study and use of the natural sciences. He suggests that the Greek Church Fathers neither ignored nature nor did they consider it too corrupt to be studied with appreciation. Patristic sources indicate that nature was studied incidental to the practice of medicine and patristic scholars had a fair appreciation for the beauties of the natural world. Wallace-Hadrill should be compared to Eric R. Dodds (see his *Pagan and Christian in an Age of Anxiety*). Dodds maintains the late ancient Christians lost interest in the material world, at least lost their feeling that the material world was inhabited and governed by divinities. The Christians' ambivalence concerning pagan educational standards is generally treated by Werner Jaeger, *Early Christianity and Greek Paideia*. Jaeger describes the development of Christian humanism combining the two traditions. Max L. W. Laistner, *Christian and Pagan Culture in the Later Roman Empire*, is a similar work. M. Spanneut, *Le Stoicisme des pères de l'église de Clement de Rome à Clement d'Alexandrie*, is a thorough study of the powerful influence that Stoicism had on some of the Christian Fathers. Part 2 reviews the Christian adoption of Stoic ideas concerning the composition and function of the human body and personality. Additional articles on the relationship between Christian and pagan culture can be found in Arnaldo Momigliano, *The Conflict between Paganism and Christianity in the Fourth Century*. The best articles include A. H. M. Jones, "The Social Background of the Struggle between Paganism and Christianity" (pp. 17–38), which describes the treatment of the aristocratic and academic opposition to Christianity, and A. A. Barb, "The Survival of Magic Arts" (pp. 100–125), on the continuing force of magic during the late Empire.

Valuable information on ancient religion can be gained through the study of skepticism. The discussion of skepticism is properly included in the history of ancient philosophy, especially the history of the Skeptics and the Epicureans. A few general treatments which focus directly on the criticism of religion are mentioned here. Anders B. Drachmann, *Atheism in Pagan Antiquity,* is an older and readable survey. Drachmann surveys the history of ancient skepticism and argues that ancient atheism made headway in overcoming popular religious superstition but could not totally uproot its supernatural base—i.e., the failure of intellectuals to establish a truly scientific world view ruined ancient atheism because orientalized religion and superstition overwhelmed the forces of reason in the late ancient period. Another old standard, Paul Decharme, *La Critique des traditions religieuses chez les grecs,* primarily covers Greek thought from the beginning to Plutarch and deals with ancient skepticism about the manner in which the gods are represented in literature and popular thought. Fritz Mauthner, *Der Atheismus und seine Geschichte in Abendlande* (4 vols.), is an excellent survey of the meaning of the word "god" in western civilization. Volume 1 concerns the ancient world. H. Ley, *Geschichte der Aufklarung und des Atheismus,* takes a different approach. Volume 1 covers the ancient world. Ley discusses the evolution of atheism in standard Marxist terms with the limitations inherent in that method.

Origen and Augustine

Space does not permit listing studies of all of the important Church Fathers, but some references must be made to Origen of Alexandria and Augustine of Hippo. Biographical and theological sketches of other figures can be found in Hans von Campenhausen, *The Fathers of the Greek Church* and *The Fathers of the Latin Church,* and George L. Prestige, *Fathers and Heretics.* Other bibliographical details are included in J. Quasten, *Patrology* (3 of 4 vols. completed).

ORIGEN (d. 254 A.D.)

See H. Musurillo, "The Recent Revival of Origen Studies," in *Theological Studies* 24 (1963):250–263, and especially Henri Crouzel's magnificent new guide, *Bibliographie critique d'Origène,* one of the Instrumenta Patristica series. Crouzel covers the important writings year by year with excellent annotations.

See H. Kraft, *Early Christian Thinkers: An Introduction to Clement of Alexandria and Origen,* for an introduction to Alexandrian theology and Origen's place in its development. Two older studies have still interesting evaluations of Origen, E. de Faye, *Origen and His Work,* and A. V. G. Allen, *Continuity of Christian Thought: A Study of Modern Theology in the Light of Its History.* De Faye asserts that Origen's thought was irreconcilable with orthodox Christian theology. Allen laments that the Christian West followed the theological lead of Augustine instead of Origen. Jean Danielou, *Origen,* is an excellent and advanced study. The several studies by Henri Crouzel are important, especially his *Théologie de l'image de Dieu chez Origène, Origène et la connaissance mystique,* and *Origène et la philosophie.* He has a unique command of scholarly work on patristic theology and he concentrates on an analysis of terminology vital to Origen's theology. See especially *Origène et la philosophie,* a discussion of Origen's use of Platonism for Christian purposes as well as his attitude toward the relationship of philosophy and theology and toward other ancient schools of thought. Henry Chadwick's edition of Origen's *Contra Celsum* has a lengthy introduction and excellent notes.

AUGUSTINE (d. 430 A.D.)

The literature on Augustine is immense. Bibliographical guides include C. Andresen, *Augustinus-Bibliographie,* combined with a collection of articles by eminent scholars as *Augustinus-Gesprach der Gegenwart,* and T. van Bavel, *Répertoire bibliographique de Saint Augustin:1950–1960,* which is topically organized. Serial bibliographies are included in *Augustiniana* (1951) and the *Revue des études augustiniennes* (1955). One of the best contributions of the latter journal is E. Lamirande, "Un Siècle et demi d'études sur l'ecclésiologie de Saint Augustin: essai bibliographique," 8 (1962):1–125. A promising new journal is published by the Augustinian Institute, *Augustinian Studies* (1970).

General studies include F. van der Meer, *Augustine the Bishop: Church and Society at the Dawn of the Middle Ages,* which discusses Augustine's life in the context of the religious culture of the fourth and fifth centuries. Van der Meer's important contribution is the fine description of the mentality of the average person of that period; see part 4 on "Popular Piety." Narrower but even better studies include Gerard Bonner, *St. Augustine—Life and Controversies* (2 vols.), and Peter Brown, *Augustine of Hippo: A Biography.* Brown's fine study follows the chronological development of Augustine's career and theology, especially his theological controversies. E. TeSelle, *Augustine the Theologian,* is also focused on the development of Augustine's theology. Eugène Portalié, *A Guide to the Thought of Saint Augustine,* first done as a contribution to the *Dictionnaire de théologie catholique,* is still useful. Portalié has a brief chronological review of Augustine's development and a topical review of the elements in his theology. Henri I. Marrou, *Saint Augustin et la fin de la culture antique,* is a classic study of Augustine's use of the rhetoric and scholarship of the late ancient period for Christian purposes.

Classical Literature

POSTSCRIPT

THIS BIBLIOGRAPHY HAS introduced the important research and reference tools and scholarly works on the history of ideas and its related fields of philosophy, science, aesthetics, and religion in antiquity. These references show that the great ideas of antiquity were chiefly the product of the amazing and ever-fertile Greek mind. Only in the religious world of late antiquity did non-Greek ideas substantially shape educated ancient thought. It is difficult to exaggerate the importance of Greek thought for western civilization. The Greeks raised most of the questions which dominated western thought until the nineteenth century, provided the vocabulary for their discussion, and proffered many of the answers—some profound, some superficial, a few even bizarre—to those questions. Most importantly, the Greeks of the classical era (600–300 B.C.) established the critical spirit necessary for the rational exploration of experience and values. They did not consider questions closed to further discussion or establish an authoritarian revelation of truth. They generally searched for ideals in this world and asserted the power of reason to comprehend the structure of reality. Finally, they firmly believed in the unity of knowledge; they sought principles which could at once explicate the truth, the beautiful, and the good.

It is true, however, that weaknesses inherent in the Greek approach to life limited their contribution to ancient civilization and promoted the late ancient disintegration of rational thought. Thinking Greeks remained tied to the polis and to their own social order. For the Greeks the polis was the natural form of social life and they thought within that frame of reference. As a result of this restricted point of view, Greek ideas were not easily applicable to different political orders. Although the Greeks contributed to the social and political thought of the post-Aristotelian world, that contribution lacked the originality and the critical spirit of the classical period. Nor did they thoroughly consider alternatives to basic inequities in their own society, the most obvious of which were the subordinate role of women and slavery. Most importantly, they did not exploit their invention of science. They did not free science entirely from philosophical (and later, religious) prejudice and develop a firm observational and experimental method. Nor did they sufficiently institutionalize science, making it a separate and properly financed profession devoted both to the comprehension of reality and to the improvement of human life. As a result, science, the finest product of the classical period, could not survive in the alien atmosphere of the late ancient world.

By the sixth century A.D. Greek civilization was moribund in the West and even in the Eastern Empire it now operated within a fundamentally religious world view. In the West, Greek thought was first substantially revived in the twelfth and thirteenth centuries. Volume 2 of this bibliography discusses the scholarship devoted to that revival in the medieval and early modern West. Like this volume, volume 2 surveys the basic fields of philosophy, science, aesthetics, and religion. It pays special attention to the revival of rationalism and the emergence of modern science to the death of Isaac Newton. Volumes 3 and 4 will survey the history of ideas from the eighteenth-century Enlightenment to the present.

Index

of Justinian. The famous French work by Alfred and Maurice Croiset, *Histoire de la littérature grecque* (5 vols.), has been translated in a condensed version, *An Abridged History of Greek Literature*.

References to Homer, Hesiod, and the archaic age prior to the fifth century B.C. are generally omitted here to allow greater attention to the dramatists and literary theory. A few basic references, however, are necessary. See Moses I. Finley, *The World of Odysseus*, on the general social and cultural background and two works by Andrew R. Burn, *The World of Hesiod* and *The Lyric Age of Greece*. The epic form of poetry found in Homer and Hesiod is covered by Gilbert Murray, *The Rise of the Greek Epic*. John A. Symond's admiring *Studies of the Greek Poets* (2 vols.) is a broader study of poetic forms, with a survey to Theocritus. C. Maurice Bowra's *Greek Lyric Poetry from Alcman to Simonides* and *Early Greek Elegists* concentrate on the period prior to the fifth century. Hermann Fränkel, *Dichtung und Philosophie des fruhen Griechentums: eine Geschichte der griechischen Epik, Lyrik, und Prosa bis zur Mitte des funften Jahrhunderts*, is a vital survey from Homer to Pindar with excellent treatment of Homer, Hesiod, and the older lyric poets (chap. 4).

GREEK TRAGIC DRAMA

The Athenians of the late sixth and fifth centuries B.C. invented drama. Exactly how they created this art form is one of the intriguing and ultimately insoluble problems of the history of ancient literature. The problem is not integral to the history of ideas as defined in the introduction, but a review of the question is in order to illustrate the scholarly energy and skill devoted to the subject. This review will focus on the careers and significance of the three great dramatists of Athens: Aeschylus, Sophocles, and Euripides.

The problems associated with Greek drama and recent literature in the field are briefly outlined by Thomas B. L. Webster, "Greek Tragedy," in *Fifty Years (and Twelve) of Classical Scholarship* (pp. 88–122). See the bibliographical notes in Schmid-Stahlin, *Geschichte der griechischen Literatur* (vols. 1–3), and Albin Lesky, *History of Greek Literature and Greek Tragedy*. The latter has a bibliography (pp. 213–224) revised to include more English titles. Also see Lesky, *Die Tragische Dichtung der Hellenen*, which contains a superb summary of the problem of the origins of the drama (pp. 11–39). There is also a bibliography and discussion of the development of tragedy in Margarete Bieber's well-illustrated *The History of the Greek and Roman Theatre*. The continuous reviews of literature on Greek tragedy in *Classical World, Lustrum, Anzeiger für Altertumswissenschaft*, and the annual *L'Année philologique* (the last named lists works separately under the names of the three great tragedians) are also vitally important references.

The handbooks and encyclopedias on the general ancient period and classical literature in general are supplemented by handbooks

Index

(An asterisk after a title indicates a paperback edition.)

List of Periodicals

Author—Title Index

Abbott, G. F. *Thucydides: A Study in Historical Reality*. London: Routledge, 1925. 76

Ackerman, James and Carpenter, Rhys, eds. *Art and Archeology*. Englewood Cliffs, NJ: Prentice Hall, 1963 128

Ackrill, J., ed. *The Categories and De Interpretatione*. Oxford: Clarendon Press, 1963. 59

Adams, C. J. *Reader's Guide to the Great Religions*. New York: Free Press, 1965. 142

Adams, F. D. *The Birth and Development of the Geological Sciences*. 1938. Reprint. New York: Dover, 1954*. 99

Adams, Sinclair M. *Sophocles The Playwright*. Toronto: Univ. of Toronto Press, 1957. 120

Adamson, J. E. *The Theory of Education in Plato's Republic*. London: Swan & Sonnenschein, 1903. 48

Adcock, F. E. *Thucydides and His History*. Cambridge, MA: Harvard Univ. Press, 1963. 76

———. *Roman Political Ideas and Practice.* Ann Arbor: Univ. of Michigan Press, 1964. 83

Adkins, Arthur W. H. *From the Many to the One: A Study of Personality and Views of Human Nature in the Context of Ancient Greek Society, Values and Beliefs.* London: Constable, 1970. 16

———. *Merit and Responsibility: A Study in Greek Values.* Oxford: Clarendon Press, 1960. 16

Agassi, J. *Towards a Historiography of Science.* The Hague: Nijhoff, 1963. 90

Allan, D. J. *The Philosophy of Aristotle.* 2d ed. London: Oxford Univ. Press, 1970. 53–54, 56, 60

Allbutt, T. C. *Greek Medicine in Rome.* London: Macmillan, 1921. 106

Allen, A. V. G. *The Continuity of Christian Thought: A Study of Modern Theology in the Light of Its History.* Boston: Houghton-Mifflin, 1884. 173

Allen, Reginald E. *Greek Philosophy: Thales to Aristotle.* New York: Free Press, 1968. 29

———, ed. *Studies in Plato's Metaphysics.* New York: Humanities Press, 1965. 45

Allsopp, B. *A History of Classical Architecture: From Its Origins to the Emergence of Hellenesque and Romanesque Architecture.* New York: Putnam, 1965. 134

Altheim, F. *A History of Roman Religion.* Trans. New York: Dutton, 1938. 148

Amaldi, Ginestra. *The Nature of Matter: Physical Theory From Thales to Fermi.* Chicago and London: Univ. of Chicago Press, 1966. 95

Amand, D. *Fatalisme et liberté dans l'antiquité grecque.* Louvain: Bibliothèque de l'université, 1945. 159

Anderson, Bernhard W. *Understanding the Old Testament.* 2d ed. Englewood Cliffs, NJ: Prentice-Hall, 1966. 154

Anderson, E. W. *A Decade of Bible Bibliography, 1957–1966.* Oxford: Blackwell, 1967. 160

Anderson, Hugh. *Jesus and Christian Origins.* New York: Oxford Univ. Press, 1964. 164

Anderson, W. D. *Ethos and Education in Greek Music: The Evidence of Poetry and Philosophy.* Cambridge, MA: Harvard Univ. Press, 1966. 138

Andresen, Carl et al. *Lexikon der alten Welt.* Tübingen and Zürich: Bartels & Huber, 1965. 13

———. *Augustinus-Bibliographie,* in *Augustinus-Gesprach der Gegenwart.* Cologne: Wienand, 1962. 174

Angus, Samuel. *The Spiritual Quests of the Graeco-Roman World.* London: Murray, 1929. 150–51, 160

———. *The Mystery Religions and Christianity: A Study in the Religious Background of Early Christianity.* London: Murray, 1925. 151

Anton, John P., and Kustas, George L., eds. *Essays in Ancient Greek Philosophy.* Albany: State Univ. of New York Press, 1971. 26, 35–36, 44

Anton, John P. *Aristotle's Theory of Contrariety.* London: Routledge & Kegan Paul, 1957. 58

Apel, Willi, ed. *Harvard Dictionary of Music.* 2d ed. Cambridge, MA: Harvard Univ. Press, 1967. 136

Apostle, Hippocrates. *Aristotle's Metaphysics.* Bloomington and London: Indiana Univ. Press, 1966. 56–57, 61

———. *Aristotle's Physics.* Bloomington and London: Indiana Univ. Press, 1969. 61

———. *Aristotle's Philosophy of Mathematics.* Chicago: Univ. of Chicago Press, 1952. 61

Armstrong, Arthur H. *The Architecture of the Intelligible Universe in the Philosophy of Plotinus: An Analytical and Historical Study.* Cambridge, UK: Cambridge Univ. Press, 1940. 73

———, ed. *The Cambridge History of Later Greek and Early Medieval Philosophy.* Cambridge, UK: Cambridge Univ. Press, 1967. 25, 67, 68

———. *Introduction to Ancient Philosophy.* 3rd ed. Westminster, England. Newman, 1963. 24, 39, 54, 68

———. "Was Plotinus a Magician?". *Phronesis,* 1 (1955), pp. 73–79. 74

———, and Marcus, R. A. *Christian Faith and Greek Philosophy.* New York: Sheed & Ward, 1960. 171

Arnim, H. *Stoicorum Veterum Fragmenta.* 4 vols. 2d ed. Leipzig: Teubner, 1921–1924. 72

Arnold, E. V. *Roman Stoicism.* New York: Cambridge Univ. Press, 1911. 71

Artelt, Walter. *Einführung in die Medizinhistorik, ihr Wesen, ihre Arbeitsweise und ihre Hilfsmittel.* Stuttgart: Enke, 1949. 104

———, and Strudel, Johannes, eds. *Index zur Geschichte der Medizin, Naturwissenschaft und Technik.* 2 vols. Munich: Urban & Schwarzenberg, 1953–1966. 104

Ashmole, B. *The Classical Ideal in Greek Sculpture.* Ann Arbor: Univ. of Michigan Press, 1964. 130

Asimov, Isaac. *A Short History of Chemistry: An Introduction to the Ideas and Concepts of Chemistry.* Garden City, NJ: Doubleday, 1965*. 98

Atkins, John W. H. *Literary Criticism in Antiquity.* 2 vols. Cambridge, UK: Cambridge Univ. Press, 1934. 111

Aubenque, P. *La Problème de l'etre chez Aristote.* 3rd ed. Paris: Presses Universitaires, 1972. 57

Aubert, Hermann and Wimmer, F. eds. *Thierkunde: Kritisch-Berichttigter Text.* 2 vols. Leipzig: Engelmann, 1868. 62

——. *Autour d'Aristote.* Louvain: Publications universitaires, 1955. 55

Badian, E. "Alexander the Great and the Unity of Mankind," *Alexander the Great: The Main Problems,* edited by G. T. Griffith. 83

Bailey, Cyril. *Epicurus: The Extant Remains With Short Critical Apparatus, Translation and Notes.* Oxford: Clarendon Press, 1926. 68–69

——. *The Greek Atomists and Epicurus.* Oxford: Clarendon Press, 1928. 36, 69–70

——. *Religion in Virgil.* Oxford: Clarendon Press, 1935. 125

Baker, Herschel. *The Image of Man: A Study of the Idea of Human Dignity in Classical Antiquity, the Middle Ages, and the Renaissance.* Cambridge, MA: Harvard Univ. Press, 1947. 4

Baldry, H. *Ancient Utopias.* Southampton: Univ. of Southampton Press, 1956. 82

——. *The Unity of Mankind in Greek Thought.* Cambridge, UK: Cambridge Univ. Press, 1965. 83

Balme, D. M. "Aristotle and the Beginnings of Zoology," *Journal of the Society for the Bibliography of Natural History,* 5 (1970), pp. 272–85. 62

Bambrough, R., ed. *Popper and Politics: Some Contributions to a Major Controversy.* New York: Barnes & Nobles, 1967. 50

Bandinelli, R. B. *Rome: The Center of Power.* Trans. New York: Braziller, 1970. 132

——. *Rome: The Later Empire.* Trans. New York: Braziller, 1970. 132

Barclay, W. *Educational Ideals in the Ancient World.* London: Collins, 1959. 20

Bargrave-Weaver, D. "The Cosmology of Anaxamander." *Phronesis,* 4 (1959), pp. 77–91. 36

Barker, Ernest, ed. *From Alexander to Constantine: Passages and Documents Illustrating the History of Social and*

Political Ideas: 336 B.C.–A.C. 337. Oxford: Clarendon Press, 1956. 81

——. *Greek Political Theory: Plato and His Predecessors.* 1918. 5th ed. Reprint. London: Methuen, 1965. 49

——. *The Political Thought of Plato and Aristotle.* 1906. Reprint. New York: Russell & Russell, 1959. 65, 80

——, ed. *The Politics.* Oxford: Clarendon Press, 1946. 65

Barnes, Harry E. *The Intellectual and Cultural History of the West.* 3 vols. 3rd ed. Reprint. New York: Dover, 1965*. 4

Baumer, Franklin L. "Intellectual History and Its Problems." *Journal of Modern History,* 21(1949), pp. 191–203. 3

Bauel, T. Van. *Répertoire bibliographique de Saint Augustin: 1950–1960.* The Hague: Nijhoff, 1963. 174

Beardsley, Monroe C. *Aesthetics From Classical Greece to the Present.* New York: Macmillan, 1966. 52, 66, 110

Beare, F. *Greek Theories of Elementary Cognition From Alcmaean to Aristotle.* Oxford: Clarendon Press, 1906. 27, 63

Beazley, J. D., and Ashmole, Bernard. *Greek Sculpture and Painting to the End of the Hellenistic Period.* 2d ed. Cambridge, UK: Cambridge Univ. Press, 1936. 129–30

Becatti, G. *The Art of Ancient Greece and Rome From the Rise of Greece to the Fall of Rome.* Trans. New York: Abrams, 1968. 129

Beck, Frederick A. B. *Greek Education: 450–350.* London, Methuen, 1964. 20

Becker, O. *Das Mathematische Denken der Antike.* Göttingen: Vandenhoeck, 1957 95

Beckwith, John. *Early Christian and Byzantine Art.* Baltimore, MD: Penguin, 1970. 132

Bekker, I., ed. *Aristoteles Opera.* 5 vols. 2d ed. Berlin: De Gruyter, 1960–1961. 54

Bengston, Hermann. *Introduction to Ancient History.* Trans. 6th ed. Berkeley, Los Angeles and London: Univ. of California Press, 1970. 13

Benson, T. W. and Prosser, M. H., eds. *Readings in Classical Rhetoric.* Boston: Allyn, 1969. 111

Berger, A. *Encyclopedic Dictionary of Roman Law.* Philadelphia: American Philosophical Society, 1953. 84

Berti, Enrico. *La Filosofia del primo Aristotele.* Padua: Cedam, 1962. 56

——. *L'Unita del Sapere in Aristotele.* Padua: Cedam, 1965. 58

Best, E. "Recent Pauline Studies," *Expository Times,* 80(1960), pp. 164–67. 167

Boyer, C. B. *A History of Mathematics.* New York: Wiley, 1968.   94

Braaten, C. E., and Harrisville, R., eds. *The Historical Jesus and the Kerygmatic Christ: Essays on the New Quest of the Historical Jesus.* New York and Nashville: Abingdon, 1964.   164

Brandon, Samuel G. F., ed. *Dictionary of Comparative Religion.* New York: Scribners, 1970.   142

———. *The Fall of Jerusalem and the Christian Church.* 2d ed. London: SCM, 1957.   166, 168

———. *Jesus and the Zealots.* Manchester: Manchester Univ. Press, 1967.   157, 166–67

Brehier, Emile. *The Philosophy of Plotinus.* Trans. Chicago and London: Univ. of Chicago Press, 1958.   73

Brett, G. B. *A History of Psychology: Ancient and Patristic.* London: Allen, 1912.   27, 47, 63, 72

Brilliant, R. *Gesture and Rank in Roman Art: The Use of Gesture to Denote Status in Roman Sculpture and Coinage.* New Haven: Connecticut Academy of Arts and Sciences, 1963.   133

Brink, C. O. *Horace on Poetry: Prolegomena to the Literary Epistles.* Cambridge, UK: Cambridge Univ. Press, 1963.   126

Brinton, Crane. *European Intellectual History.* New York: Macmillan, 1964*.   2

———. *Ideas and Men: The Story of Western Thought.* 2d ed. New York: Prentice-Hall, 1963.   3–4

Brochard, V. *Les Sceptiques grecs.* 2d ed. Paris: Vrin, 1959.   68

Bronowski, Jacob, and Mazlish, Bruce. *The Western Intellectual Tradition From Leonardo to Hegel.* New York: Harper & Row, 1960.   5

Brown, F. E. *Roman Architecture.* New York: Braziller, 1961.   134

Brown, Peter. *Augustine of Hippo: A Biography.* Berkeley and Los Angeles: Univ. of California Press, 1967.   169, 174

Brumbaugh, Robert S. *The Philosophers of Greece.* New York: Crowell-Collier, 1964.   25

———. *Plato for the Modern Age.* New York: Crowell-Collier, 1962.   37, 39, 46

———. *Plato on the One.* New Haven and London: Yale Univ. Press, 1960.   45

———. *Plato's Mathematical Imagination: Passages in the Dialogues and Their Interpretation.* Bloomington and London: Indiana Univ. Press, 1954.   46–47

Brunius, T. "Catharsis." *Dictionary of the History of Ideas.* Vol. 1, pp. 264–70.   67

Buchanan, Emerson. *Aristotle's Theory of Being.* Cambridge, MA: Harvard Univ. Press for the Univ. of Mississippi, 1962.   57

Buckdahl, Gerd. "A Revolution in the Historiography of Science?" *The History of Science.* 4(1965), pp. 55–70.   90

Bultmann, Rudolph. *Primitive Christianity in Its Contemporary Setting.* Trans. Cleveland and New York: World, 1956*.   152, 163–64

———. *Theology of the New Testament.* 2 vols. Trans. New York: Scribners, 1954–55.   152, 164–65, 168

———. *The Gospel of John: A Commentary.* Trans. Philadelphia: Westminster, 1970.   152

Burkert, Walter. *Lore and Science in Ancient Pythagoreanism.* Trans. Cambridge, MA: Harvard Univ. Press, 1972.   33

Burn, A. R. *The World of Hesiod.* London: Kegan Paul, 1936.   114

———. *The Lyric Age of Greece.* New York: St. Martin's, 1970.   114

Burnet, John. *Greek Philosophy. Part I: Thales to Plato.* London: Macmillan, 1914.   25, 29, 39

———. *Early Greek Philosophy.* 4th ed. New York: Barnes & Noble, 1958.   29–30

———, ed. *Platonis Opera.* Oxford: Clarendon Press, 1899–1906.   38

Bury, John B., ed. *The Ancient Greek Historians.* 1908. Reprint. New York: Dover, 1957*.   75

———. *Cambridge Ancient History,* 12 vols. and 5 supp. vols. Cambridge, UK: Cambridge Univ. Press, 1923–28.   11, 86, 109–10, 140

Busolt, G. and Swoboda, H. *Griechische Staatskunde.* 2 vols. Munich: Beck, 1920–26.   81

Butcher, Samuel H. *Aristotle's Theory of Poetry and the Fine Arts.* 1894. Reprint. New York: Dover, 1951*.   66

———. *Some Aspects of the Greek Genius.* London: Macmillan, 1891.   14

Buttrick, George A., ed. *The Interpreter's Bible.* 12 vols. New York and Nashville: Abingdon, 1951–57.   162

———. *The Interpreter's Dictionary of the Bible.* 4 vols. New York and Nashville: Abingdon, 1962.   162

Clark, Kenneth. *The Nude: A Study in Ideal Form.* New York: Pantheon, 1956. 128–29

Clarke, Martin L. *Higher Education in the Ancient World.* London: Routledge & Kegan Paul, 1971. 20

———. *Rhetoric at Rome: A Historical Survey.* London: Cohen, 1953. 112

———. *The Roman Mind: Studies in the History of Thought From Cicero to Marcus Aurelius.* 2d ed. Cambridge, MA: Harvard Univ. Press, 1968. 18, 71

Clemen, C. *Primitive Christianity and Its Non-Jewish Sources.* Trans. Edinburgh: Clark, 1912. 152

Clendening, L., ed. *Source Book of Medical History.* New York: Schuman, 1942. 105

Cleve, Felix M. *The Giants of Pre-Sophistic Philosophy.* 2 vols. The Hague: Nijhoff, 1965. 29

———. *The Philosophy of Anaxagoras: An Attempt at Reconstruction.* New York: Columbia Univ. Press, 1949. 35

Coates, W. H., and White, H. V. *Western Intellectual History.* 2 vols. New York: McGraw-Hill, 1968. 5

Cochrane, Charles N. *Christianity and Classical Culture: A Study of Thought and Action From Augustus to Augustine.* New York: Oxford Univ. Press, 1944. 19–20, 172

———. *Thucydides and the Science of History.* Oxford: Clarendon Press, 1929. 77

Cohen, Morris R. *Reason and Nature: An Essay on the Meaning of the Scientific Method.* 2d ed. Glencoe: Free Press, 1953. 90

———, and Drobkin, Israel. *A Source Book in Greek Science.* Cambridge, MA: Harvard Univ. Press, 1948. 87, 93, 105

Cole, F. J. *Early Theories of Sexual Generation.* Oxford: Clarendon Press, 1930. 103

———. *A History of Comparative Anatomy: From Aristotle to the Eighteenth Century.* London: Macmillan, 1944. 103

Cole, Thomas. *Democritus and the Source of Greek Anthropology.* Cleveland: The Press of Western Case Reserve, 1967. 36

Collingwood, Robin G. *The Idea of History.* New York: Oxford Univ. Press, 1946. 75

Collison, Robert J. *Bibliographies: Subject and National: A Guide to Their Contents, Arrangement and Use.* 3rd ed. London: Crosby & Lockwood, 1968. 8–9

Commager, S., ed. *Virgil: A Collection of Critical Essays.* Englewood Cliffs, NJ: Prentice-Hall, 1966*. 125

Conacker, D. J. *Euripidean Drama: Myth, Theme and Structure.* Toronto: Univ. of Toronto Press, 1967. 121

Cook, A. B. *Zeus: A Study in Ancient Religion.* 5 vols. Cambridge, UK: Cambridge Univ. Press, 1914 ff. 145

Cook, R. M. *Greek Art: Its Development, Character and Influence.* New York: Farrar, Straus & Giroux, 1972. 130

Cooper, Lane, and Gudeman, A. *Aristotle and the Art of Poetry.* 2d ed. Ithaca, NY: Cornell Univ. Press, 1947. 66

———. *A Bibliography of the Poetics of Aristotle.* New Haven: Yale Univ. Press, 1928. 66

———. *The Poetics of Aristotle: Its Meaning and Influence.* 1927. Reprint. New York: Cooper Square Press, 1963. 66

Copleston, Frederick. *A History of Philosophy.* 8 vols. Westminster, UK: Newman Press, 1946–66. 24–25, 38–39, 43, 47, 49, 52, 54, 56, 59, 63, 66–68

Copley, F. O. *Latin Literature From the Beginnings to the Close of the Second Century.* Ann Arbor: Univ. of Michigan Press, 1969. 123

Cornford, Francis M. *From Religion to Philosophy: A Study of the Origins of Western Speculation.* London: Arnold, 1912. 30

———. "The Marxist View of Ancient Philosophy." *The Unwritten Philosophy and Other Essays.* Cambridge, UK: Cambridge Univ. Press, 1950. 51

———. *Plato and Parmenides.* London: Harcourt-Brace, 1939. 45

———. *Plato's Cosmology: The Timaeus of Plato Translated With a Running Commentary.* New York: Humanities Press, 1937. 46

———. *Plato's Theory of Knowledge: The Theaetetus and Sophist of Plato Translated With a Running Commentary.* New York: Harcourt-Brace, 1935. 43

———. *Principium Sapientiae: The Origins of Greek Philosophical Thought.* Cambridge, UK: Cambridge Univ. Press, 1951. 30

———. *Thucydides Mythistoricus.* London: Arnold, 1907. 77

Costa, C. D. N., ed. *Horace.* London: Routledge & Kegan Paul, 1973. 127

Croiset, A., and Croiset, M. *An Abridged History of Greek Literature.* Trans. New York: Macmillan, 1905. 114

————. *Time in Greek Tragedy.* Ithaca, NY: Cornell Univ. Press, 1968.   116

Derry T. K. and Williams, T. I. *A Short History of Technology From the Earliest Times to A.D. 1900.* Oxford and New York: Oxford Univ. Press, 1961.   100

De Witt, Norman J. *Epicurus and His Philosophy.* Minneapolis: Univ. of Minnesota Press, 1954.   69

Diano, C. "Epicure: La philosophie du plaisir et la société des amis." *Les études philosophiques,* n.s. 22(1967).   70

Dickinson, Goldsworthy, L. *The Greek View of Life.* 1896. Reprint. Ann Arbor: Univ. of Michigan Press, 1966*.   14

Dicks, D. R. *Early Greek Astronomy to Aristotle.* Ithaca, NY: Cornell Univ. Press, 1970.   97

————. "Solstices, Equinoxes and the Presocratics." *Journal of Hellenic Studies,* 86(1966), pp. 26–40.   32

Diels, Hermann, and Kranz, Walther. *Die Fragmente der Vorsokratiker.* 3 vols. 12th ed. Zurich: Weidmann, 1966–1967.   28

Dill, Samuel. *Roman Society From Nero to Marcus Aurelius.* 2d ed. London: Macmillan, 1905.   19

————. *Roman Society in the Last Century of the Western Empire.* 2d ed. London: Macmillan, 1899.   19

Diller, H., ed. *Sophokles.* Darmstadt: Wissenschaftliche, 1967.   119

Dinsmoor, W. B. *Architecture of Ancient Greece.* 3rd ed. London and New York: Botsford, 1950.   134

Dirlmeier, F., ed. *Nikomachische Ethik.* Berlin: De Gruyter, 1969.   64

————. "Zum gegenwärtigen Stand der Aristotelesforschung." *Wiener Studien,* 76(1963), pp. 54–67.   53

Dodd, Charles H. *The Interpretation of the Fourth Gospel.* Cambridge, UK: Cambridge Univ. Press, 1953.   167

————. *The Parables of the Kingdom.* 2d ed. New York: Scribners, 1961.   165

Dodds, Eric R. *The Ancient Concept of Progress and Other Essays on Greek Literature and Belief.* Oxford: Clarendon Press, 1973.   17, 73, 119–22

————, ed. *The Bacchae.* 2d ed. Oxford: Clarendon Press, 1963.   122

————. *The Greeks and the Irrational.* Berkeley and Los Angeles: Univ. of California Press, 1956.   17–18, 74

————. *Pagan and Christian in an Age of Anxiety.* Cambridge, UK: Cambridge Univ. Press, 1965.   160, 172

————, et al. *Les Sources de Plotin.* Geneva: Vandoeuvres, 1957.   74

Dorigo, W. *Late Roman Painting: A Study of Pictorial Records, 30 B.C.—A.D. 500.* Trans. New York: Praeger, 1971.   133

Drabkin, E. T. "An Approach to Greek Science." *Toward Modern Science,* edited by Robert Palter, Vol. 1, pp. 123–41.   85

Drachmann, A. B. *Atheism in Antiquity.* Trans. London: Gyldenal, 1922.   173

Du Bourguel, Pierre. *Early Christian Art.* Trans. New York: Reynal & Morrow, 1971.   132

Duckles, V. "Music Literature, Music and Sound Recordings." *Library Trends,* 15 (1967), pp. 494–521.   135

————. *Music Reference and Research Materials: An Annotated Bibliography.* 2d ed. New York: Free Press, 1967.   136

Dudley, Donald R. *History of Cynicism.* London: Methuen, 1937.   70

————. *Virgil.* New York: Oxford Univ. Press, 1969.   125

————. *The World of Tacitus.* London: Secker & Warburg, 1968.   78

Duff, J. W. *A Literary History of Rome From the Origins to the Close of the Golden Age.* 2 vols. 3rd ed. 1909. Reprint. London: Benn, 1964.   123–24, 126

Duhem, Pierre. *Le Système du monde: Histoire des doctrines cosmologiques de Platon à Copernic.* 10 vols. Paris: Hermann, 1913–1959.   97

Dumézil, G. *Archaic Roman Religion.* 2 vols. Trans. Chicago and London: Univ. of Chicago Press, 1970.   148

Dunn, John. "The Identity of the History of Ideas." *Philosophy,* 43 (1968), pp. 85–104.   3

Düring, Ingemar, and Owen, G. E. L. *Aristotle and Plato in the Mid-Fourth Century.* Göteborg: Almqvist & Wiksell, 1957.   43, 55–56, 59

Düring, Ingemar. *Aristoteles: Darstellung und Interpretation seines Denkens.* Heidelberg: Winter, 1966.   53–54, 56, 59, 60, 63, 66

————. *Aristotle's De Partibus Animalium: Critical and Literary Commentaries.* Gothenburg: Almqvist, 1945.   62

————. *Aristotle in the Ancient Biographical Tradition.* Göteborg: Almqvist & Wiksell, 1957.   55

————. "Greek Music: Its Fundamental Features and Its Significance." *Journal of World History,* 3(1956), pp. 302–30.   138

————. *Naturphilosphie bei Aristoteles und Theophrast.* Heidelberg: Stiehm, 1969.   58, 61

Ferguson, John. *Aristotle*. New York: Twayne, 1972. 54
———. *The Heritage of Hellenism: The Greek World From 323–31 B.C.* New York: Science Library, 1973. 18–19
———. *Moral Values in the Ancient World*. London: Methuen, 1958. 26
———. *A Companion to Greek Tragedy*. Austin: Univ. of Texas Press, 1972. 115
———. *Religions in the Roman Empire*. Ithaca, NY: Cornell Univ. Press, 1970. 150–51
Festugière, André-Jean. *Epicurus and His Gods*. Trans. Cambridge, MA: Harvard Univ. Press, 1956. 69
———. *Hermetisme et mystique paienne*. Paris: Aubier, 1967. 153
———. *Personal Religion Among the Greeks*. Berkeley and Los Angeles: Univ. of California Press, 1954. 150, 160
———. *La Revelation d'Hermes Trismegiste*. 4 vols. Paris: Vrin, 1944–1954. 153, 159–60
Field, Guy G. *The Philosophy of Plato*. Rev. ed. New York: Oxford Univ. Press, 1949. 39
———. *Plato and His Contemporaries: A Study in Fourth Century Life and Thought*. 3rd ed. New York: Barnes & Noble, 1967. 39
———. "Plato and Natural Science." *Philosophy*, 8(1933), pp. 131–41. 46
Finley, John H. *Four Stages of Greek Thought*. Stanford: Stanford Univ. Press, 1966. 14
———. *Thucydides*. Cambridge, UK: Cambridge Univ. Press, 1942. 76
Finley, M. I. *The Greek Historians*. New York: Viking Press, 1959. 75
———. "Utopianism: Ancient and Modern." *The Critical Spirit: Essays in Honor of Herbert Marcuse*, edited by K. H. Wolff and Barrington Moore, pp 3–27. Boston: Beacon Press, 1967. 82
———. *The World of Odysseus*. London: Chatto & Windus, 1956. 114
Fletcher, Bannister. *A History of Architecture on the Comparative Method*. 17th ed. New York: Scribners, 1961. 134
Fliche, Augustin, and Martin, Victor, eds. *Histoire de la èglise*. Paris: Bloud & Gay, 1934 ff. 169
Foakes-Jackson, F. J., and Lake, Kirsopp, eds. *The Beginnings of Christianity*. 5 vols. New York: Macmillan, 1920–1933. 166
Foester, W., ed. *Gnosis: A Selection of Gnostic Texts*. 2 vols. Trans. Oxford: Clarendon Press, 1972. 153

Forbes, R. J. *Man the Maker: A History of Technology and Engineering*. London and New York: Abelard-Schuman, 1958. 100
———. *Studies on Ancient Technology*. 9 vols. Leiden: Brill, 1955–1964. 99–100
Fosdick, Harry Emerson. *A Guide to Understanding the Bible*. New York: Harper & Row, 1938. 154
Fowler, W. Wade. *The Religious Experience of the Roman People*. London: Macmillan, 1911. 125, 148
Fraenkel, Eduard. *Agamemnon*. 2 vols. Trans. Oxford: Clarendon Press, 1950. 117–19
———. *Horace*. Trans. Oxford: Clarendon Press, 1959. 126–27
Fränkel, H. *Dichtung und Philosophie des fruhen Griechentums: Eine Geschichte der Griechischen Epik, Lyrik und Prosa bis zur Mitte des funften Jahrhunderts*. 2d ed. Munich: Beck, 1962. 114
Frank, Tenny. *Life and Literature in the Roman Republic*. Berkeley and Los Angeles: Univ. of California Press, 1956. 123
———. *Vergil: A Biography*. 1922. Reprint. New York: Russell & Russell, 1965. 124
Frankfort, H. *Kingship and the Gods: A Study of Ancient Near Eastern Religion as the Integration of Society and Nature*. Chicago: Univ. of Chicago Press, 1948. 79
Freeman, Kathleen. *Ancilla to the Pre-Socratic Philosophers: A Complete Translation of the Fragments in Diels' "Fragmente der Vorsokratiker."* Cambridge, MA: Harvard Univ. Press, 1948. 28
———. *The Pre-Socratic Philosophers: A Companion to Diels' "Fragmente der Vorsokratiker."* 2d ed. Oxford: Blackwell, 1959. 28
Frick, Karl. "Einführung in die alchimiegeschichtliche Literatur." *Sudhoffs Archiv*, 45(1961), pp. 147–63. 98
Friedländer, Paul. *Introduction to Plato*. 3 vols. Trans. Princeton: Princeton Univ. Press, 1964–68. 38, 40
Fritz, Kurt Von. *Die Griechische Geschichtsschreibung*. 3 vols. Berlin: De Gruyter, 1967 ff. 75–77
———. *Grundprobleme der Geschichte der antiken Wissenschaft*. Berlin and New York: De Gruyter, 1971. 93
———. *The Theory of the Mixed Constitution in Antiquity: A Critical Analysis of Polybius's Political Ideas*. New York: Columbia Univ. Press, 1959. 77–78

------. *By Light, Light: The Mystic Gospel of Hellenized Judaism.* New Haven: Yale Univ. Press, 1935. 158

------. "Paul and the Hellenization of Christianity." *Religions in Antiquity: Essays in Memory of Erwin Ramsdell Goodenough,* pp. 23–71. Leiden: Brill, 1968. 168

------. "The Political Philosophy of Hellenistic Kingship." *Yale Classical Studies,* 1(1928), pp. 55–102. 83

Gorce, Maxime, and Mortier, Raoul, eds. *Histoire générale des religions.* 4 vols. 2d ed. Paris: Quillet, 1965. 141

Gordon, B. L. *Medicine Throughout Antiquity.* Philadelphia: Davis, 1949. 105

Gould, J. *The Development of Plato's Ethics.* Cambridge, UK: Cambridge Univ. Press, 1955. 48

------. *Platonic Love.* New York: Free Press, 1963. 48

Grabar, A. *Early Christian Art: From the Rise of Christianity to the Death of Theodosius.* New York: Braziller, 1969. 132

Grant, Frederick C., ed. *Ancient Roman Religion.* New York: Liberal Arts Press, 1957. 149

------. *An Introduction to New Testament Thought.* New York and Nashville: Abingdon, 1950. 163, 165

------, ed. *Hellenistic Religions: The Age of Syncretism.* New York: Liberal Arts Library, 1957. 149

------. *Roman Hellenism and the New Testament.* New York: Scribners, 1962. 149

Grant, Michael. *The Ancient Historians.* New York: Scribners, 1970. 75

------. *Myths of the Greeks and the Romans.* New York: World, 1964. 149

------. *Roman Literature.* Cambridge, UK: Cambridge Univ. Press, 1954. 123

------. *Roman Myths.* London: Weidenfeld & Nicolson, 1971. 149

Grant, Robert M. *Augustine to Constantine: The Thrust of the Christian Movement into the Roman World.* New York: Harper & Row, 1970. 169

------. *Gnosticism and Early Christianity.* New York: Harper & Row, 1959. 153

------, ed. *Gnosticism: A Sourcebook of Heretical Writings From the Early Christian Period.* New York: Harper & Row, 1961. 152–53

------. *The Letter and the Spirit.* London: SPCK, 1957. 170

Graves, Robert, "The Virgil Cult." *Virginia Quarterly Review* (1962), pp. 13–35. 125

Gray, R. A. *A Guide to Book Review Citations: A Bibliography of Sources.* Columbus: Ohio State Univ. Press, 1968. 10

Green, M. J. R. *A History of Botany: 1860–1900.* Oxford: Clarendon Press, 1909. 102

Greene, E. L. *Landmarks of Botanical History.* Washington, D.C.: Smithsonian Institute, 1909. 102

Greene, William C. *Moira: Fate, Good and Evil in Greek Thought.* Cambridge, MA: Harvard Univ. Press, 1944. 16, 74

------. "Platonism and Its Critics." *Harvard Studies in Classical Philology,* 61(1953), pp. 39–71. 50

------. "Plato's View of Poetry." *Harvard Studies in Classical Philology* (1928), pp. 1–75. 52

Greenwood, L. H. *Aspects of Euripidean Tragedy.* Cambridge, UK: Cambridge Univ. Press, 1953. 122

Grene, Marjorie. "Aristotle and Modern Biology." *Journal of the History of Ideas* 33 (1972), pp. 395–424. 62

------. *A Portrait of Aristotle.* Chicago and London: Univ. of Chicago Press, 1963. 53–54, 60, 62

Griffin, A. K. *Aristotle's Psychology of Conduct.* London: Williams & Norgate, 1931. 63

Griffith, G. T., ed. *Alexander the Great: The Main Problems* New York: Barnes & Noble, 1966. 83

Grimal, Pierre. *Guide de l'étudiant latiniste.* Paris: Presses Universitaires, 1971. 13

Groningen, G. Van. *First Century Gnosticism: Its Origins and Motifs.* Leiden: Brill, 1967. 152

Gross, J. *La Divinization du chrètien d'aprés les pères Grecs.* Paris: Galbalda, 1938. 160

Grote, George. *Plato and the Other Companions of Sokrates.* 4 vols. 2d ed. London: Murray, 1888. 40

Grout, Donald J. *A History of Western Music.* Rev. ed. New York: Norton, 1973. 137

Grube, G. M. *The Drama of Euripides.* New York: Barnes & Noble, 1947. 122–23

------. *The Greek and Roman Critics.* London: Methuen, 1965. 66, 111

------. *Plato's Thought.* London: Methuen, 1935. 40, 52

Grundy, G. B. *Thucydides and the History of His Age.* 2 vols. Oxford: Blackwell, 1948. 76–77

Gschnitzer, F., ed. *Zur Griechischen Staatskunde.* Darmstadt: Wissenschaftliche, 1969. 81

Guignebert, C. *Jesus.* Trans. New York: Universal Books, 1931. 165

Gulley, Norman. *The Philosophy of Socrates.* London: Macmillan, 1968. 37

———. *Plato's Theory of Knowledge.* New York: Barnes & Noble, 1961. 43

Gunkel, W., and Gunkel, H. G. *Astrologumena: Die astrologische Literatur in der Antike und ihre Geschichte.* Wiesbaden: Steiner, 1966. 159

Guthrie, William K. C. "The Development of Aristotle's Theology." *Classical Quarterly,* 27(1933), pp. 162–71; (1934), pp. 90–98. 58

———. *The Greek Philosophers From Thales to Aristotle.* London: Methuen, 1950. 25

———. *The Greeks and Their Gods.* London: Methuen, 1950. 144, 146

———. *History of Greek Philosophy.* 3 vols. Cambridge, UK: Cambridge Univ. Press, 1962–69. 25, 28–29, 31, 33, 35–36

———. *In the Beginning: Some Greek Views on the Origins of Life and the Early State of Man.* Ithaca, NY: Cornell Univ. Press, 1957. 16–17

———. *Orpheus and Greek Religion.* London: Methuen, 1935. 146

Gwiney, T., and Dickinson, F. *Greek and Roman Authors: A Checklist of Criticism.* Metuchen, NJ: Scarecrow Press, 1973. 12

Haardt, R., ed. *Gnosis: Character and Testimony: An Anthology of Hellenistic Gnosticism.* Trans. Leiden: Brill, 1971. 31, 153

Hack, Roy K. *God in Greek Philosophy to the Time of Socrates.* Princeton: Princeton Univ. Press, 1931. 31

Hadas, Moses *Hellenistic Culture: Fusion and Diffusion.* New York: Columbia Univ. Press, 1959. 18

———. *A History of Greek Literature.* New York: Columbia Univ. Press, 1962. 113

———. *A History of Latin Literature.* New York: Columbia Univ. Press, 1952. 123–24, 126

Hager, F. P., ed. *Metaphysik und Theologie von Aristoteles.* Darmstadt: Wissenschaftliche, 1969. 57–58

Hahn, H. F. *The Old Testament in Modern Research.* London: SCM, 1956. 154

Hall, R. W. *Plato and the Individual.* The Hague: Nijhoff, 1963. 49

Hall, Thomas S. *Ideas of Life and Matter: Studies in the History of General Physiology* 2 vols. Chicago: Univ. of Chicago Press, 1967. 103

Hallie, P.P., ed. *Scepticism, Man and God: Selections From the Writings of Sextus Empiricus.* Middletown, CT: Wesleyan Univ. Press, 1964. 68

Hamburger, Max. *Morals and Law: The Growth of Aristotle's Legal Theory.* 2d ed. New York: Biblio & Tannen, 1965. 65–66

Hamilton, Edith. *The Greek Way to Western Civilization.* New York: Norton, 1931. 14

———. *The Roman Way to Western Civilization.* New York: Norton, 1932. 18

———, and Huntington Cairns eds. *The Collected Dialogues of Plato Including the Letters.* Princeton: Princeton Univ. Press, 1961. 38

Hamlin, T. *Architecture Through the Ages.* 1895. Reprint. New York: Putnam, 1953. 134

Hammond, M. *The City in the Ancient World.* Cambridge, MA: Harvard Univ. Press, 1972. 80

———. *City State and World State in Greek and Roman Political Theory Until Augustus.* Cambridge, MA: Harvard Univ. Press, 1951. 80

Hammond, N.G.L. and Scullard, eds. *Oxford Classical Dictionary.* 2d ed. London: Oxford Univ. Press, 1970. 13, 140

Hammond, W. *A Bibliography of Aesthetics and of the Philosophy of the Fine Arts for 1900–1932.* New York: Longmans, Green, 1934. 110

Hanfmann, George M. *Roman Art: A Modern Survey of the Art of Imperial Rome.* Greenwich: New York Graphics, 1964. 132

Hanson, R.P.C. *Allegory and Event: A Study of the Sources and Significance of Origen's Interpretation of Scripture.* London: SPCK, 1959. 170

Hardie, W.F.R. *Aristotle's Ethical Theory.* Oxford: Clarendon Press, 1968. 64–65

———. *A Study in Plato.* Oxford: Clarendon Press, 1936. 44

Harnock, Adolph Von. *History of Dogma.* 4 vols. New York: Dover, 1961. 170–71

———. *The Mission and Expansion of Christianity in the First Three Centuries.* Trans. New York: Putnam, 1905.   171

Harrison, Jane. *Prolegomena to the Study of Greek Religion.* 3d ed. Cambridge, UK: Cambridge Univ. Press, 1922.   146

———. *Themis: A Study of the Social Origins of Greek Religion.* 2d ed. Cambridge, UK: Cambridge Univ. Press, 1927.   146

Harsh, P. W. *A Handbook of Classical Drama.* Stanford: Stanford Univ. Press, 1944.   115

Harvey-Gibson, R. J. *Outlines of the History of Botany.* London: Black, 1917.   102

Hastings, James, ed. *Dictionary of the Bible.* 1909. Revised by F. C. Grant and H. H. Rowley. New York: Oxford Univ. Press, 1963.   162

———. *Encyclopedia of Religion and Ethics.* 13 vols. New York: Scribner's, 1908.   142

Hatch, Edwin H. *The Influence of Greek Ideas and Usages Upon the Christian Church.* 1891. Revised by F. C. Grant. New York: Harper & Row, 1956*.   171

Hauser, Arnold. *The Social History of Art.* 2 vols. Trans. New York: Knopf, 1951.   129

Havelock, Eric A. *The Crucifixion of Intellectual Man.* Boston: Beacon Press, 1950.   118

———. *The Liberal Temper in Greek Politics.* New Haven, CT: Yale Univ. Press, 1957.   82

———. *Preface to Plato.* Cambridge, MA: Harvard Univ. Press, 1963.   41, 48–49

Havelock, C. M. *Hellenistic Art: The Art of the Classical World From the Death of Alexander the Great to the Battle of Actium.* Greenwich: New York Graphics, 1969.   130

Heath, T. *Aristarchus of Samos: The Ancient Copernicus.* 1913. Reprint. Oxford: Clarendon Press, 1959.   97

———. *Greek Astronomy.* London: Dent, 1932.   97

———. *History of Greek Mathematics.* 2 vols. Oxford: Clarendon Press, 1921.   95

———. *A Manual of Greek Mathematics.* Oxford: Clarendon Press, 1931.   95

———. *Mathematics in Aristotle.* Oxford: Clarendon Press, 1949.   61

Heiberg, J. L. *Mathematics and Physical Science in Classical Antiquity.* Trans. Oxford: Clarendon Press, 1922.

Heidel, W. A. *The Heroic Age of Science: The Conception, Ideals and Methods and Science Among the Ancient Greeks.* Baltimore, MD: Williams & Wilkins, 1933.   85

Heinimann, Felix. *Nomos und Physis: Herkunft und Bedeutung einer Antithese in griechischen Denken des 5. Jahrhunderts.* Basel: Reinhardt, 1945.   26, 81

Heinze, Richard. *Virgils epische Technik.* Leipzig: Teubner, 1903.   124

Hengel, M. *Die Zeloten: Untersuchungen zur judischen Freiheitsbewegung in der Zeit von Herodes I bis 70 nach Christus.* Leiden: Brill, 1961.   157

———. *Was Jesus a Revolutionist?.* Philadelphia: Fortress, 1971*.   157

Henry, Paul. *Études Plotiniennes.* Vol. I: *Les États du texte du Plotin.* Paris: Desclèe et Brouwer, 1938.   73

———. *Les Manuscripts de Ennéades.* Rev. ed. Paris: Desclée et Brouwer, 1948.   73

———, and Schwyzer, eds. *Plotini Opera.* 2 vols. Paris and Brussels: Museum Lessianum, 1951–1958.   73

———. *Plotin et l'occident.* Louvain: Specilegium Sacrum Lovaniense, 1934.   73

Herford, R. T. *The Pharisees.* London: Allen & Unwin, 1924.   155

Herr, Frederich. *The Intellectual History of Europe.* Trans. London: Weidenfeld & Nicholson, 1966.   4

Herter, H., ed. *Thukydides.* Darmstadt: Wissenschaftliche, 1968.   77

Hicks, R. D. *Stoic and Epicurean.* 1910. Reprint. New York: Russell & Russell, 1962.   70

Highet, Gilbert. *The Classical Tradition: Greek and Roman Influences on Western Literature.* Oxford: Clarendon Press, 1949.   112

———. *Poets in a Landscape.* New York: Knopf, 1957.   123, 126

Higham, John. "Intellectual History and Its Neighbors." *Ideas in Cultural Perspective,* edited by Philip Wiener and Aaron Noland, pp. 81–93. New Brunswick: Rutgers Univ. Press, 1962.   3

Hinnells, J. R. "Christianity and the Mystery Cults." *Theology,* 571(1968), pp. 20–26.   150

Hodges, H. W. M. *Technology in the Ancient World.* New York: Knopf, 1970.   100

Hofmann, J. E. *Geschichte der Mathematik.* 4 vols. Berlin: De Gruyter, 1953–1957.   94

Holborne, Hajo. "The History of Ideas." *American Historical Review,* 73(1968), pp. 683–95.   3

———. "The Thesis of Parmenides." *Review of Metaphysics*, 22(1969), pp. 700–25. 34

Kapp, E. *Greek Foundations of Traditional Logic*. New York: Columbia Univ. Press, 1942. 26, 59

Kee, H., Young, F., and Froehlich, K. *Understanding the New Testament*. 3rd ed. Englewood Cliffs, NJ: Prentice-Hall, 1973. 163

Keller, O. *Die antike Tierwelt*. 2 vols. Leipzig: Engelmann, 1909–1913. 103

Kelley, J. N. D. *Early Christian Doctrine*. 3rd ed. New York: Harper & Row, 1965. 170

Kennedy, G. *The Art of Persuasion in Greece*. Princeton: Princeton Univ. Press, 1963. 112

———. *The Art of Rhetoric in the Roman World*. Princeton: Princeton Univ. Press, 1972. 112

Kerfeld, G. B. "Recent Works on Presocratic Philosophy." *American Philosophical Quarterly*, 2(1965), pp. 1–11. 28

Kern, O. *Die Religion der Griechen*. 2 vols. Berlin: Weidmann, 1926–1938. 145

Kiernan, Thomas. *Aristotle Dictionary*. New York: Philosophical Library, 1962. 54

Kirk, Geoffrey S., and Raven, J. E. *The Presocratic Philosophers*. Cambridge, UK: Cambridge Univ. Press, 1962. 28, 33

Kirk, Geoffrey. *The "Bacchae" by Euripides*. Englewood Cliffs, NJ: Prentice-Hall, 1970. 122

———. "Some Problems in Anaximander." *Classical Quarterly*, N.S. 5(1955), pp. 21–38. 33

———. *Heraclitus: The Cosmic Fragments*. Cambridge, UK: Cambridge Univ. Press, 1954. 34

Kittel, G., and Friedrich, G., eds. *Theological Dictionary of the New Testament*. 7 vols. Trans. Grand Rapids, MI: Eerdmans, 1964. 162

Kitto, Humphrey D. F. *The Greeks*. Baltimore, MD: Penguin, 1951*. 14

———. *Greek Tragedy: A Literary Study*. London: Methuen, 1961. 115

———. *Sophocles: Dramatist and Philosopher*. Oxford: Clarendon Press, 1958. 120

Klausner, Joseph. *Jesus of Nazareth: His Life, Times and Teachings*. Trans. New York: Macmillan, 1925. 164–65

Klein, R., ed. *Prinzipat und Freiheit*. Darmstadt: Wissenschaftliche, 1969. 84

———, ed. *Das Staatsdenken der Römer*. Darmstadt: Wissenschaftliche, 1966. 84

Kline, Morris. *Mathematical Thought From Ancient to Modern Times*. New York: Oxford Univ. Press, 1972. 93–94

———. *Mathematics in Western Culture*. New York: Oxford Univ. Press, 1953. 94

Kneale, William, and Kneale, Martha. *The Development of Logic*. Oxford: Clarendon Press, 1953. 26–27, 59, 72

Knight, W. Jackson. *Roman Vergil*. 3rd ed. New York: Barnes & Noble, 1970. 124–25

Knox, B. M. *The Heroic Temper: Studies in Sophoclean Tragedy*. Berkeley and Los Angeles: Univ. of California Press, 1964. 120

Knox, Wilfred L. *St. Paul and the Church of Jerusalem*. Cambridge, UK: Cambridge Univ. Press, 1927. 167

———. *St. Paul and the Church of the Gentiles*. Cambridge, UK: Cambridge Univ. Press, 1939. 167–68

Kohler, H. *Musik und Dichtung in alten Griechenland*. Bern and Munich: Francke, 1963. 138

Koren, Henry J. *Research in Philosophy: A Bibliographical Introduction to Philosophy*. Pittsburg: Duchesne Univ. Press, 1966. 24

Koyré, Alexander. *Discovering Plato*. Trans. New York: Columbia Univ. Press, 1945. 39

Krämer, Hans J. *Arete bei Platon und Aristoteles: Zum Wesen und zur Geschichte des platonischen Ontologie*. Heidelberg: Winter, 1965. 42

———. *Platonismus und hellenistischen Philosophie*. Berlin: De Gruyter, 1971. 72

———. *Ursprung der Geistmetaphysik: Untersuchungen zur Geschichte des Platonismus zwischen Platon und Plotin*. Amsterdam: Schippers, 1964. 72

Krautheimer, R. *Early Christian and Byzantine Architecture*. Baltimore, MD: Penguin, 1965. 135

Kraft, H. *Early Christian Thinkers: An Introduction to Clement of Alexander and Origen*. London: Lutterworth, 1964. 173

Krieger, Leonard. "The Autonomy of Intellectual History." *Journal of the History of Ideas*, 34(1973), pp. 499–517. 3

Kristeller, Paul O. "The History of Philosophy and the History of Ideas." *The Journal of the History of Philosophy*, 2(1964), pp. 1–14. 3

———. "The Role of Medical and Biological Analogies in Aristotle's Ethics." *Phronesis*, 13(1968), pp. 68–83. 65

Lloyd-Jones, H. "Zeus in Aeschylus." *Journal of Hellenic Studies*, (1956), pp. 55–67. 118

———, ed. *Agamemnon*. Englewood Cliffs, NJ: Prentice-Hall, 1970. 117

———, ed. *The Libation Bearers*. Englewood Cliffs, NJ: Prentice-Hall, 1970. 117

———, ed. *The Eumenides*. Englewood Cliffs, NJ: Prentice-Hall, 1970. 117

Lodge, Rupert C. *The Philosophy of Plato*. London: Routledge & Kegan Paul, 1956. 39, 47, 52

———. *Plato's Theory of Art*. New York: Humanities Press, 1953. 52

———. *Plato's Theory of Education*. London: Kegan Paul, Trench & Trubner, 1947. 48

———. *Plato's Theory of Ethics*. New York: Harcourt-Brace, 1928. 47–48

Lone, T. *Aristotle's Research in Natural Science*. London: Newman, 1912. 62

Long, A. A. *Problems in Stoicism*. London: Athlone, 1971. 72

Long, H. S. "A Bibliographical Survey of Recent Work on Aristotle." *Classical World*, 51(1958), p. 47 ff. 53

Longrigg, J. "Philosophy and Medicine: Some Early Interactions." *Harvard Studies in Classical Philology*, 67. Cambridge, MA: Harvard Univ. Press, 1963. 106

L'Orange, H. P. *Art Forms and Civic Life in the Later Roman Empire*. Trans. Princeton: Princeton Univ. Press, 1965. 132–33

———. *Likeness and Icon: Studies in Classical and Early Medieval Art*. Odense: Odense, 1973. 133

———. *Studies on the Iconology of Cosmic Kingship in the Ancient World*. Cambridge, MA: Harvard Univ. Press, 1953. 133

Lowrie, W. *Art in the Early Church*. New York: Pantheon, 1947. 132

Lovejoy, Arthur O., and Boas, George. *Primitivism and Related Ideas in Antiquity*. Baltimore, MD: Johns Hopkins, 1935. 17

Lovejoy, Arthur O. *Essays in the History of Ideas*. Baltimore, MD: Johns Hopkins, 1948. 2

———. *The Great Chain of Being*. Cambridge, MA: Harvard Univ. Press, 1936. 2, 4, 52

Lucas, D. *The Greek Tragic Poets: Their Contribution to Western Life and Thought*. Boston: Beacon Press, 1952. 115

Lucas, E. L. *Art Books: A Basic Bibliography*. Greenwich: New York, 1968. 127

Lucas, F. L. *Euripides and his Influence*. 1923. Reprint. New York: Cooper Square, 1963. 121

Luccioni, J. *La Pensée politique de Platon*. Paris: Presses Universitaires, 1958. 50

Lukasiewicz, J. *Aristotle's Syllogism From the Standpoint of Modern Formal Logic*. 2d ed. Oxford: Clarendon Press, 1957. 59

Lullies, R., and Hirmer, Max. *Greek Sculpture*. Trans. Rev. ed. New York: Abrams, 1960. 130

Lutoslawski, W. *The Origin and Growth of Plato's Logic*. Trans. New York: Longmans, 1897. 44

Lynch, W. F. *An Approach to the Metaphysics of Plato Through the Parmenides*. Washington, D.C.: Georgetown Univ. Press, 1959. 45

McColl, M. H., ed. *Aeschylus: A Collection of Critical Essays*. Englewood Cliffs, NJ: Prentice-Hall, 1972. 118

MacColl, N. *The Greek Sceptics: Pyrrho to Sextus*. London: Macmillan, 1899. 68

MacDonald, W. L. *The Architecture of the Roman Empire*. New Haven and London: Yale Univ. Press, 1965. 135

———. *Early Christian and Byzantine Architecture*. New York: Braziller, 1962. 135

McGuire, Martin R. P. *Introduction to Classical Scholarship*. Rev. ed. Washington, D.C.: Catholic Univ. Press, 1961. 11–12, 109

McIlwain, Charles H. *The Growth of Political Thought in the West*. New York: Macmillan, 1932. 65, 78

McIntyre, Alisdair. *A Short History of Ethics: A History of Moral Philosophy From the Homeric Age to the Twentieth Century*. New York: Macmillan, 1966 26, 47, 64

Mackail, J. W. *Virgil and His Meaning to the World of Today*. 1922. Reprint. New York: Cooper Square, 1963. 124

MacKendrick, Paul. "Herodotus: 1954–1963." *Classical World*, 56(1962–63), p. 269 ff. 76

MacKenna, Stephen, ed. *The Enneads*. 5 vols. 4th ed. London: Faber, 1969. 73

McKeon, Richard. "Aristotle's Concept of the Development of the Nature of Scientific Method." *Journal of the History of Ideas*, 8(1947), pp. 3–45. 60

Maclès, L. N. *Manuel de bibliographie*. 2d ed. Paris: Presses Universitaires, 1969. 9

Fourth Century. Oxford: Clarendon Press, 1963. 172

———. "Freedom of Speech in Antiquity." *Dictionary of the History of Ideas,* Vol. 2, pp. 252–63. 82

Monan, J. D. *Moral Knowledge and Its Methodology in Aristotle.* Oxford: Clarendon Press, 1968. 64–65

Montefiore, Claude G. *The Synoptic Gospels.* 2 vols. London: Macmillan, 1927. 166

———, and Loewe, H., eds. *A Rabbinic Anthology.* Philadelphia: Jewish Publications Society, 1960. 156

Moore, George Foote. *Judaism in the First Centuries of the Christian Era.* 3 vols. Cambridge, MA: Harvard Univ. Press, 1927–1930. 156

Moraux, Paul, ed. *Aristoteles in der neueren Forschung.* Darmstadt: Wissenschaftliche, 1968. 53

———. *Aristote et son ecole.* Paris: Presses Universitaires, 1962. 55

Moravcsik, J. M. E., ed. *Aristotle: A Collection of Critical Essays.* Garden City, NJ: Doubleday, 1967. 55

More, Paul E. *The Religion of Plato.* 1921. Reprint. Princeton: Princeton Univ. Press, 1956. 51

Morgenbesser, S., ed. *Philosophies of Science Today.* New York: Basic Books, 1967. 91

Morris, C. *Western Political Thought.* Vol. 1: *Plato to Augustine.* New York: Basic Books, 1967. 78

Morris, R. P. *A Theological Book List.* 3rd ed. Naperville, IL: Allenson, 1968. 141

Morrow, Glenn R. *Plato's Cretan City: A Historical Interpretation of the Laws.* Princeton: Princeton Univ. Press, 1960 51

Moulinier, L. *Orphée et l'orphisme à l'époque classique.* Paris: Belles Lettres, 1955. 146

Mourelatos, Alexander. *The Route of Parmenides.* New Haven and London: Yale Univ. Press, 1970. 34

Mowry, L. *The Dead Sea Scrolls and the Early Church.* South Bend, IN: Notre Dame Univ. Press, 1966. 156

Multhauf, R. *The Origins of Chemistry.* New York: Watts, 1966. 99

Murphy, N. R. *The Interpretation of Plato's Republic.* Oxford: Clarendon Press, 1951. 48

Murray, Gilbert. *Aeschylus: The Creator of Tragedy.* Oxford: Clarendon Press, 1940. 117

———. *Euripides and His Age.* 2d ed. Oxford: Clarendon Press, 1946. 121

———. *Five Stages of Greek Religion.* 3rd ed. Boston: Beacon Press, 1951. 143–44, 146, 150

———. *The Rise of the Greek Epic.* 4th ed. New York: Oxford Univ. Press, 1934. 114

Musurillo, H. "The Recent Revival of Origen Studies." *Theological Studies,* 24(1963), pp. 250–63. 173

Myres, J. L. *Herodotus: Father of History.* Oxford: Clarendon Press, 1953. 76

———. *The Political Ideas of the Greeks: With Special Reference to Early Notions About Law, Authority and Natural Order in Relation to Human Ordinance.* New York: Abingdon Press, 1927. 81

Nagel, E. *The Structure of Science: Problems in the Logic of Scientific Explanation.* New York: Harcourt, Brace & World, 1961. 90–91

Needham, Joseph. *A History of Embryology.* 2d ed. New York: Abelard-Schuman, 1959. 103

Neill, Stephen. *The Interpretation of the New Testament: 1861–1961.* New York: Oxford Univ. Press, 1966. 162–63

Nestle, D. *Eleutheria: Studien zum Wesen der Freiheit bei den Griechen un im Neuen Testament.* Tübingen: Mohr, 1967. 82

Nettleship, R. L. *Lectures on the Republic of Plato.* 1897. Reprint. London: Macmillan, 1962. 42

———. *The Theory of Education in the Republic of Plato.* 1906. Reprint. New York: Teacher's College Press, 1968. 48

Neuburger, O. *The Technical Arts and Sciences of the Ancients.* New York: Barnes & Noble, 1960. 100

Neugebauer, Otto. *The Exact Sciences in Antiquity.* 2d ed. Providence, RI: Brown Univ. Press, 1957. 94, 96

Neusner, Jacob. *The Formation of the Babylonian Talmud: Studies in the Achievements of Late Nineteenth and Twentieth Century Historical and Literary-Critical Research.* Leiden: Brill, 1970. 156

———. *From Politics to Piety: The Emergence of Pharisaic Judaism.* Englewood Cliffs, NJ: Prentice-Hall, 1973. 156

———. *The Rabbinic Traditions About the Pharisees Before 70.* 3 vols. Leiden: Brill, 1971. 156

Newman, James. *The World of Mathematics.* 4 vols. New York: Simon & Schuster, 1956. 94

Newman, W. L. *The Politics of Aristotle.* 4 vols. Oxford: Clarendon Press, 1887–1902. 65

Nilsson, Martin P. *Dionysiac Mysteries of the Hellenistic and Roman Age.* Lund: Gleerup, 1957. 146

——. *Geschichte der griechischen Religion.* 2 vols. 2d ed. Munich: Beck, 1961. 144, 149–51, 159

——. *Greek Piety.* Trans. Oxford: Clarendon Press, 1948. 144, 159

——. *History of Greek Religion.* Trans. 2d ed. Oxford: Clarendon Press, 1948. 144

——. *Minoan-Mycenaean Religion and Its Survival in Greek Religion.* 2d ed. Lund: Gleerup, 1950. 146

Nock, Arthur Darby. *Conversion: The Old and the New in Religion From Alexander the Great to Augustine of Hippo.* Oxford: Clarendon Press, 1933. 151

——. *Early Gentile Christianity and Its Hellenistic Background.* New York: Harper & Row, 1957*. 151

——. *Essays on Religion in the Ancient World.* 2 vols. Cambridge, MA: Harvard Univ. Press, 1972. 150

——, and Festugiere, A. J. *Corpus Hermeticum.* 4 vols. Paris: Les Belles Lettres, 1945–1954. 153

Norden, E. *Aeneis: Buch VI.* 3d ed. Leipzig and Berlin: Teubner, 1934. 125

Nordenskiöld, Eric. *The History of Biology: A Survey.* Trans. New York: Tudor, 1928. 101

Norwood, G. *Essays on Euripidean Drama.* Berkeley and Los Angeles: Univ. of California Press, 1954. 121

Noyes, A. *Horace: A Portrait.* New York: Sheed & Ward, 1947. 126

Nuyens, F. *L'Evolution de la psychologie d'Aristote.* Louvain: Institute Superieur, 1948. 63–64

Oates, Whitney J. *Plato's View of Art.* New York: Scribner, 1972. 52

——. *Aristotle and the Problem of Value.* Princeton: Princeton Univ. Press, 1963. 65

O'Brien, D. O. *Empedocles' Cosmic Cycle: A Reconstruction From the Fragments and Secondary Sources.* Cambridge, UK: Cambridge Univ. Press, 1969. 35

O'Brien, Michael J. *The Socratic Paradoxes and the Greek Mind.* Chapel Hill: Univ. of No. Carolina Press, 1967. 48

——, ed. *Twentieth Century Interpretation of Oedipus Rex: A Collection of Critical Essays.* Englewood Cliffs, NJ: Prentice-Hall, 1965. 119

O'Connor, M. B. *Religion in the Plays of Sophocles.* Menesha: Banta, 1923. 121

Ogilvie, R. M. *The Romans and Their Gods.* London: Chatto & Windus, 1969. 149

Onians, Richard B. *The Origins of European Thought About the Body, the Individual, the Soul, the World, Time and Fate. New Interpretations of Greek, Roman and Kindred Evidence, also of some Basic Jewish and Christian Beliefs.* Cambridge, UK: Cambridge Univ. Press, 1951. 15–16

Opstelten, J. C. *Sophocles and Greek Pessimism.* Trans. Amsterdam: No. Holland, 1952. 121

Organ, T. W. *An Index to Aristotle in English Translation.* Princeton: Princeton Univ. Press, 1949. 54

Ormson, J. O. *The Concise Encyclopedia of Western Philosophy and Philosophers.* New York: Hawthorne, 1960. 23–24

Ostwald, Martin. *Nomos and the Beginnings of Athenian Democracy.* Oxford: Clarendon Press, 1969. 81

——. "Ancient Greek Ideas of Law." *Dictionary of the History of Ideas,* Vol. 2, pp. 673–85. 81

Otis, Brooks. *Virgil: A Study in Civilized Poetry.* Oxford: Clarendon Press, 1964. 125

Owen, Geoffrey E. L. "Eleatic Questions." *Classical Quarterly,* 54(1960), pp. 84–102. 34

——. "Logic and Metaphysics in Some Earlier Works of Aristotle." *Aristotle and Plato in the Mid-Fourth Century,* edited by I. Düring and G.E.L. Owen, pp. 163–90. 59

Owens, Joseph. *The Doctrine of Being in the Aristotelian Metaphysics: A Study in the Greek Background of Medieval Thought.* 2d ed. Toronto: Univ. of Toronto Press, 1963. 57

——. "The Grounds of Universality in Aristotle." *American Philosophical Quarterly,* 3(1966), pp. 162–69. 57

——. *A History of Ancient Western Philosophy.* New York: Appleton-Century-Crofts, 1959. 24, 39, 54

——. "Recent Footnotes to Plato." *Review of Metaphysics,* 20(1967), pp. 646–61. 38

Page, D., and Denniston, J. D. *Agamemnon*. Oxford: Clarendon Press, 1957. 118

Palanque, J. R., Bardy, G., De Labriolle, P., De Plinval, G., and Brehier, Louis. *The Church in the Christian Roman Empire*. 2 vols. Trans. New York: Macmillan, 1953. 169

Palter, Robert. *Toward Modern Science*. 2 vols. New York: Noonday, 1952. 85

Pannekoep, A. *A History of Astronomy*. London: Allen & Unwin, 1961. 97

Parks, George, and Temple, Ruth Z. *The Greek and Latin Literatures*. New York: Ungar, 1968. 14

Partington, James R. *A History of Chemistry*. 4 vols. London: Macmillan, 1961–70. 97, 99

Patrick, M. M. *The Greek Sceptics*. New York: Columbia Univ. Press, 1929. 68

Patzig, G. *Aristotle's Theory of the Syllogism: A Logico-Philological Study of Book A of the "Prior Analytics."* Trans. 2d ed. New York: Humanities Press, 1969. 59

Pedech, P. *La Méthode historique de Polybe*. Paris: Les Belles Lettres, 1964. 78

Pelikan, Jaroslav. *The Emergence of Catholic Tradition: 100–600*. Chicago and London: Univ. of Chicago Press, 1970. 170

Pemberton, J. E. *How To Find Out in Mathematics*. New York: Macmillan, 1963. 93

Perret, J. *Horace*. Trans. New York: New York Univ. Press, 1964. 126

Perrin, Norman. *The Kingdom of God in the Teachings of Jesus*. Philadelphia: Westminster, 1963. 165

Peters, F. E. *Greek Philosophical Terms*. New York: New York Univ. Press, 1967. 24

Petit, G. and Theodorides, J. *Histoire de la zoologie des origines à Linné*. Paris: Hermann, 1962. 103

Petit, P. *Guide de l'étudiant en histoire ancienne*. Paris: Presses Universitaires, 1962. 13

Pevsner, Nicholas. *An Outline of European Architecture*. Baltimore, MD: Penguin, 1961. 133–34

Pfeiffer, Robert. *History of Classical Scholarship: From the Beginning to the End of the Hellenistic Age*. Oxford: Clarendon Press, 1968. 112

Pfeiffer, R. *Introduction to the Old Testament*. New York: Harper & Row, 1948. 154, 160

Philip, J. A. *Pythagoras and Early Pythagoreanism*. Toronto: Univ. of Toronto Press, 1967. 33–34

Philippe, M. D. *Aristoteles*. Bern: Franck, 1948. 53

Phillips, E. D. *Aspects of Greek Medicine*. New York: St. Martins, 1973. 105

Picard, C. *Les religions préhellenique: Crete et Mycènes*. Paris: Presses Universitaires, 1948. 146

Pickard-Cambridge, A. W. *Dithyramb, Tragedy and Comedy*. Revised by T.B.L. Webster. Oxford: Clarendon Press, 1962. 117

Pinard de la Boullaye, H. *L'Etude comparée des religions*. Vol. 1: *Son histoire dans le monde occidental*. Paris: Beauchesne, 1929. 142

Platnauer, Maurice, ed. *Fifty Years (and Twelve) of Classical Scholarship*. Rev. ed. Oxford: Blackwell, 1968. 12, 74–75

Pistorius, P. V. *Plotinus and Neo-Platonism: An Introductory Study*. Cambridge, UK: Bowes & Bowes, 1952. 73

Plochmann, G. K. "Nature and the Living Thing in Aristotle's Biology." *Journal of the History of Ideas*, 14(1953), pp. 167–91. 63

Podlecki, A. J. *The Political Background of Aeschylean Tragedy*. Ann Arbor: Univ. of Michigan Press, 1966. 118

Pohlenz, Marx. *Freedom in Greek Life and Thought: The History of an Ideal*. Trans. New York: Humanities Press, 1966. 82

———. *Die Griechische Tragödie*. 2 vols. 2d ed. Göttingen: Vandenhoeck, 1954. 116

———. *Hippocrates und die Bergrundung der wissenschaftlichen Medizin*. Berlin: De Gruyter, 1938. 107

———. *Die Stoa: Geschichte einer geistigen Bewegung*. 2 vols. 2d ed. Göttingen: Vandenhoeck, 1955–59. 71

Poincaré, Henri. *The Foundations of Science. Science and Hypothesis. The Values of Science*. Trans. New York: Science Press, 1929. 90

Pollitt, J. J. *Art and Experience in Classical Greece*. Cambridge, UK: Cambridge Univ. Press, 1972. 131

———. *Sources and Documents in the History of Art*. 2 vols. Englewood Cliffs, NJ: Prentice-Hall, 1965–66. 129, 131

Popper, Karl. *Conjectures and Refutations: The Growth of Scientific Knowledge*. 3rd ed. London: Routledge & Kegan Paul, 1969. 91

———. *The Open Society and Its Enemies*. 2 vols. Princeton: Princeton Univ. Press, 1950. 50

Portalie, E. *A Guide to the Thought of Saint Augustine.* London: Burns & Oates, 1960. 174

Pöschl, Victor. "The Poetic Achievement of Virgil." *Classical Journal,* 56(1960–61). 125

———, ed. *Tacitus.* Darmstadt: Wissenschaftliche, 1969. 78

Post, Gaines. "The Ancient Roman Idea of Law." *Dictionary of the History of Ideas,* Vol. 2, pp. 685–90. 84

Prescott, H. W. *The Development of Virgil's Art.* 1927. Reprint. New York: Russell & Russell, 1965. 124

Prestige, G. L. *Fathers and Heretics.* London: SPCK, 1940. 173

Preus, A. "Science and Philosophy in Aristotle's 'Generation of Animals.'" *Journal of the History of Biology,* 3(1970), pp. 1–52. 62–63

Prumm, K. *Religionsgeschichtliches Handbuch.* 2d ed. Freiburg: Herder & Herder, 1954. 150

Quasten, J. *Patrology.* 3 vols. Westminster: Newman, 1950–60. 161, 173

Quinn, K. *Virgil's Aeneid: A Critical Description.* Ann Arbor: Univ. of Michigan Press, 1968. 125

Quispel, G. *Gnosis als Weltreligion.* Zurich: Origo, 1951. 152

Rad, G. von. *Old Testament Theology.* 2 vols. Trans. New York: Harper & Row, 1962–65. 155

Radl, Emanuel. *The History of Biological Theories.* Trans. London: Oxford Univ. Press, 1909. 102

Rahner, H. *Greek Myth and Christian Mystery.* Trans. London: Burns & Oates, 1963. 150

Rohner, Karl, ed. *Sacramentum Mundi: An Encyclopedia of Theology.* 8 vols. New York: Herder & Herder, 1968. 142

Rand, E. K. *The Magical Art of Virgil.* Cambridge, MA: Harvard Univ. Press, 1931. 124

Randall, John Herman. *Aristotle.* New York: Columbia Univ. Press, 1960. 55

———. *The Making of the Modern Mind.* Rev. ed. Boston: Houghton-Mifflin, 1954. 5

———. *Plato: Dramatist of the Life of Reason.* New York and London: Columbia Univ. Press, 1970. 40–41

Rankin, H. D. *Plato and the Individual.* New York: Barnes & Noble, 1964. 49

Raschini, M. A. *Interpretazioni socratiche.* Milan: Marzorati, 1970. 37

Raven, J. E. "The Basis of Anaxagoras's Cosmology." *Classical Quarterly,* 48(1954), pp. 123–37. 36

———. *Plato's Thought in the Making: A Study of the Development of His Metaphysics.* Cambridge, UK: Cambridge Univ. Press, 1965. 44

———. *Pythagoreans and Eleatics.* Toronto: Univ. of Toronto Press, 1948. 34

Read, John. *Through Alchemy to Chemistry.* London: Bell, 1957. 99

———. *The Alchemists in Life, Literature and Art.* London: Nelson, 1947. 99

Reckford, Kenneth. *Horace.* New York: Twayne, 1969. 126

Reed, H. S. *A Short History of the Plant Sciences.* Waltham, MA: Chronica Botanica, 1942. 102

Reesor, M. E. "The Problem of Anaxagoras." *Essays in Ancient Greek Philosophy,* edited by J. Anton and G. Kustas, pp. 81–87. 36

Reinhardt, Karl. *Aischylos als Reisseur und Theologe.* Bern: Francke, 1949. 119

———. *Parmenides und die Geschichte der griechischen Philosophie.* 2d ed. Frankfurt: Klosterman, 1959. 34

———. *Sophokles.* 3rd ed. Frankfurt: Klosterman, 1947. 121

Reitzenstein, Richard. *Die Hellenistische Mysterienreligionen nach ihrer Grundgedanke und Wirkungen.* 3rd ed. Leipzig: Teubner, 1927. 151–52, 168

Rey, A. *La Science dans l'antiquité.* 4 vols. Rev. ed. Paris: Michel, 1942–1948. 92–93

Richardson, A. *A Theological Word Book of the Bible.* New York: Macmillan, 1951. 161–62

Richter, Gisela. *A Handbook of Greek Art.* 6th ed. New York: Praeger, 1969. 129

———. *The Sculpture and Sculptors of the Greeks.* New Haven: Yale Univ. Press, 1950. 130

Rider, K. J. *History of Science and Technology: A Selected Bibliography for Students.* 2d ed. London: Library Association, 1970. 87

Ringgren, H. *The Faith of Qumran: Theology of the Dead Sea Scrolls.* Trans. Philadelphia: Fortress, 1963. 156

Rist, John. *Epicurus: An Introduction.* Cambridge, UK: Cambridge Univ. Press, 1972. 69

———. *Plotinus: The Road to Reality.* Cambridge, UK: Cambridge Univ. Press, 1967. 73

————. *Stoic Philosophy*. Cambridge, UK: Cambridge Univ. Press, 1969.   71

Ritter, Joachim, ed. *Historisches Wörterbuch der Philosophie*. 3 vols. Basel and Stuttgart: Schwabe, 1971.   24

Rivoira, G. T. *Roman Architecture and its Principles of Construction Under the Empire*. Trans. Oxford: Clarendon Press, 1925.   134

Robert, W. Rhys. *Greek Rhetoric and Literary Criticism*. 1922. Reprint. New York: Cooper Square, 1963.   111

Roberts, J. D. *Philosophie et science: Eléments de bibliographie*. Paris: Beauchesne, 1968.   90

Robertson, D. S. *A Handbook of Greek and Roman Architecture*. 2d ed. Cambridge, UK: Cambridge Univ. Press, 1954.   134

Robin, Leon. *Greek Thought and the Origins of the Scientific Spirit*. Trans. 1928. Reprint. New York: Russell, 1967.   31

Robinson, John M. *An Introduction to Early Greek Philosophy*. Boston: Houghton-Mifflin, 1968.   28–29, 34

Robinson, R. *Plato's Earlier Dialectic*. Oxford: Clarendon Press, 1953.   44

Robinson, T. M. *Plato's Psychology*. Toronto: Univ. of Toronto Press, 1970.   47

Rohde, E. *Psyche: The Cult of Souls and Belief in Immortality Among the Greeks*. Trans. New York: Harcourt-Brace, 1925.   146–47

Rook, Arthur. *The Origin and Growth of Biology*. Baltimore, MD: Penguin, 1964*.   102

Rose, Herbert J. *A Commentary on the Surviving Plays of Aeschylus*. 2 vols. Amsterdam: No. Holland, 1957–58.   117

————. *The Ecologues of Vergil*. Berkeley and Los Angeles: Univ. of California Press, 1942.   125

————. *A Handbook of Greek Literature*. 4th ed. London: Methuen, 1951.   113

————. *A Handbook of Latin Literature*. London: Methuen, 1966.   123–24, 126

————. *Religion in Greece and Rome*. New York: Harper & Row, 1959*.   143, 147–48

————, ed. *Vergil's Messianic Ecologue: Its Meaning, Occasion and Sources*. London: Murray, 1907.   125

Rosenberger, F. *Die Geschichte der Physik in Grunzugen mit synchronistischen Tabellen*. Hildesheim: Olms, 1965.   96

Rosenmeyer, T. G. "Platonic Scholarship: 1945–1955." *Classical Weekly*, 50(1957), p. 173 ff.   38

Ross, W. David. *Plato's Theory of Ideas*. Oxford: Clarendon Press, 1957.   44

————. *Aristotle*. 5th ed. New York: Barnes & Noble, 1953.   54, 56, 60, 63

————, ed. *The Metaphysics*. 2 vols. New York: Oxford Univ. Press, 1924.   56

————, ed. *The Prior and the Posterior Analytics*. Oxford: Clarendon Press, 1949.   60

————, ed. *Aristotle's Physics*. Oxford: Clarendon Press, 1936.   61

————, ed. *Aristotle: De Anima*. London: Oxford Univ. Press, 1956.   63

Roth, Cecil, ed. *Encyclopedia Judaica*. 16 vols. Jerusalem: KTER, 1971.   142

Rowland, Benjamin. *The Classical Tradition in Western Art*. Cambridge, MA: Harvard Univ. Press, 1963.   128

Rowley, H. H. *The Old Testament and Modern Scholarship*. Oxford: Oxford Univ. Press, 1951.   154

————. *Eleven Years of Bible Bibliography: 1946–1956*. Indian Hills: Falcon Press, 1957.   160

————, and Black, ʌ , eds. *Peake's Commentary on the Bible*. 1919. Rev. ed. New York: Nelson, 1962.   162

Rudolph, K. "Gnosis und Gnosticismus." *Theologische Rundschau*, 34(1969), p. 121 ff.; 26(1971), p. 1 ff.   154

Runciman, W. G. *Plato's Later Epistemology*. Cambridge, UK: Cambridge Univ. Press, 1962.   43

Russell, D. A., and Winterbottom, M. (eds.) *Ancient Literary Criticism: The Principal Texts in New Translations*. Oxford: Clarendon Press, 1972.   111

Russell, D. S. *The Methods and Message of Jewish Apocalyptic*. Philadelphia: Westminster, 1964.   156

Russo, Francois. *Eléments d'histoire des sciences et des techniques: Bibliographie*. 2d ed. Paris: Hermann, 1969.   87

Ryle, Gilbert. *Plato's Progress*. Cambridge, UK: Cambridge Univ. Press, 1966.   40–41

Sabine, George. *A History of Political Theory*. 4th ed. New York: Holt, Rinehart & Winston, 1973.   78

Sachs, Curt. *The Rise of Music in the Ancient World: East and West*. New York: Norton, 1943.   138

Sachs, Julius von. *History of Botany*. Trans. Oxford: Clarendon Press, 1907.   102

Saintsbury, George. *A History of Art and Literary Tastes in Europe From the Earliest*

——. *Greek Architecture*. New York: Braziller, 1965. 134

Scully, Vincent. *The Earth, The Temple and the Gods: Greek Sacred Architecture*. Rev. ed. New York: Praeger, 1969. 131–32

Sedgwick, H. D. *Horace: A Biography*. Cambridge, MA: Harvard Univ. Press, 1947. 126

Segal, Eric, ed. *Euripides: A Collection of Critical Essays*. Englewood Cliffs, NJ: Prentice-Hall, 1968. 122

Seligman, Paul. *The Apeiron of Anaximander: A Study of the Origins and Function of Metaphysical Ideas*. London: Athlone, 1962. 32

Selincourt, Aubrey De. *The World of Hesiod*. Boston and Toronto: Little Brown, 1962. 76

Sellars, W. D. *The Roman Poets of the Augustan Age: Horace and the Elegiac Poets*. 1892. Reprint. New York: Biblo & Tanner, 1962. 124, 126

Senn, G. *Die Entwicklung de biologischen Forschungsmethode in der Antike und ihrer Grundsatzliche Föderung durch Theophrast von Erasos*. Aaran: Sauerländer, 1933. 102

Sheppard, J. T. *Aeschylus and Sophocles: Their Work and Influence*. New York and London: Green, 1927. 117, 120

Shiel, J., ed. *Greek Thought and the Rise of Christianity*. London: Longmans, 1968. 171

Shorey, Paul. "The Origins of the Syllogism." *Classical Philology*, 19 (1924), pp. 1–25. 60

——. *The Unity of Plato's Thought*. Chicago: Univ. of Chicago Press, 1904. 39, 47

——. *What Plato Said*. Chicago: Univ. of Chicago Press, 1933. 39

Shotwell, J. T. *An Introduction to the History of History*. Revised by J. W. Swain. New York: Columbia Univ. Press, 1961. 75

Showerman, G. *Horace and His Influence*. New York: Longmans, Green, 1931. 126

Shute, C. *The Psychology of Aristotle: An Analysis of the Living Being*. 1941. Reprint. New York: Russell & Russell, 1964. 63

Siegel, R. E. *Galen on Sense Perception*. Basel: Karger, 1970. 107

——. *Galen's System of Physiology and Medicine*. New York: Karger, 1968. 107

Sigerist, H. *A History of Medicine*. 2 vols. New York: Oxford Univ. Press, 1951. 103, 105–06

Simon, Maurice. *Jewish Sects in the Time of Jesus*. Trans. Philadelphia: Westminster, 1967. 155

Simpson, F. M. *A History of Architectural Development*. 3 vols. Rev. ed. London: Longmans, Green, 1954–1958. 134

Sinclair, T. A. *A History of Greek Political Thought*. 2d ed. Cleveland and New York: World, 1968. 49, 81

Singer, Charles. *A Short History of Scientific Ideas to 1900*. Oxford: Clarendon Press, 1959. 88–89

——, ed. *A History of Technology*. 5 vols. Oxford: Clarendon Press, 1954–1958. 100

——. *A History of Biology to About the Year 1900*. 3rd rev. ed. London: Abelard-Schuman, 1960. 101–02

——. *Studies in the History and Method of Science*. 2 vols. Oxford: Clarendon Press, 1921. 102

——. *A Short History of Anatomy from the Greeks to Harvey*. New York: Dover, 1957*. 102

——, and Underwood, E. Ashworth. *A Short History of Medicine*. 2d ed. Oxford: Clarendon Press, 1962. 105

Sinnige, Theo G. *Matter and Infinity in the Presocratic Schools and Plato*. Assen: Van Gorcum, 1968. 32

Sirks, M. J., and Zirkle, C. *The Evolution of Biology*. New York: Ronald, 1964. 100–01

Skinner, Quentin. "Meaning and Understanding in the History of Ideas." *History and Theory*, 8(1969), pp. 3–53. 3

Smith, D. E. *History of Mathematics*. 2 vols. Boston: Ginn, 1923. 94

Smith, J. A., and Ross, W. David, eds. *The Works of Aristotle Translated into English*. 12 vols. London: Oxford Univ. Press, 1908–1952. 53, 62, 64

Smith, Preserved. *A History of Modern Culture*. 2 vols. 1930–1934. Paperback reprint. New York: Collier, 1962. 5

Smyth, H. W. *Aeschylean Tragedy*. 1924. Reprint. New York: Biblo & Tannen, 1969. 117

Snaith, N. *The Distinctive Ideas of the Old Testament*. London: Epworth, 1955 154

Snell, Bruno. *The Discovery of the Mind: The Greek Origins of European Thought*. Trans. Cambridge, MA: Harvard Univ. Press, 1953. 16

Solmsen, Friedrich. "Aristotle's Syllogism and Its Platonic Background." *Philosophical Review*. 60(1951), pp. 563–71. 59–60

———. *The Mind of Plato*. 1922. Reprint. Ann Arbor: Univ. of Michigan Press, 1960. 39

———. *Plato: The Man and His Work*. 6th ed. New York: Meridian, 1949. 39

———. *Socrates*. London: Davies, 1932 37

Taylor, F. Sherwood. *The Alchemists*. New York: Schuman, 1949. 99

Taylor, Lili Ross. *The Divinity of the Roman Emperor*. Urbana, IL: American Philological Association, 1931. 83

Tcherikover, V. A. *Hellenistic Civilization and the Jews*. Trans. Philadelphia: Jewish Publications Society, 1957. 157–58

Tempkins, O., and Tempkins, C. L., eds. *Ancient Medicine: Selected Papers of Ludwig Edelstein*. Baltimore, MD: Johns Hopkins, 1967. 106

Te Selle, E. *Augustine the Theologian*. New York: Herder & Herder, 1970. 174

Thomson, George. *Aeschylus and Athens*. 2d ed. London: Lawrence & Wishart, 1948. 117–18

Thompson, J. W. *History of Historical Writings*. 2 vols. New York: Macmillan, 1942. 75

Thompson, D'Arcy. "Aristotle the Naturalist." *Science and the Classics*, pp. 37–78. Oxford: Oxford Univ. Press, 1940. 62

Thompson, O., ed. *The International Cyclopedia of Music and Musicians*. 9th ed. New York: Dodd & Mead, 1964. 136–37

Thorndike, Lynn. *A History of Magic and Experimental Science*. 8 vols. New York: Columbia Univ. Press, 1923–1958. 89, 159

Thornton, J. L., and Tulley, R.I.J. *Science Books, Libraries and Collections*. 2d ed. London: Library Association, 1962. 87

Thornton, J. L. *A Select Bibliography of Medical Biography*. 2d. ed. London: Library Association, 1970. 104

Thorson, T. L., ed. *Plato: Totalitarian or Democrat?* Englewood Cliffs, NJ: Prentice-Hall, 1963*. 50

Tixeront, J. *History of Dogmas*. 3 vols. Trans. St. Louis: Herder & Herder, 1910–1916. 171

Tóth, I. "Non Euclidean Geometry Before Euclid." *Scientific American*, 221(1969), pp. 87–102. 61

Totok, Wilhelm. *Handbuch der Geschichte der Philosophie I: Das Altertum*. Frankfurt: Klostermann, 1964. 22, 27, 37, 53, 67

———, Weitzel, R., and Weimann, K. N. *Handbuch der bibliographischen Nachschlagewerke*. 4th ed. Frankfurt: Klosterman, 1972. 9

Toulmin, Stephen. *The Philosophy of Science: An Introduction*. London: Hutchinson, 1953. 90

———, and Goodfield, Jane. *The Architecture of Matter: The Physics, Chemistry, and Physiology of Matter*. New York: Harper & Row, 1962. 95, 98

———. *The Discovery of Time*. London: Hutchinson, 1965. 95

———. *The Fabric of the Heavens: The Development of Astronomy and Dynamics*. New York: Harper & Row, 1961. 96–97

Ueberweg, Friedrich, and Praechter, Karl. *Grundriss des Geschichte der Philosophie*. 8 vols. Reprint. Basel: Schwabe, 1960 22, 28, 53, 66

Ulrich's International Periodicals Directory. 15th ed. New York: Bowker, 1973. 9

Underwood, E. Ashworth, ed. *Science, Medicine and History: Essays on the Evolution of Scientific Thought and Medical Practice Written in Honor of Charles Singer*. 2 vols. Oxford: Clarendon Press, 1953. 106

Untersteiner, Mario. *The Sophists*. Trans. New York: Philosophical Library, 1954. 336

Usher, S. *The Historians of Greece and Rome*. London: Hamilton, 1969. 75

Van Der Meer, F. *Early Christian Art*. Trans. London: Faber & Faber, 1967. 132

———. *Augustine the Bishop: Church and Society at the Dawn of the Middle Ages*. Trans. New York: Harper & Row, 1965. 169, 174.

Van Der Waerden, B. L. *Science Awakening*. 2d ed. Groningen: Noordhoff, 1954. 95

Van Ess, D. H. *The Heritage of Musical Style*. New York: Holt, Rinehart & Winston, 1970. 137

Vanhoutte, M. *La Philosophie politique de Platon dans les "Lois"*. Louvain: Publications Universitaires, 1954. 51

Varet, Gilbert. *Manuel de bibliographie philosophique*. 2 vols. Paris: Presses Universitaires. 1956. 11, 21–22, 53, 86, 109, 140

Verdenius, W. J. *Parmenides: Some Comments on His Poem*. Groningen: Batavia, 1942. 34

————. "Traditional and Personal Elements in Aristotle's Religion." *Phronesis,* 5(1960), pp. 56–70. 58

Vermes, G., ed. *The Dead Sea Scrolls in English.* Baltimore, MD: Penguin, 1962. 15

Verrall, A. W. *Euripides the Rationalist: A Study in the History of Art and Religion.* Cambridge, UK: Cambridge Univ. Press, 1913. 122

Versenyi, L. G. "Plato and His Liberal Opponents." *Philosophy,* 46(1971), pp. 222–36. 51

Vigouroux, Fuleran G., and Pirot, Louis, eds. *Dictionnaire de la Bible.* 12 vols. Paris: Letouzey, 1907–63. 162

Vlastos, Gregory. "Equality and Justice in Early Greek Cosmologies." *Classical Philology,* 42(1947), pp. 156–78. 33

————. "Ethics and Physics in Democritus." *Philosophical Review,* 54(1945), pp. 578–92; 55(1946), pp. 53–64. 36

————, ed. *The Philosophy of Socrates: A Collection of Critical Essays.* Garden City, NJ: Doubleday, 1971. 37

————. "The Physical Theory of Anaxagoras." *American Philosophical Review,* 59(1950), pp. 31–57. 35–36

————, ed. *Plato: A Collection of Critical Essays.* 2 vols. Garden City, NJ: Doubleday, 1970. 37–38, 42–43, 45, 51

Vogel, Cornelia de. *Greek Philosophy: A Collection of Texts Selected and Supplemented With Some Notes and Explanations.* 3 vols. Leiden: Brill, 1950–64. 27–28

————. *Pythagoras and Early Pythagoreanism: An Interpretation of Neglected Evidence on the Philosopher Pythagoras.* Assen: Van Gorcum, 1966.

Volbach, W. F. *Early Christian Art.* New York: Abrams, 1961. 132

Wagenvoort, H. *Roman Dynamism: Studies in Ancient Roman Thought, Language and Custom.* Oxford: Blackwell, 1947. 148

Wagner, Hans. "Zum Problem der Aristotelischen Metaphysik Begriffs." *Philosophische Rundschau,* 7(1959), pp. 511–21. 57

Walbank, F. W. *A Historical Commentary on Polybius.* 3 vols. Oxford: Clarendon Press, 1957–1967. 77

Waldock, Arthur John Alfred. *Sophocles the Dramatist.* Cambridge, UK: Cambridge Univ. Press, 1951. 120

Walford, A. J. *Guide to Reference Materials.* 3 vols. London: Library Association, 1966–1970. 8

Walker, K. *The Story of Medicine.* New York: Oxford Univ. Press, 1955. 105

Wallace-Hadrill, D. S. *The Greek Patristic View of Nature.* New York: Barnes & Noble, 1968. 172

Wallis, R. T. *Neo-Platonism.* London: Duckworth, 1972. 72

Walsh, J. J. *Aristotle's Concept of Moral Weakness.* New York: Columbia Univ. Press, 1963. 64

————, and Shapiro, H. L., eds. *Aristotle's Ethics: Issues and Interpretations.* Belmont, CA: Wadsworth, 1967. 67

Walton, A. "The Cult of Asklepios." *Cornell Studies in Classical Philology,* 3(1894). Reprint. New York: Johnson, 1965. 107

Walzer, R. *Galen on Medical Experience.* New York: Oxford Univ. Press, 1946. 107

Warry, J. G. *Greek Aesthetical Theory.* New York: Barnes & Noble, 1967. 52, 66, 110

Wassermann, F. M. "Thucydidean Scholarship: 1942–1956." *Classical World,* 55(1956–57), pp. 65 ff. 76

Watson, G. *The Stoic Theory of Knowledge.* Belfast: Queens Univ. Press, 1916. 72

Watterson, J. *Architecture: A Short History.* Rev. ed. New York: Norton, 1968. 134

Wesbter, T. B. L. *Art and Literature in Fourth Century Athens.* London: Athlone, 1956. 113

————. *Greek Art and Literature: 700–530 B. C.* New York: Praeger, 1960. 113

————. *Greek Art and Literature: 530–400 B. C.* Oxford: Clarendon Press, 1939. 113

————. *Hellenistic Poetry and Art.* London: Methuen, 1964. 113

————. *An Introduction to Sophocles.* Oxford: Clarendon Press, 1969. 113

————. *The Tragedies of Euripides.* London: Methuen, 1917. 121

Wedberg, Anders. *Plato's Philosophy of Mathematics.* Stockholm: Almqvist, 1955. 47

Wegner, M. *Das Musikleben der Griechen.* Berlin: De Gruyter, 1949. 138

Weil, E. "La Place de la logique dans la pensée Aristotelicienne." *Revue de Metaphysique et morale,* 56(1951), pp. 283–315. 59

Weiss, Johannes. *Earliest Christianity: A History of the Period A. D.30–150.* 2 vols.

Trans. New York and Evanston, IL: Harper & Row, 1959. 163, 165, 168

Wenley, R. M. *Stoicism and Its Influence.* 1924. Reprint. New York: Cooper Square, 1963. 70

Werner, Martin. *The Formation of Christian Dogma.* 1941. Trans. London: Black, 1957. 170

West, M. L. *Early Greek Philosophy and the Orient.* Oxford: Clarendon Press, 1971. 29–30

Westrup, J. A. *An Introduction to Music History.* 4th ed. London: Hutchinson, 1963. 137

Wheeler, M. *Roman Art and Architecture.* New York: Praeger, 1964. 134–35

Wheelwright, Philip. *Heraclitus.* Princeton: Princeton Univ. Press, 1959. 34

———. ed. *The Presocratics.* New York: Odyssey, 1966*. 28

Whibley, Leonard, ed. *A Companion to Greek Studies.* 4th éd. New York and London: Hafner, 1963. 13, 140

White, G. W. *Annotated Bibliography for the History of Geology.* Urbana: Univ. of Illinois Press, 1964. 99

Whiteley, D. E. H. *The Theology of Paul.* Oxford: Blackwell, 1964. 168

Whitford, R. H. *Physics Literature.* 2d ed. Metuchen, NJ: Scarecrow Press, 1968 93

Whitman, Cedric H. *Sophocles: A Study in Heroic Humanism.* Cambridge, MA: Harvard Univ. Press, 1951. 120

Whittaker, T. *The Neo-Platonists: A Study in the History of Hellenism.* 2d ed. Cambridge, MA: Harvard Univ. Press, 1928. 72

Wieland, Wolfgang. *Die Aristotelische Physik.* 2d ed. Göttingen: Vandenhoeck, 1970. 61

Wiener, Philip, and Noland, Aaron, eds. *Ideas in Cultural Perspective.* New Brunswick: Rutgers Univ. Press, 1962. 2–3

Wightman, W. P. D. *The Growth of Scientific Ideas.* London: Oliver & Boyd, 1959. 89

Wilamowitz-Moellendorff, Ulrich von. *Aristoteles and Athens.* 2 vols. 1893. Reprint. Berlin: Weidmann, 1966. 66

———. *Der Glaube der Hellenen.* 2 vols. Berlin: De Gruyter, 1931–32. 144–45

Wild, J. *Plato's Modern Enemies and the Theory of Natural Law.* Chicago: Univ. of Chicago Press, 1953. 51

———. *Plato's Theory of Man: An Introduction to the Realistic Philosophy of Culture.* Cambridge, MA: Harvard Univ. Press, 1946. 50–51

Wiles, Maurice. *The Making of Christian Doctrine.* Cambridge, UK: Cambridge Univ. Press, 1967. 170

———. *The Christian Fathers.* New York and Philadelphia: Hodden & Stoughton, 1966. 170

Wilkinson, L. P. *Horace and His Lyric Poetry.* Cambridge, UK: Cambridge Univ. Press, 1945. 126

Williams, Gordon. *The Nature of Roman Poetry.* London: Oxford Univ. Press, 1970*. 123

———. *Tradition and Originality in Roman Poetry.* Oxford: Clarendon Press, 1968. 123–24

Willoughby, H. *A Study of Mystery Initiations in the Graeco-Roman World.* Chicago: Univ. of Chicago Press, 1929. 151

Wilson, J. R., ed. *Euripides Alcestis.* Englewood Cliffs, NJ: Prentice-Hall, 1968. 122

Wilson, R. M. *Gnosticism and the New Testament.* Oxford: Blackwell, 1968. 153

———. *The Gnostic Problem: A Study of the Relations Between Hellenistic Judaism and the Gnostic Heresy.* London: Mowbray, 1958. 153, 158

Wimsatt, W. K., and Brooks, Cleanth. *Literary Criticism: A Short History.* New York: Vintage, 1967. 111

Winchell, Constance. *Guide to Reference Books.* 8th ed. Chicago: American Library Association, 1967. 8

Windelband, Wilhelm. *A History of Ancient Philosophy.* Trans. 1899. Reprint. New York: Dover, 1956*. 24, 39, 43, 54

Winnington-Ingram, R. P. "Ancient Greek Music: 1932–1957." *Lustrum,* 3(1958), pp. 5–58. 138

———. *Mode in Ancient Greek Music.* Cambridge, UK: Cambridge Univ. Press, 1936. 138

Winspear, A. D. *The Genesis of Plato's Thought.* New York: Dryden, 1940. 50

Wirzubski, Chaim. *Libertas as a Political Ideal at Rome During the Later Republic and Early Principate.* Cambridge, UK: Cambridge Univ. Press, 1950. 84

Wissowa, Georg. *Religion und Kultus der Romer.* 2d ed. Munich: Beck, 1912. 148–49

Wolf, Eric. *Griechisches Rechtsdenken.* 6 vols. Frankfurt: Klosterman, 1950–1970. 49, 81–82

Wolff, Philippe. *The Awakening of Europe.* Baltimore, MD: Penguin, 1968*. 4

Wolfson, Harry A. "The Knowability of and Describability of God in Plato

The History of Ideas, vol. 1, was copy edited by Amanda Clark Frost, and proofed by John R. "Jack" Raup. Text design by Shelly Lowenkopf, composition using Palatino for text and display by Chapman's Phototypesetting, Fullerton, Calif. Printing and binding by Edwards Brothers, Inc., Ann Arbor, Mich.